Energy Security

The geopolitics of oil and gas have made a spectacular return to the international political agenda. The European Union (EU) has recognized the importance of incorporating energy security more systematically into foreign policy. It has committed itself to pursuing an energy security policy based on market interdependence, European unity and long-term governance improvements in producer states. In offering the first broad, global assessment of the foreign policy dimensions of EU energy security, this book considers how far these commitments have been implemented.

Examining how the EU's general approach to energy security has played out in the specific political contexts of different countries and regions, distinctive features of the book include:

- a thorough analysis of current EU strategies towards energy security, assessing the EU as an international actor
- a key focus on the governance structures of producer states including the Middle East, Russia, Central Asia and the Caspian, and Sub-Saharan Africa
- a major addition to debates surrounding markets and geopolitics, informing both international relations and international political economy

This book will be of interest to students, scholars and policy-makers in the fields of European/EU politics, energy politics, foreign policy and international relations.

Richard Youngs is Associate Professor at the Department of Politics and International Studies at the University of Warwick, UK and Director of the Democratization programme at FRIDE in Madrid, Spain.

Routledge Advances in European Politics

Energy Security

Europe's new foreign policy challenge

Richard Youngs

Routledge
Taylor & Francis Group

LONDON AND NEW YORK

First published 2009
by Routledge
2 Park Square, Milton Park, Abingdon, Oxon OX14 4RN

Simultaneously published in the USA and Canada
by Routledge
270 Madison Avenue, New York, NY 10016

Routledge is an imprint of the Taylor & Francis Group, an informa business.

Typeset in Times New Roman
by Taylor & Francis Books
Printed and bound in Great Britain
by TJI Digital, Padstow, Cornwall

British Library Cataloguing in Publication Data
A catalogue record for this book is available from the British Library

Library of Congress Cataloging in Publication Data
Youngs, Richard, 1968-
Energy security: Europe's new foreign policy challenge / Richard Youngs.
    p. cm. – (Routledge advances in European politics)
  Includes bibliographical references and index.
  1. Energy policy – European Union countries. 2. Energy industries –
European Union countries. 3. European Union countries – Foreign policy.
4. Power resources – European Union countries. I. Title.
  HD9502.E852Y68 2009
  337.1'42 – dc22
                        2008033904

ISBN 978-0-415-47804-5 (hbk)
ISBN 978-0-203-88262-7 (ebk)

Contents

Illustrations

Map

Tables

Acknowledgements

Several dozen interviews were carried out for this book on a non-attributable basis with policy-makers in Brussels, European capitals and a number of producer states: the author is grateful to all those who provided information and answered questions. Jos Boonstra, Ed Burke, Stuart Croft, Ana Echagüe, Christian Egenhofer, Michael Emerson, Amelia Hadfield, Giacomo Luciani, Neil Melvin, Gerd Nonneman, Natalia Shapovalova and Robert Springborg offered highly useful comments on different parts of the text. Ana Martiningui and Kimana Zulueta helped in preparing the text and tables. The author is grateful for funding from the German Marshall Fund and the European Commission for supporting energy-related research projects at FRIDE upon which this book draws.

Abbreviations

ACP	Africa, Caribbean and Pacific countries
AEI	Advanced Energy Initiative
AFRICOM	United States Africa Command
ALNG	Australian Liquefied Natural Gas
BP	British Petroleum
BTC	Baku–Tblisi–Ceyhan
BTE	Baku–Tblisi–Erzurum
CEO	chief executive officer
CFSP	Common Foreign and Security Policy
CITIC	China International Trust and Investment Corp
CNPC	China National Petroleum Corporation
CPC	Caspian Pipeline Consortium
CSR	corporate social responsibility
DCI	Development Cooperation Instrument
DfID	Department for International Development
DG RELEX	Directorate-General for External Relations
DG TREN	Directorate-General for Energy and Transport
EC	European Commission
ECT	Energy Charter Treaty
EDF	European Development Fund
EIB	European Investment Bank
EIDHR	European Initiative on Democracy and Human Rights
EIF	European Investment Fund
EITI	Extractive Industry Transparency Initiative
EMP	Euro-Mediterranean Partnership
ENP	European Neighbourhood Policy
ENPI	European Neighbourhood Partnership Instrument
EP	European Parliament
EPA	Economic Partnership Agreements
ESDP	European Security and Defence Policy
ESS	European Security Strategy
ETS	Emissions Trading Scheme
EU	European Union

FCO	Foreign and Commonwealth Office
FDI	foreign direct investment
FSB	Federal'naya Sluzhba Bezopasnosti
FTA	free trade agreement
GCC	Gulf Cooperation Council
GDP	gross domestic product
GGESS	Gulf of Guinea Energy Security Strategy
GNP	gross national product
IAEA	International Atomic Energy Agency
IEA	International Energy Agency
IMF	International Monetary Fund
IMU	Islamic Movement of Uzbekistan
IOC	international oil company
JESS	Joint Energy Security of Supply Working Group
KGB	Komityet Gosudarstvennoy Bezopasnosti
LNG	liquefied natural gas
MEDA	Mesures d'Accompagnement
MEDREG	Mediterranean Working Group on Electricity and Natural Gas
MEND	Movement for the Emancipation of the Niger Delta
MEP	Member of the European Parliament
MP	Member of Parliament
MNC	multinational corporation
MFN	most-favoured nations
MoU	memorandum of understanding
MPLA	Popular Movement for the Liberation of Angola – Party of Labour
NATO	North Atlantic Treaty Organization
NEGP	Northern European Gas Pipeline
NGO	non-governmental organization
NNPC	Nigerian National Petroleum Corporation
NOC	national oil company
NRCI	National Resistance Council of Iran
ODA	Official Development Assistance
OECD	Organization for Economic Cooperation and Development
OGP	oil and gas producers
OIDHR	Office for Democratic Institutions and Human Rights
OPEC	Organization of the Petroleum Exporting Countries
OSCE	Organization for Security and Cooperation in Europe
PCA	Partnership and Cooperation Agreement
PCD	Policy Coherence Development
PDP	People's Democratic Party
PDVSA	Petróleos de Venezuela Sociedad Anónima
PMOI	People's Mujahedeen Organization of Iran
PSA	production sharing agreement
RECAMP	Reinforcement of African Peace-Keeping Capabilities

SPDC	Shell Petroleum Development Company of Nigeria
SPLA	Sudan People's Liberation Army
SPLM	Sudan People's Liberation Movement
TACIS	Technical Aid to the Commonwealth of Independent States
TCA	Trade and Cooperation Agreement
TRACECA	Transport Corridor to Connect Europe via the Caucasus to Asia
UAE	United Arab Emirates
UNDP	United Nations Development Programme
UNICE	Union of Industrial and Employers' Confederations of Europe
UNITA	National Union for the Total Independence of Angola
US	United States
WMD	weapon of mass destruction
WTO	World Trade Organization

1 Introduction

After the attacks of 11 September 2001 (9/11) international relations were dominated by debates about terrorism and then by events in Iraq. However, while the West's strategic glance was thus preoccupied, the issue of energy security stole its way onto the international agenda. By the mid-2000s, many analysts and diplomats concurred that new concerns over energy security represented the most pre-eminent of international issues. This was a remarkable change from the decade following the 1991 Gulf War, in which Western diplomats had sanguinely 'paid very little attention to oil security issues'.[1] One respected analysis judged that 'oil has made a spectacular return to the international political agenda'.[2] The *Financial Times* observed, 'Energy security, a dead issue in the 1990s, has emerged as a pressing concern of governments and business'.[3]

The energy challenge

Concerns over energy security rose on the back of a number of events and trends. Oil and gas prices more than trebled between 2002 and 2007, peaking at over $140 a barrel during the summer of 2008, before dropping back to below $100 a barrel in the first week of September. The whittling down of spare production capacity made this the tightest oil market in three decades. Alarm bells sounded when California suffered a series of power blackouts. They intensified as the stand off between the West and Iran over the latter's nuclear programme led Tehran to threaten a cut in energy supplies. Attacks became more frequent and damaging on oil facilities in Nigeria, while politically driven interruptions increased to Venezuelan oil production. Iraq's slide into civil anarchy involved a failure to return the country's oil production levels even back to their modest Saddam-era levels. In 2005 Hurricane Katrina rendered inoperable significant amounts of US production capacity. Signalling a linkage with post-9/11 concerns, terrorist attacks on energy facilities were regularly threatened or rumoured.

In perhaps the most sobering episode for European policy-makers, in early 2006 Russia cut gas supplies to Ukraine in the midst of a dispute over pricing, causing a temporary 30 per cent decline in gas flows to European Union

(EU) states. Moscow then more than doubled gas prices to Georgia, and in January 2007 cut gas supplies through Belarus in relation to another pricing dispute, this time with President Lukashenko. In January 2008 a further dispute flared between Russia and Ukraine. Protests over high fuel prices took place in European cities in the early summer of 2008, before Russia's invasion of South Ossetia further intensified concerns.

Underlying these events, warnings grew louder that a peak of oil and gas production was imminent. Predictions of when 'peak oil' would occur differed, but it was widely agreed that beyond 2015 maintaining energy-supply levels would constitute an increasingly acute challenge. Experts also predicted an increasing concentration of supplies from countries with a high risk of internal instability – Russia, the Persian Gulf, Algeria and increasingly West Africa.[4] In 2005, of overall European Union gas supplies, 25 per cent came from Russia and 14 per cent from North Africa; of oil supplies, 31 per cent came from the Middle East and North Africa and 27 per cent from Russia. Variation existed between member states: France benefited from relatively low external dependency, for example, while 75 per cent of Spanish oil and gas supplies originated from unstable or undemocratic regimes.[5] In general, however, while reserves were set to decrease, demand for oil and gas was predicted to rise exponentially. It was estimated that in 2035 global energy consumption would be double that of 2005, with fast-developing economies such as those of China and India hungry for ever-increasing supplies of oil and gas. And all this while the imperative of slowing climate change pointed to exactly the opposite conclusion, that hydrocarbon consumption should be dramatically reduced.

In short, a combination of high oil prices, demand and supply trends and the nature of political developments in a number of crucial energy providers rendered energy security an urgent concern within European foreign-policy deliberations. The EU was already the world's largest importer of energy and there was widespread agreement that its external energy dependency would deepen. The EU's import dependency for oil was set to increase from 52 per cent in 2003 to 95 per cent in 2030, and for gas from 36 to 84 per cent over the same period.[6] In comparison, the US's energy import was predicted to rise more modestly to 60 per cent in 2025.[7] In absolute terms EU import requirements would double by 2030.[8] With North Sea production dwindling, the UK found itself on the brink of losing a hundred years of energy self-sufficiency, while the Dutch government also fretted over the prospect of a new external vulnerability. By 2007 European citizens listed climate change and energy dependency as their top two security concerns, above international terrorism.[9]

The International Energy Agency (IEA) estimated that $200 billion worth of investment per year – equivalent to 2 per cent of global gross domestic product – would be needed in increases to production capacity to meet energy requirements by 2030. It was also calculated that by 2012 the EU would face a 30 per cent shortfall in its gas-import requirements. In its January 2007

Strategic Energy Review the European Commission asserted that urgent action was needed to diversify energy supplies, in particular away from Russia and the Middle East and towards Central Asia and West Africa.[10]

Implications for European foreign policy

In March 2006 the European Commission issued a new Green Paper on energy security. This concluded that, 'Europe has entered into a new energy era' and that the 'increasing dependence on imports from unstable regions and suppliers presents a serious risk ... [with] some major producers and consumers ... using energy as a political lever'.[11] This paper asserted that growing concerns over international energy security required a rethink of some of the core aspects of European foreign policy in several areas of the world and lamented that hitherto European coordination on energy-related challenges had been negligible. Experts argued that incorporating the issue of future resource scarcity into a broader concept of security presented the EU with one of its most pressing foreign-policy challenges.[12] Energy policy required multi-faceted reforms *within* Europe itself – the development of renewable energy sources, reform of the internal EU energy market – but the need for a *foreign-policy* reassessment also occupied a prominent place in a series of new European strategy papers.

These commitments left open the question of exactly what form this foreign-policy reassessment would take. That is the issue addressed by this book, which charts the European Union's response to the challenge of energy security during the mid-2000s. The book focuses very specifically on the foreign-policy dimensions of energy security, as opposed to internal energy-market issues or the development of alternative and renewable sources of energy. It examines how the EU's general (proclaimed) approach to energy security played out in the specific political contexts of different producer countries and regions. It seeks to explain and illuminate such policy evolution through reference to both analytical explanations of the EU as a foreign-policy actor and broader international relations (and international political economy) frameworks.

In so doing, the book addresses six key questions:

- whether the energy security imperative in practice had a notable impact on European foreign policy, or in contrast drove the most notable changes in the internal aspects of energy policy;
- whether the pursuit of energy security strengthened or weakened cooperation between European governments;
- whether competition for energy security displaced quintessentially European 'soft power' approaches in favour of a drift back towards nineteenth-century style power politics;
- whether the EU exercised effective influence over international energy matters or conversely was increasingly sidelined by what some posited as

a new energy-driven 'Great Game' involving the United States, Russia and China as principal players;

- whether the conventional wisdom that energy security encourages consumer governments to be less critical of autocratic regimes indeed captured the way in which European foreign policy changed; and
- whether the priority attached to energy security accorded European oil multinationals greater influence over EU foreign policies.

Summary of findings

The book's analysis leads towards a number of main conclusions, related to these six main research concerns.

First, energy security did gain central importance to Common Foreign and Security Policy (CFSP) deliberations and many new initiatives took shape during the mid-2000s. At the same time many proposals for deepening cooperation were rejected by member states. Less attention was given to the foreign-policy dimensions of energy security than to the internal aspects of energy policy or climate change; indeed, tensions often arose between these different strands of energy strategy. The depth of commitment varied between regions; energy concerns had most impact on policy towards Russia, least on policy in Africa.

Second, energy engendered some high-profile divisions between member states. Some emergent dynamics of convergence were witnessed partly as a result of spill-over from internal European cooperation, partly in response to particularly acute external challenges linked to assertive producer state actions. However, the dynamics of socialization were more limited than in most other areas of CFSP coordination. The most conspicuous prioritization of national interests occurred in Russia, although undercutting and preferential bilateral deals were also a feature of policy in the Middle East, Central Asia and Africa.

Third, the EU stressed a strong commitment to market-based approaches to external energy security, and many of its policies did accord substance to this declared preference. At the same time, member-state behaviour became more geopolitical and cut across some of the basic principles enshrined within internal market rules. The EU eschewed a hard-power securitization of its energy policies, but neither was its strategy confined to a replication of 'market-governance' or soft-power norms and values.

Fourth, across the different producer regions the EU struggled to match the US's direct security engagement, while it also risked losing out to rising powers such as China. In some places – especially in Sub-Saharan Africa – the EU remained slow to react to this increased strategic competition. In other areas, the EU's weak influence owed more to competing powers such as China and Russia out-competing Europe by providing more direct political benefits to producer states.

Fifth, the EU proclaimed an approach to energy security predicated on support for governance reforms in producer states. In practice, it was highly inconsistent on this issue. There were clear cases where energy interests overrode support for democracy and human rights reforms. In other instances, the focus on governance transparency increased as a result of energy concerns. In general, however, the most striking feature was the extent to which energy- and democracy-related decisions were disconnected from each other.

Sixth, European energy companies were not highly engaged in the development of EU external energy-related policies and many remained ambivalent about what a Europeanized strategy could provide in terms of short-term concrete benefit. Energy companies most commonly espoused free-market solutions, which pushing in practice for their own preferential long-term deals and geopolitical backing from national governments. Oil companies came to support the export of EU governance standards to producer states as a means of facilitating their own exploration and production, but the quality of democratic process in these countries played no determinant role in investments decisions or in lobbying efforts at the EU level.

As debates on energy have raged, the issue of energy security has remained virtually absent from studies of EU foreign policy. Standard volumes on CFSP or EU security policy have offered little systematic coverage of energy security.[13] There appears to be an increasing mismatch between intensifying concerns over energy at the policy level and the paucity of its coverage in academic studies of EU foreign and security policy. Energy security remains a subject studied by energy (political) economists, and not integrated into the normal purview of work on CFSP; and where it is addressed as a foreign-policy concern it increasingly tends to be through a Russia-specific lens. This book aims to correct these shortcomings, and better link the energy and CFSP debates. The following chapter introduces the main analytical debates relevant to this aim, before the details of EU energy policies are examined across the main producer countries and regions.

2 Concepts of energy security and EU foreign policy

This book's focus on European approaches to energy security bridges three areas of debate. First, it relates to and draws from debates that juxtapose market-based and geopolitical strategies – debates that in turn have relevance for the broader analytical frameworks of international relations and international political economy. Second, a central focus is on the relationship between energy security and producer states' structures of governance. And third, the book contributes to longstanding debates over the European Union's (EU) characteristics as an international actor. A central aim of the book is to link together these three areas of analysis that have invariably been pursued as very separate areas of enquiry. This introductory chapter introduces these three areas of deliberation, in order to provide a framework for the subsequent detailed assessment of European energy policies in different producer states and regions. In outlining the 'state of the art' in debates over 'markets versus geopolitics', energy and governance, and EU foreign-policy coordination, the chapter suggests that a number of core questions remain undetermined – and thus guide this book's analysis of EU energy security strategies.

Markets and geopolitics

As concerns over energy security intensified, it was suggested that debate amongst energy experts could be structured around two alternative 'story-lines', that of 'markets and institutions' and that of 'regions and empires'.[1] From the former perspective, many energy analysts argued that the key change since the oil crises of the 1970s had been the growing role of international markets. Some experts judged that the international energy economy had been fundamentally transformed by the expansion of commodity and financial markets, rendering oil more susceptible to market dynamics than to the hitherto politically influenced oligopolistic linkages between producer states, consumer governments and energy national champions.[2] In 2001, one much-cited study asserted that the gradual development of 'a connected set of commodity markets where competition is the rule and economics works' had made obsolete the geopolitics that dominated energy security thinking in the 1970s and 1980s. Bilateral deals between govern-ments to guarantee supply were a thing of the past, and the imbalance of power was if anything now to the disfavour of exporting states. Consequently, these experts concluded, 'energy security' in a 1970s-geopolitical sense was now 'a footnote ... an empty phrase', as archaic as 'medieval mystery plays'.[3]

Mitigating some of the fear over energy insecurity, those with a faith in market mechanisms argued that post-2003 high oil prices were the result of a 'catching-up' after two decades of declining demand for oil, and that these high prices would in their turn engender changes in government policies and consumer behaviour, as substitution strategies took shape. Future prices would be less stable, but the key was to find mechanisms to temper the nat-ural ebb and flow of market adjustment. It was suggested that the commonly used image of an imminent 'oil peak' – the source of so many energy secur-ity worries – was mistaken. Rather, the extent of 'reserves' depended on price: the more prices rose the more reserves would become economically recoverable. Oil would not suddenly run out, as market corrections would occur well before serious depletion came about. It was more likely that a more or less sustainable 'plateau' of oil production would be reached.[4] For some trenchant critics the geopolitical panic associated with 'peak oil' was based on a Malthusian-like error of 'geological determinism'; a failure to recognize that a natural resource 'frontier' had always existed; and some highly imprecise methods for calculating reserves.[5] Some analysts recalled that in the 1970s there were predictions that oil production would peak around 2000, but then market development, new discoveries and technolo-gical advances had fostered two (apparently) benign decades in energy security.

An important factor underlying the pertinence of market dynamics was the incipient development of international gas markets. Hitherto gas prices had largely tracked oil prices, but as gas became a more staple fuel the pro-spect arose of more competitive international gas markets developing, with gas 'disconnecting' itself from oil markets and developing at the expense of oil to a far greater extent. As gas moved from being a marginal to central fuel there would likely be a shift from regionally isolated to internationally interdependent gas markets, exposing both producing and consuming states to shocks in any other part of the system. Traditional 'point-to-point' approaches, focusing on bilateral supply relationships, would prove increas-ingly less effective as gas markets came to resemble the current commodity oil market.[6] Many saw the incipient development of Liquefied Natural Gas (LNG) as already engendering market-based dynamics within the gas sector.[7]

Some experts argued sanguinely that, 'Policies of reducing import depen-dence are unnecessary' and advocated 'market-extending energy policies'. They offered the comfort that, 'Economics will protect consumers against extortionate prices' and the political use of national energy resources.[8] Oil was a fungible commodity, for which markets cleared at a common price.[9] Even those stressing that the geopolitical dimension of energy security required

a more comprehensive approach, including enhanced surveillance and protection of transport routes, most centrally cautioned against the growing
tendency to 'micromanage markets in the face of political pressure'.[10] Free
trade consequently represented the 'best route to national energy security for
most countries'. Most critical for security was the general health of the world
trading system, not its 'specifically ... energy component'. The US was in a
unique position, as guarantor of last resort for international security, and
hence its policy mix would have to include a 'hard security' element. For other
(and especially European) states the US's own dependence on guaranteeing
the international market was the guarantee of their own security.[11]

It was argued that market-based solutions would involve international
coordination, based around international good governance standards, multilateral institutions and cooperation. With supplies locked into international
markets, the loss in foreign-policy manoeuvrability would be relatively limited. The political challenge was the more subtle one of designing policies
that would encourage competition without discouraging long-term investment in infrastructure and productive capacity. Consumer states would need
primarily to avoid conflating policies aimed at the security of the international market *system* with efforts simply to increase their own investment
opportunities in producer states – it was such an error that would unnecessarily
politicize energy security by leaving producer states frustratingly feeling that
they were the targets of others' energy strategies, while enjoying little say over
the redesign of multilateral architecture.[12]

In contrast to this emphasis on international markets, other analysts suggested that the defining change to energy security was – and would increasingly be – its *geopolitical* dimension. The 'regions and empires' storyline would
place greater stress on strategic alliances; the search for 'exclusive backyards';
military power to protect supplies; intra-Western rivalry and undercutting;
and Western oil companies taking control of production capacity through
buy outs and mergers in producer states.[13]

A common theme of analysis within the geopolitical storyline was the suggestion that Western consumer countries had long neglected systematically
to incorporate energy security concerns into the design of their foreign
policies. They had, it was widely claimed, been lulled into a false sense of
complacency by the international oil markets that had been benign for consumers since the 1980s. The gradual politicization of energy had consequently
gone unnoticed. In 1998 it was the severe dip in oil prices that had triggered
protests, political instability and even regime changes in Nigeria, Indonesia
and Venezuela. These were the roots of sellers' more aggressive postures less
than a decade later, and the introduction of more political dynamics into the
panorama of energy security.

As one analyst averred, it constituted 'a huge leap of faith to assume that
since markets functioned in 1990, they will be able to cope with a future
crisis in today's changing political backdrop'.[14] It was widely pointed out
that markets suffered from the twin problems of 'inertia' – oil producers have

such high sunk costs that they are slow to respond to price signals that should encourage them expeditiously to switch away from hydrocarbons – and 'hidden costs' – ranging from environmental impacts to the cost of maintaining military protection for production sites and pipelines – that are not reflected in the market prices for oil and gas.

It was suggested that geopolitics became pivotal in the absence of any agreement on the basic 'governance structure' of international energy, meaning that 'the conflict-laden history of international oil in the twentieth century [was] bound to continue'.[15] Moreover, one critic opined that Western states were still in practice not inclined seriously to act to reduce external energy dependencies and hydrocarbon consumption, and that 'energy security' continued to be understood in terms of securing alliances with producer states that were more favourable than those struck by competitor consumer states.[16]

Some analysts suggested that the new feature of energy security by the mid-2000s was that 'circumstances [could now] be imagined in which supply and demand will not balance in a desirable manner'. Actions of producers, as well as competitor purchasers such as China, were increasingly linked to the broader geopolitical context. Many producer states rejected the democratic norms of the Western-dominated international system and tended towards a philosophy of 'weak globalization'. Producers' move away from market-based solutions was hastened by the rising demand for energy of China and India, with whom secure deals could now be sown up circumventing 'Western norms'.[17] An emerging 'Asia–Gulf nexus' might increasingly be expected to 'spawn political dimensions'.[18] The West would have to reverse powerful current trends to ensure that China and India veered towards cooperative solutions, based on international markets, rather than mercantalism and zero-sum competition.[19]

In short, it was argued that energy policy could not be understood other than in the context of an emerging 'quadripolar' world, divided between US, European, Asian and Middle Eastern power blocs.[20] These geopolitical realities were compounded by the growing concentration of energy supplies. After 2010, growth in oil supplies would come from a much smaller number of states, ensuring conditions distorting of free-market dynamics. Just four states, Russia, Iran, Turkmenistan and Qatar, accounted for more than half global gas reserves. Many doubted the extent to which gas would be subjected to market dynamics, with fixed, structural dependence on a small number of producers actually increasing – particularly in the cases of Russia and Algeria – and lamented that the much heralded take-off of LNGs was proving illusive. Indeed, at the end of 2007 nearly all LNG was being traded on the basis of long-term contracts, shadowing the standard oil and gas market.[21] The implications of such concentrated dependency led one high-level report to warn that the US administration had retreated too much from the energy sector, leaving decisions to de-monopolized private companies when a more 'comprehensive strategic approach' needed to be pursued through national champions.[22]

Another deepening concern was with 'energy poverty' in the third world engendering resource-related conflict. The more the West sought to take energy supplies out of the third world, in pursuit of its own supposed energy security, the worse this poverty and tension would become. In short, geopolitical tension might grow in the event of either of two outcomes: if developing countries did grow and gain access to energy then global reserves would not be sufficient; if they did not gain access to supplies then energy-related conflict was likely to be a feature of future international relations.

In consequence of all these political factors, by the mid-2000s it was commonly predicted that energy would henceforth have much greater impact on foreign policy. One noted expert warned that the current 'paradigm of energy security is too limited and must be expanded to include many new factors ... energy security does not stand by itself but is lodged in the larger relations among nations and how they interact with one another'.[23] Another cautioned that the challenge could no longer be addressed only through energy-specific policies but must rather be related to broader foreign policy, including through an understanding of how internal market liberalization within the West itself conditioned this external dimension.[24]

Energy, governance and the multinationals

A vitally important question cut across the markets and geopolitical story-lines: what was the relationship between Western energy interests and political developments in producer states? It was widely suggested that a central aspect of the geopolitical dimension would be a diminishing Western focus on human rights and democracy. Received wisdom was that oil and democracy appeared not to mix. No major oil and gas producer in the developing world was a consolidated democracy, and all had levels of corruption disproportionately high for their respective levels of development. The presence of oil and gas reserves were associated with weak state structures, the over-centralization of executive power, higher military spending, and a natural resource dependency that militated against broader social and economic modernization.[25] According to one study, oil hindered democracy by both facilitating repression and choking modernization.[26]

The well-established 'rentier state' argument had both a demand and supply logic: first, oil income meant that regimes did not have to raise revenues from their citizens; second, it meant citizens could be bought off for disenfranchisement with oil largesse. One trenchant view was that a 'first law of petropolitics' determined that 'the price of oil and the pace of freedom always move in opposite directions in oil-rich petrolist states'. It was suggested that those Arab states that had liberalized to some degree were precisely those with the least oil. With energy prices rising and supplies dwindling, the 'tide of democratization that followed the fall of the Berlin Wall seem[ed] to have met its match in the black tide of petro-authoritarianism'.[27]

Table 2.1 Political and civil rights in key producer states (Freedom House scores 2007)

Producer	Political rights	Civil rights	Status
Algeria	6	5	Not free
Angola	6	5	Not free
Azerbaijan	6	5	Not free
Cameroon	6	6	Not free
Chad	6	6	Not free
Colombia	3	3	Partially free
Congo	6	5	Not free
Egypt	6	5	Not free
Equatorial Guinea	7	6	Not free
Gabon	6	4	Partially free
Iran	6	6	Not free
Iraq	6	6	Not free
Kazakhstan	6	5	Not free
Kuwait	4	4	Partially free
Libya	7	7	Not free
Nigeria	4	4	Partially free
Oman	6	5	Not free
Qatar	6	5	Not free
Russia	6	5	Not free
Saudi Arabia	7	6	Not free
Sudan	7	7	Not free
Turkmenistan	7	7	Not free
United Arab Emirates	6	5	Not free
Uzbekistan	7	7	Not free
Venezuela	4	4	Partially free
Averages	5.9	5.2	

Source: Freedom House 2007

The standard critical view was that any Western commitment to support democracy and human rights in producer states was entirely disingenuous. And even where the West did focus on such values it was only as a cloak for pursuing oil interests. So, for example critics argued that Western action against president Milosevic in the 1990s was a calculated strategy of freeing the way for pipelines across the Balkans from Russia; that a peace deal in Sudan was 'imposed' by the West in such a way as to facilitate international access to oil in the south of the country; that removing the Taleban was also really about opening new pipeline routes; and that new pro-democracy policies in the Middle East were no more than a ruse for 'US and British control of world oil and gas assets'.[28]

One view was that producer states' more aggressive push for higher oil prices was the result of too much political liberalization already having emerged in leading Organization of Petroleum Exporting Countries (OPEC) states.[29] The US's imposition of sanctions against producing states for other foreign-policy objectives was now seen as an 'outmoded' policy, no longer viable with the demise of slack oil markets.[30] The whole democracy-spreading agenda stood in precarious limbo confronted with Russian and Chinese strategies to block Western democracy assistance; the apparently strong economic performance of semi-autocratic regimes; and doubts over whether Western democracy support now enjoyed any meaningful leverage. If the 'victory' of Western liberal values had been too easily assumed in the 1990s, many now observed a more finely balanced, and unresolved, battle between 'state-based pluralism' and the notion of global normative values.[31] Others saw the 'utopianism' of the democracy agenda as already comprehensively defeated and power 'floating away' from Western liberal states as 'ongoing resource war' loomed.[32]

However, another side of this argument was that sustainable energy security required a greater, not diminished, focus on political reform in producer states. It was argued that over the longer term, indeed, producer and consumer countries would have a common interest in stable and predictable international markets. Neither were consumer countries quite so powerless to encourage democratic reform in producer states: many pointed out that leverage was more balanced between consumer and producer countries due to the latter's increasing search for 'security of demand'.

For some experts, the kind of durable stability needed for energy security would be best guaranteed through greater political accountability in the still largely autocratic producer states, to the extent that conflict over the distribution of oil revenues tended to be greater where governance systems were weaker.[33] Stability in energy supply for the EU would, it was asserted, depend upon the 'comprehensiveness of political participation in the periphery countries'.[34] Regimes' distribution of oil rent – invariably seen as the disincentive to democratic change in oil-rich states – clearly had not sufficed to 'buy off' popular discontent in, for example, Middle Eastern producer states, where growing numbers of people agitated for political liberalization. In countries such as Iran, Venezuela, Nigeria and Algeria authoritarian populism had produced spurts of public spending that were the root of instability. Autocratic regimes in producer states had increasingly subsidized domestic fuel prices to shore up their own legitimacy, this limiting export capacity.[35] Whatever the uncertainties of democratic change, recent history showed that prioritizing strategic bilateral relationships with autocratic regimes, to the detriment of more open governance and multilateral commitments, was no guarantor of energy security.[36]

Additionally, to the extent that energy poverty and conflict over natural resources fed into the mix of factors engendering 'failing states', their mitigation became a matter of self-interest for Western powers. Such conflicts were judged to raise the spectre of increasingly prevalent 'new oil wars'. These were distinct from the 'old oil wars' in which the Great Powers battled between themselves for control over energy producing territories. Instead, the 'new oil wars' were drawing international actors into producer states' internal conflicts in an aim to stem the instability prejudicial to their own strategic interests. In this sense, the state-building agenda would increasingly form part of the energy security calculus, it was argued.[37] It was suggested that governance reforms were necessary to stem the increasingly common phenomenon of insurgencies being sustained and motivated by the theft of oil resources.[38]

Still others doubted that political conditions counted for very much one way or the other. Oil was a cyclical product with high production costs and long maturity periods, beyond the vagaries of short-term politics. Periods of over-investment were followed by periods of under-investment as dictated by market prices: prices rose after 2002–3 because of the lack of investment in the 1990s, when prices were low. Some experts asserted that the economic needs and interdependencies of producer states would mean that changes in governments or even regimes would have little impact on energy policies – whichever 'side' the West backed and whether it had a military presence or not in oil producing regions.[39]

Significantly, traditional international relations analytical frameworks – corresponding closely to each side of the markets-geopolitics divide – left underdetermined this relationship between energy interests and producer states' governance structures. The traditional realist vision would be of Western states seeking to 'counterbalance' the rise of powerful new producer states; more 'defensive' forms of realism favoured by some theorists might predict rather a 'bandwagoning' with such countries. Neither version saw important impact deriving from variation in producer countries' domestic political structures. Analysis based on market-interdependency either saw international cooperation as most important, regardless of states' internal political systems; or assumed that interdependence would be managed around universally accepted governance standards. In short, from both analytical perspectives the relationship between democracy and international energy security merited further specification.

These issues were in turn closely related to the role and interests of Western oil companies. The latter were routinely seen as primarily responsible for undermining human rights and democracy, and as a determining influence over Western energy-related foreign policies. Debates indeed continued over the influence exerted by multinationals on 'home' government foreign policies. Strikingly, however, issues related to the strategic perspectives and actions of European multinational corporations (MNCs) have not formed any notably central part of work on EU foreign-policy cooperation. More general conceptual frameworks have either pointed to the increasing diplomatic-strategic significance of the private sector; or suggested that collective action problems associated with MNCs continue to give governments the stronger bargaining power.[40] But, in the analysis of EU foreign-policy dynamics, the application and exploration of such dynamics has been conspicuously absent.

In respect of energy, some analysts predicted that MNCs' role was set to become increasingly important, in the correction of capacity shortfalls. With the exception of Saudi Aramco, no national (producer state) oil company had a good record in exploration or development, their resources having been dispersed across a wide range of politically-motivated activities and not focused in an efficient way on increasing production capacity.[41] The future would, consequently, see further moves towards big, international energy companies, with weaker national bases, and this would ensure that 'infrastructure development [would] increasingly be driven by commercial interests rather than national energy security objectives'.[42]

One common view argued that MNCs had pushed Western governments into supporting the emergence of 'low intensity' or 'limited' democracy in developing markets. Companies enjoyed the formal trappings of democracy, while these regimes retained overwhelming state power that was used to pursue liberalization and create amenable investment conditions for foreign capital. Limited democracy, or in some cases liberalized authoritarianism, was perceived to combine stability and control over anti-market elements, on the one hand, with clear rules-based economies, on the other hand.[43] Others saw international business as a more positive force for democratic development, as MNCs searched for more transparent and predictable political environments, better-educated workforces and more open sources of information. Some statistical studies suggested that institutional transparency and respect for human rights were positively correlated to the size of host countries' foreign direct investment (FDI) receipts.[44]

One study concluded that MNCs had since the 1990s not in practice been strongly engaged in determining geopolitical strategies related to good governance questions, often unsure how their own interests related to political structures in host countries. Significant variation existed between different firms and between private-sector actions in different host countries: in some states, some MNCs clearly sought to prop up authoritarian regimes; in others, the low intensity democracy thesis was more apposite; while in some markets, some firms judged that their interests would be better served by more transparent and predictable, high-quality democracy.[45]

These debates spoke to the question of *whose* interests lay behind the advocacy of different energy security strategies. Had energy security constraints been pushed onto the agenda – and possibly exaggerated – by private-sector actors seeking foreign-policy changes to shore up their own narrow commercial interests? Market discourses were, in this sense, increasingly interrogated by more critical analysts. For some, certain economic and political interests had been empowered through a discourse emphasizing the deepening of international constraints, this deployed as a means of making particular EU-level policy responses more likely.[46] Globalization and market discourse were to this end themselves used as 'soft' geopolitics.[47] Others saw the key role as being played by transgovernmental networks of technocrats that had pushed forward the agendas of cross-border regulatory harmonization in different sectors in a way that 'disaggregated' the whole notion of national interests.[48]

In sum, an over-arching 'markets versus geopolitics' debate was ongoing and intensified as energy security climbed the list of foreign-policy priorities. It remained unclear exactly how this debate related to the contested linkage between Western energy interests, on the one hand, and the nature of governance in producer states, on the other hand. These areas of debate raised a set of strategy-related questions for international energy security; at a level more specific to the European Union, the question was how they related to the characteristics and development of the Common Foreign and Security Policy (CFSP).

Europe as international energy actor

Where did European policies fit in this conceptual panorama? What kind of international energy actor was the EU emerging as, and towards which story-line would we expect the EU to approximate? How did the EU conceive the relationship between democratic norms and security-commercial interests?

The early history of European energy strategies was imbued with very obvious geopolitical dimensions. Much of military strategy in the two world wars was conditioned by the need to secure oil supplies. This was why, for instance, the battle at El Alamein in Egypt was so pivotal to the course of World War II. In 1953, it was Prime Minister Mohammed Mossadeq's attempt to nationalize the Anglo-Persian Oil Company that triggered British involvement in the CIA-orchestrated coup in Iran. Oil also lay behind the Anglo-French Suez intervention in 1956: Nasser's nationalization of the Suez Canal threatened to double the distance of supply routes from the Persian Gulf to Europe.

Fierce transatlantic competition over energy supplies also had a long history. Shell and Royal Dutch joined forces in 1903 specifically to compete against US giant Standard Oil.[49] Standard Oil in turn fought against its exclusion from contracts awarded on a privileged basis within the confines of European colonial structures. The UK's manoeuvres to block US access to its Middle Eastern territories occasioned some of the most serious differences between London and Washington, with particularly bitter rivalry ensuing in Saudi Arabia in the immediate aftermath of the Second World War. Baku had been the site of some of the earliest and most vicious competition, from the battle between the Rockefellers, Nobels and Rothschilds in the initial oil boom of the late 1800s until the city was 'lost' to the West as a result of the Russian revolution.

Energy security had also been a highly divisive issue in the early days of European foreign policy cooperation. The international oil politics of the 1970s had driven debilitating wedges between European states, when OPEC reduced supplies to Germany and the Netherlands for being 'too soft' on Israel, while Arab states successfully courted France as counter-balance both to these two European governments and to the United States.

Notwithstanding this long history of division and often violent struggle to protect European access to energy supplies, by the end of the twentieth century much debate focused on the claim that the EU had developed into an international actor that was quintessentially civilian and which had transcended traditional power politics. One influential study asserted that while the US had moved to a 'regions and empires' approach to energy policy, the EU was wedded to the 'markets and institutions' framework.[50] Yet it also predicted that, faced with the new imperative of energy security, member states would increasingly 'break ranks' and engage in mercantile geopolitics, prioritizing their own 'well-to-pump' partnerships with producer governments and oil companies.[51] To the extent that such predictions were made with little detailed substantiation, it was necessary to marry debates over energy security to a fuller appreciation of the EU's characteristics as a foreign-policy actor.

Economic and trade instruments were the core of European power. The EU had become a tough, united and effective trade negotiator. Its international projection was founded upon a powerful and increasingly integrated business sector. The euro was increasingly establishing itself as an international currency. And after enlargement to 25 member states in 2004 (and to 27 in 2007) the EU became the world's largest single economic space.

Of crucial relevance to international energy policy, the EU was widely seen as predisposed towards the export of economic and regulatory norms, as its key means of influence in pursuit of foreign-policy objectives. Reflecting its own experience of market integration, the EU had assumed a lead role in developing a 'deep' trade agenda that sought to address 'behind-the-border' issues by seeking agreements on the making of domestic rules over investment and regulation in non-European states.[52] The EU itself was about the transposing of laws into different national contexts, giving EU foreign policy a tendency to replicate the same logic externally. The influential concept of 'EU external governance' captured this notion of the EU seeking to transfer its own rules and legal norms to other countries and organizations as a form of 'external Europeanization'.[53] It was suggested that energy policy fitted such a model, to the extent that the EU sought to export internal market rules as a means 'to liberate energy supply from the control ... of unstable elites and cartels'.[54]

From a different perspective to such rationalist explanations, increasingly heard was the contention that the EU's unity and international influence derived from its representing a set of values rather than from a purposive set of strategies adopted in pursuit of material self-interest. One writer described the EU as an emergent 'liberal superpower', whose 'latent power' – or power by example and positive incentive – rendered it more in tune with a 'postmodern international system': the post-material EU had, it was held, 'rejected realist interpretations of the international system' and represented 'the new pole in a post-modern bipolar international order'.[55] The increasing tendency to posit the EU as a 'deliberative' political space suggested that strategies for material self-interest had to be argued out in terms of embedded norms, identities and principles.[56] For one theorist, European foreign-policy cooperation could in this sense be explained as an international 'civilizing process'.[57] The EU was said to be instinctively drawn to 'search for settled frameworks', mirroring its own internal cooperation.[58]

Many analysts were concerned with showing how European influence and unity flowed from the fact that the EU had become an international actor that could not be fully explained through material interest-driven rationalism – either in terms of the dynamics that governed its internal coordination or the nature of its external policy preferences. Conceptual accounts of European foreign policy cooperation most commonly argued that the EU's Common Foreign and Security Policy had come to transcend the minimalist cooperation of realist bargaining between member states, and was rather subject to the dynamics of normative socialization and discursive persuasion.

From this perspective, analysts argued that national interests were now 'constructed' within common EU forums and constantly adapted to a dynamic of 'shared problem solving', as opposed to being separately predetermined and fought out within standard realist-style competitive negotiation. This, analysts contended, had generated a process of 'social learning', underpinning the emergence of common European identity.[59] 'Institutionalization' had exerted 'an almost insidious impact on the way EU states define and pursue their foreign policies', creating a 'social rule' that militated against defections from common positions.[60] From the different perspective of foreign-policy analysis, the CFSP, national foreign policies and Commission-managed economic dimensions of EU external dimensions were seen as increasingly moulded together in a deeply interconnected 'European foreign policy system'.[61] In short, security was seen as increasingly defined in common European terms, in accordance with internally embedded EU norms.

Increasingly, the concept of governance, used to explain the convergent impact of loose and non-hierarchical policy networks in the European Union, was extended to the analysis of CFSP.[62] Indeed, it was specifically suggested that the concept of 'security governance' could be employed to explain European policies, with security strategies reflecting the both formal and informal coordination between multiple (including private) actors, structured by discourse and norms. Experts asserted that, 'the European level is emerging as a necessary framework for the elaboration of security policy, without this necessarily implying integration as traditionally understood', to the extent that, '[t]he Europeanization of security has been the great political revolution of the late twentieth and early twenty-first centuries'.[63] Crucial to the concept of security governance was the notion of the EU seeking to draw 'outsiders' into its own networks, in contrast to the firm inclusion–exclusion dichotomy of traditional approaches to security.[64]

Traditionally concerned with explaining the paucity of European unity, neo-realists also increasingly suggested reasons why deepening EU cooperation could be traced to reasons of instrumental self-interest – tying down Germany, counteracting US hegemony, gaining influence for small states. Complementing the dynamics of socialization, it was argued that national governments had engaged in 'collusive delegation', themselves seeing merit in centralizing foreign-policy decisions at the European level as a means of eluding domestic responsibility for difficult policy choices.[65] To some analysts, realism and institutionalization increasingly pulled in the same direction towards European cooperation, around established patterns of EU interaction with the international system and global economy – even if neorealist accounts still struggled to capture the depth and institutionalization of foreign-policy cooperation that had developed within the European Union.[66]

Other analysts placed emphasis on how the EU was itself heading slowly towards adopting a more military strategic culture. The first European Security Strategy (ESS) agreed in December 2003 committed the EU to 'rapid ... and robust intervention'[67] where necessary for its own security. The European Security and Defence Policy (ESDP) was by the mid-2000s moving, if somewhat haltingly, towards strengthening coordinated military capabilities. In 2005 a European Defence Agency was created, and Spain, Italy, France, Portugal and the Netherlands agreed to set up a European gendarmerie force. By 2008 17 ESDP missions had been undertaken and rapidly deployable 'battle-groups' became operational in 2007. The EU's overall military spend rose to nearly $250 billion a year. One expert argued that the EU's claim to be a distinctive 'normative power' had weakened after 9/11, with a drift towards 'martial potency' reflecting member states' increasing view of EU collaboration as a route to their becoming 'bigger and better great powers'.[68] A prominent realist view saw the ESS as driven by an aim to strengthen European international presence through militarization. One analyst argued that realist impulses were pre-eminent in the incipient development of ESDP, with national governments motivated to cooperate in order to enhance 'coalitional coercive diplomacy'.[69] By 2008 French president Nicolas Sarkozy was pushing for ESDP to enshrine a commitment to collective defence and for a revamped European Security Strategy capable of enhancing the projection of European strategic power.[70] One of the most influential EU foreign-policy diplomats famously pushed the EU to acknowledge that the 'laws of the jungle' ruled beyond its own 'post-modern' paradise, requiring more geopolitical forms of engagement.[71]

Many critics increasingly condemned the EU's espousal of democratic norms as a new form of geopolitical 'imperialism' rather than welcoming its positive ethical potential. Some contended that the EU's 'civilian power' increasingly resembled 'soft imperialism', or a form of 'soft power applied in a hard way', under whose cloak asymmetrically applied norms were a strategy of rationalized self-interest.[72] One analyst argued that many EU actions looked like the 'prototype of imperial politics', with power and control being pursued through a 'neo-medieval' rather than 'neo-Westphalian' form of empire: that is, one focused on the conditioned strengthening of governance in weak states rather than the counter-balancing of strong states.[73] The *Wall Street Journal* termed the EU's aim to extend its own legal and administrative structures 'regulatory imperialism'.[74]

One critic railed against the easy assumption that 'what is good for Europe is good for the world' and argued that, contrary to much normative rhetoric, European foreign policy was in practice still determined by the structural constraints of the international system.[75] For another analyst, the EU's legal *acquis* was self-servingly kept 'unsettled and flexible' to be more useful as a means of furthering the Union's external foreign-policy goals.[76] There might then be bilateral political negotiations with third-country states around a degree of 'mutual adaptation' necessary to strike a more politically flavoured deal on the incorporation of some elements of EU legislation.[77] It was pointed out that European governments had often constructed commitments to 'norms' in a way that favoured their own respective former colonies and 'client' states.[78]

Fiercer competition was also predicted with the United States, with the Cold War strategic umbrella no longer mitigating transatlantic tensions as it had after the 1970s oil shocks.[79] Indeed, the broader development of autonomous European security capacity was interpreted as one of the most striking cases of 'leash-slipping', a new form of counter-balancing US hegemony not through hard power confrontation but through differentiated approaches to global challenges.[80] An interesting variation on these geopolitical arguments suggested that the EU was being – and indeed should be – drawn to its own distinctive model of a regional 'geo-energy space', within which energy issues were addressed through strategic and formalized alliances with producer states on Europe's periphery, this in preference to pure market principles.[81] Conversely, despite growing anti-American rhetoric, some analysts suggested that the EU was in practice increasingly beholden to the US's hard security power in places such as the Middle East and Central Asia being deployed to safeguard the interests of the market-democracy West as a whole.[82]

In sum, the view was increasingly prevalent that European foreign policies were conditioned by a powerful convergence of preferences and normative identities; while other experts observed an incipient trend towards more instrumental, hard-power strategies. In fact it was striking that such conceptual debates over European 'actorness' rarely shed light specifically on approaches to energy security. Analysts of European foreign policy increasingly lamented that the 'to militarize or not to militarize' question had obscured a focus on the deeper and more pervasive changes in the nature of EU power. Debates applying different analytical explanations to the supposed emergence of a common European 'strategic culture' overwhelmingly took the latter concept to refer solely to the conditions and legitimacy of military intervention.[83] It was noted that in both analysis and formal institutional development, ESDP had been 'fenced off' from the broader challenges of European security.[84] General studies of European security typically identified energy security as a key challenge but then entirely excluded the topic from their own remit.[85]

Debates were still most commonly framed around the aged concept of 'civilian power' when this provided little analytical guidance to the relationship between EU instruments and the new complexities of international challenges.[86] This in turn reflected a traditional tendency to conceive the development of European foreign policy as a sui generis and self-contained domain unduly neglecting its increasing meshing with broader trends in international relations.[87] Analysis of European foreign policy often seemed fixated with the longstanding question of how to define the nature of the EU as a political body, rather than with critically assessing the substantive European contribution to concrete international challenges.

Conclusion

The implications of these three areas of on-going debate – markets versus geopolitics; energy and governance; and the EU's nature as a foreign policy actor – for the evolution of energy security strategies remained distinctly unclear. A key question was whether energy security imperatives would indeed push the EU back towards a realist-style prioritization of exogenous material interests and undermine its oft-proclaimed distinctiveness from the United States. For some, the structural underpinnings of realism were likely to militate against European cooperation, while others saw them as pushing EU member states into deeper, self-protecting coordination. EU coordination would in the future be both more necessary, to protect individual governments from supply uncertainty, and more difficult to achieve, due to an increasing asymmetry of 'energy exposure' between different European economies.[88] With a variety of security paths now opening up vis-à-vis the United States, the ramifications were unclear for (what some still saw as) the whole normative justification for European coordination as counterbalance to US strategies.[89] Indeed, energy security was but one issue caught in the broader, identity-related competition between 'Euroatlanticism' and 'Eurogaullism'.[90]

In conclusion, it is from these conceptual debates that the cluster of questions emerges that forms the central subject matter of this book:

1   Was energy really set to become a priority for CFSP? Or was it the internal dimensions of energy security that were addressed with greater urgency?
2   Would EU policies be based on constructed norms, of economic and political values? Was EU policy more like the 'markets and institutions' storyline, or that of 'regions and empire'?
3   Was the EU united as an international actor in this sphere? Did it act as a united security community, each member state concerned to advance the energy security of other EU countries? And if so, was it united around a common European orientation towards 'soft power' and norms-oriented approaches? Or would internal divisions grow, and this lead to no more than shallow and sporadic cooperation on external energy strategy?
4   Would, in contrast, realism dictate growing EU unity around more strategic power, and this diminish the defence of human rights and democratic

values? Has the challenge of energy security indeed led to a more undiluted dynamic of alliance-building with authoritarian regimes?

5 Would the EU have the capacity at all to rival the US and other powers in the field of energy security?

6 What role did European oil companies play in the evolution of EU energy policy? Were European MNCs part of a 'security governance network', or excluded and/or at odds with CFSP diplomacy?

The book proceeds to offer a general overview of new European energy initiatives, investigating the latter's balance between market and geopolitical philosophies; the degree of unity between member states over key policy developments; and the relationship between energy strategy and support for democratic governance in producer states – the three issues outlined in this chapter. The book then examines each of these questions in greater detail in studies of EU policies in four countries/regions, namely the Middle East, Russia, Central Asia and the Caucasus, and Sub-Saharan Africa. The account then focuses on the role played in recent policy changes by the major European energy companies, before a final assessment is offered of Europe's evolving external policies of energy security. Each regional/country case study is structured around the three areas of debate explored in this chapter; these debates are revisited in the concluding chapter to assess what light the study of EU energy security policies shines on this collection of issues.

3 The policy response

European energy initiatives

Energy policy was not formally incorporated within the scope of the Common Foreign and Security Policy (CFSP) and no legal base existed for the development of a common external energy policy. When the Commission published a Green Paper entitled 'Towards a European strategy for the security of energy supply' in November 2000, this elicited little interest and produced no concrete policy advance. The 2003 European Security Strategy (ESS) included one sentence noting Europe's increasing energy dependency, but this was not linked in any specific sense to the European Union's (EU) strategic objectives, which were rather identified as emanating from terrorism, nuclear proliferation, failed states, crime and regional conflicts.[1] Energy was not the subject of one of the 'sub-strategies' drawn up in 2004 to implement the Security Strategy. Council officials lamented that even by 2004 as they drafted new papers on the topic, it was impossible to convince senior figures in either Brussels or national capitals that there was any systematic relationship between energy security and the rightful scope of CFSP.

This situation then appeared to change dramatically. An aura of neglect was replaced by a battery of new European energy initiatives that promised to put energy security at the heart of EU foreign policy. This chapter provides an overview of these initiatives. It examines how far these new policies represented an advance over existing commitments; how far European member states' policy preferences approximated to a shared vision of energy security; and how the new initiatives related to the 'markets versus geopolitics' framework and the debates over democratic governance norms outlined in the previous chapter. The chapter finds that significant new energy initiatives were agreed, but that the priority attached to the foreign-policy dimensions of energy concerns was equivocal; that beneath strong rhetorical commitment to basing energy policy on the outward expansion of EU internal market norms in practice, European governments adhered to more geopolitical tenets; and that a striking disconnect persisted between energy deliberations and policy-making on good governance issues in producer states.

Energy boost

A range of energy initiatives was gradually established on a low-profile and ad hoc basis within the EU's different international partnerships. An EU–Russia energy dialogue commenced in 2000. November 2004 saw the launch of a Black Sea and Caspian Sea cooperation initiative, aimed at the progressive integration of this region into the European energy market. In October 2005, the Energy Community South East Europe Treaty was signed, with the aim of incorporating Balkan states into the European regional market for gas and petroleum products; this initiative would extend the EU energy acquis to the Balkans and coordinate infrastructure linkages, with World Bank financial support.[2] Balkan states were due to open their gas and power markets fully to the EU in 2008. A Memorandum of Understanding on energy cooperation was signed with Ukraine in December 2005, reflecting Kiev's aspiration to join the Energy Community South East Europe Treaty. Similar bilateral energy partnerships were signed in 2006 with Azerbaijan and Kazakhstan.

Sub-regional energy dialogues developed with the Maghreb and Mashreq from the late 1990s under the Euro-Mediterranean Partnership (EMP). The incipient European Neighbourhood Policy (ENP) also contained an energy component. A notably reinforced programme of such energy cooperation began under the rubric of Algeria's EMP association agreement. Outside the scope of formal EU frameworks, after 2003 efforts were made to initiate energy dialogue with Libya. In December 2004, bilateral political dialogue between the EU and Organization of Petroleum Exporting Countries (OPEC) was formally established and developed from 2005.

If policy-makers recognized that such initiatives had developed in a fragmented fashion, deliberation then (apparently) moved to a more overarching strategic level. Discussion was pushed in particular by the UK presidency in the second half of 2005. The October 2005 EU summit at Hampton Court agreed a formal commitment to move towards the definition of a common European energy policy. A first set of proposals was set out in the European Commission's March 2006 Green Paper. This paper started from the premise that, 'Acting together, [the EU] has the weight to protect and assert its interests.'[3] The paper identified a number of practical, technical priorities in relation to the internal dimensions of energy policy. The most significant new departure was, however, at the international and strategic level. The Commission argued that the EU needed a 'coherent external energy policy', agreement on which would represent 'a break from the past' – a past characterized by a conspicuous lack of unity and coordination. The paper proposed a Strategic EU Energy Review, with regular follow-up political discussions; a network of 'energy correspondents' to facilitate coordination between member states; 'a better integration of energy objectives into broader relations with third countries'; coordinated response mechanisms in relation to crises in energy supplies; and the development of inter-connecting energy systems between different geographical areas, as a means of transcending the so far partial technical cooperation pursued separately with individual partner states.[4]

Responding to the Green Paper, member state representatives in the European Council accepted that 'foreign and development policy aspects are gaining increasing importance to promote energy policy objectives with other countries'. They backed the Commission's calls for better coordination, and more specifically for a comprehensive Strategic Energy Review, 'addressing in particular the aims and actions needed for an external energy policy over the medium-to long-term'.[5] In a follow up note to the Council, the Commission stated that energy security policy 'must also be consistent with the EU's broader foreign policy objectives such as conflict prevention and resolution, non-proliferation and promoting human rights'.[6] Such linkages were pushed inter alia by the Benelux states, who urged the Political and Security Committee to drop its reluctance to engage in energy matters and argued that European leverage would be strengthened by 'embedding energy in a wider range of subjects'.[7]

External-relations commissioner Benita Ferrero-Waldner revealed that the aim to bolster the foreign-policy dimensions of energy policy was the key driving force behind the ENP. She admitted that the Russia–Ukraine gas dispute at the beginning of 2006 was 'a wake up call, reminding us that energy security needs to be even higher on our political agenda'.[8] Indeed, some analysts saw energy security concerns as the only factor in practice linking the diverse regions included within the ENP, and the main issue according the latter some logical rationale.[9] At the first high-level European Neighbourhood Policy conference held on 3 September 2007, commissioner Ferrero-Waldner listed energy as a top priority and floated the idea of a new 'neighbourhood energy agreement'.[10]

Further initiatives commenced to deepen energy cooperation with Turkey, in recognition of the latter's importance as a transit route into the EU and Ankara's influence in the wider Black Sea and Caspian regions. By 2007 energy was a prominent issue in nearly all external political dialogues, where it had been barely mentioned five years previously – this, according to one official, requiring member states to look at energy from a common European perspective and not only through the lens of their national policies. Twenty-two million euros of one of the Commission's post-2007 external relations budgets, the development cooperation instrument (or DCI) was allocated to energy projects, representing 7 per cent of funding. Eurobarometer polls suggested a clear majority of the European population wished to see a more common EU energy policy (although in a number of central and eastern European states and Finland the balance of opinion was against such deeper cooperation).[11]

Rhetorical commitments incrementally intensified. At the end of 2006, Commission president José Manuel Barroso declared that energy had been 'until recently a forgotten subject in the European agenda. Now it is back at the heart of European integration, where it began with the creation of the Coal and Steel Community. And where it belongs.' He was confident that by this stage a 'quick revolution' had taken place, with member states dropping their nationally centred approaches and genuinely agreeing on the desirability of a common European energy strategy.[12] He committed the EU to making energy a priority topic in all summits with third countries. During his stint as external-relations commissioner, that ended in 2004, Chris Patten had engaged little with energy issues; for his successor, Ferrero-Waldner, energy became a staple part of diplomatic activity. Indeed, the latter was reportedly pushed by several member states (including the UK) into engaging more on energy issues as part of the EU 'getting its act together' on energy security. The deputy director general for energy at the European Commission railed that, 'Those who try to hide the fact that energy has moved into the realm of foreign policy are trying to forget reality ... Why can't Europe bring energy politics into the core of external policies?'[13]

A number of institutional innovations reflected the new priority attached to energy issues. The network of 'energy correspondents' was launched in May 2007, linking together the key personnel covering energy issues in member states and the Brussels institutions. This was conceived as the core of 'an energy crisis management system'.[14] An energy unit was created within the Commission's external-relations department, with instructions from commissioners that energy be woven into policies in each geographical area: this unit was charged with ensuring that henceforth geographical departments assessed and justified policies in terms of how these contributed towards energy security. A number of member states advocated moving all decisions on energy security to qualified majority voting – they contrasted the stagnation of unanimity-bound foreign-policy making with the qualified majority voting that had, they argued, ensured more productive debate in the area of climate change.

On 10 January 2007 the Commission published its eagerly awaited Strategic Energy Review. This reiterated the main principles and objectives that had taken shape during 2006: the need for greater 'capability to react in times of external energy security pressure'; the importance of international partnerships based on 'shared rules or principles derived from EU [internal] energy policy'; the desirability of 'comprehensive partnerships based on mutual interest, transparency, predictability and reciprocity'; the need for some form of energy supply solidarity mechanism, especially for states dependent on a single gas supplier; the intention to make available increased funding for energy projects through the EU's new financial instruments; the need to promote 'transparent legal frameworks' in producer states; and the idea of European coordinators to represent EU interests in key international energy projects.[15]

The March 2007 EU summit agreed an energy action plan for 2007–9. This reiterated a series of core principles, based around the need for diversification; crisis-response mechanisms; transparency both between member states and within producer states' governance structures; and an assessment of current patterns of energy imports into different member states.[16] The June 2007 summit, at which the new Lisbon treaty was hammered out between European leaders, included a number of developments pertinent to energy. A new legal base was introduced in the treaty for EU legislation in the field of energy, along with provisions for qualified majority voting in some areas of energy policy. Poland insisted on a new energy solidarity clause, this representing one of its threats to veto a new treaty mandate – although the reference to energy policy needing to be in accordance with 'a spirit of solidarity between member states' was less committal and specific than Poland had wanted. Some of the more general reforms agreed also had relevance for energy security. The powers of the high representative to speak on behalf of the EU were enhanced, fusing powers hitherto falling to a number of different commissioners (although the UK insisted that the post would not be called a 'foreign minister' and that there was reference to the fact that these new powers would not cut-across national foreign policies). Some member-state representatives reported that they supported this revision thinking in particular of energy policy. In mid-2008 preparations began for a new strategic review that would consider the need for additional energy security policy instruments.

A number of European governments also introduced new energy security initiatives at the national level. In 2006 the Dutch government committed itself to addressing energy security as a part of its broad foreign-policy agenda of 'peace and security'; the Dutch Energy Council pushed the government to go a step further and establish energy security as a separate priority with its own institutional resources and new instruments.[17] The British government established an inter-ministerial Joint Energy Security of Supply Working Group (JESS) in 2001, and energy security was identified as one of eight strategic priorities for UK foreign policy.[18] The 2004 Energy Act committed the government to deliver annual reports to parliament on Britain's energy security preparedness. A seminal Energy White Paper stated that as the UK moved towards becoming an energy importer, this 'requires us to take a longer strategic international approach to energy reliability'.[19] UK documents suggested that the ESS needed to be fully harnessed for energy security objectives.[20] Prime Minister Tony Blair's 2006 Lord Mayor's (that is, principal foreign-policy) speech singled out energy security as one of the issues where more effective European coordination was most apposite. A number of energy advisors were brought into the Foreign and Commonwealth Office from oil companies. A cross-departmental energy security action plan was agreed, under whose auspices a new Energy Group was charged with raising awareness of energy security challenges across Whitehall. Links between this group and, for example, the FCO's Engaging with the Islamic World initiative reflected an aim to improve the strategic specificities of energy planning in individual producer states. The commitment to linking climate change and international energy security policy within a more holistic strategy was reiterated in a further UK energy White Paper published in May 2007.[21]

Foreign policy versus climate change?

Notwithstanding these new commitments and institutional changes, many doubted whether the external dimension of energy security had indeed been given a significant boost. A number of proposals floated from different quarters within the European Parliament, the Council Secretariat, the Commission or member states did not prosper. These included proposals for an EU special representative for energy; for the EU to be provided with stronger formal legal competence over external energy issues; for a mandatory 'energy clause' to be inserted into third-country agreements, in parallel to existing human rights, counter-terrorism and non-proliferation clauses; and for the application of 'reinforced cooperation' to create what some labelled 'an energy Schengen'. An influential member-state diplomat likened the EU's formal energy dialogues with third countries to 'a toolbox with no tools inside'. One Commission official suggested, evasively, that any 'solidarity clause' would be balanced against the diversity of member states' external interests. Commonly, member-state diplomats rejected the notion of an 'energy clause' requiring cooperation of third countries as 'neo-imperial'.

The EP lamented that the absence of this range of initiatives indicated that the external dimension of energy policy was still not accorded any significant priority.[22] As negotiations began for the new strategic review in 2008, most member states insisted that they remained to be convinced that major new supranational competences or instruments were merited in the energy sphere. In December 2007 the European Council mandated a revision of the European Security Strategy; as of mid-2008, insiders agreed that it was unlikely that the Strategy would be widened more systematically to include energy security issues.

The standard foreign-policy dimensions of energy security were clearly and increasingly over-shadowed by the climate-change agenda. The relationship between the internal, environmental and geostrategic aspects of energy policy was less than entirely harmonious. European debate focused increasingly on the internal and environmental dimensions of energy security. Many experts and practitioners argued that a focus on the 'demand' side should not be diluted by concerns over the international, 'supply' side of energy security. As one put it, investing in domestic energy efficiency *was* now the best form of foreign policy.[23] Despite all the formal rhetoric to the contrary, many policy-makers in energy ministries still argued in private that energy security was a matter of reducing external dependencies, rather than strengthening interdependencies; of reducing the pressures on foreign policy, rather than incorporating foreign policy as an integral part of energy policy. In 2005 the Swedish government even created a 'Commission against oil dependency'. In several foreign ministries there was scarcely hidden resistance to and criticism of the increasing prominence of environment ministries in relation to energy issues.

The Commission's 2007 Strategic Review proposed that the EU commit unilaterally to a 20 per cent reduction of carbon emissions by 2020. European policy-makers emphasized that the EU's distinctive lead role in energy issues emanated most significantly from its commitment to the Kyoto protocol, and its pioneering Emissions Trading Scheme. As far back as 2001 the EU's Renewables Directive had made a commitment to double the share of renewable sources in European energy production by 2010. New European Investment Bank funding was now made available for the development of renewable energy technologies. A new European Strategic Energy Technology Plan was introduced to increase and coalesce investment in alternative energy sources. The EU played a firm and high-profile role in the Bali climate change conference in December 2007.

The 2007 Review's coverage of external policies was strikingly thin compared to its focus on the internal market, climate change and the development of renewable energy resources. Many observers criticized the limits to the EU's Emissions Trading Scheme and its Kyoto commitments; but it could not be doubted that the EU had emerged as a 'player' in climate change debates in a way that it had not in relation to the geopolitics of energy security. One member state's energy representative bemoaned the fact that within the Council the external dimension was, after the initial shock of the Russia–Ukraine dispute, now read as 'less acute' and less in need of fundamentally new policies. Barroso's launch of the document focused almost solely on the proclaimed urgency of Europe moving towards a 'low carbon economy'. At least in terms of discourse, and the (im)balance in the document between internal and external dimensions, some policy-makers intuited a nuanced shift: the stress by 2007 appeared to be not quite so much on a coherent incorporation of energy security into CFSP, and slightly more on reducing external energy dependency in order to temper the impact on foreign policies.

Climate change was a discrete issue that had captured public attention and driven policy changes in a way that the more diffuse external-geopolitical challenges of energy security had failed to do.[24] One senior EU diplomat lamented that by the autumn of 2007 energy debates in Brussels were 'all about climate change.' David Miliband's inaugural speech as British Foreign Secretary in July 2007 mentioned *only* climate change as the energy security challenge facing the UK.[25] The UK government committed itself to investing 100 million pounds in renewable energy development between 2008–13. One critic argued that if an 'external' issue conditioned policy it was that the fear of short-term supply cut-offs – a topic much beloved of the media but one that distracted attention from the more real challenge of designing a longer-term vision for sustainable supplies.[26] The opening in October 2007 of a new Norwegian gas field capable, it was estimated, of meeting 20 per cent of UK market demand for the next forty years was seen by some as relaxing the urgency for such a long-term vision for extra-European supplies.

The focus on climate change during 2007 culminated in the Commission releasing in January 2008 its more detailed plans for how the EU's ambitious targets were to be met. The overarching framework was labelled the '20/20/ by 2020' plan: by 2020 the EU would reduce greenhouse gas emissions by 20 per cent; obtain 20 per cent of its energy from renewable sources; and increase energy efficiency by 20 per cent. Existing ETS sectors (power and industry) would face a tougher cap and the initiative would be widened to more sectors of economic activity to bring overall coverage to around 50 per cent of total CO2 emissions. Member states would be set varying targets for renewables, extending from a high of 40 per cent of total energy use in Sweden to a low of 10 per cent in Malta – differences that occasioned fierce tensions between governments. Significantly, this phase of policy development began to raise questions over the link to external policies. The Commission claimed that its '20/20/20' plan would save 50 billion euros a year in reduced oil and gas exports.[27] Others detected signs of 'renewables' themselves becoming part of EU foreign-policy bargaining: the EU would support the development of alternative sources in places like North Africa, if European companies were able to lay the pipelines to import such power back into EU markets.[28] One observer distinguished Europe's 'climate change-led' energy policy to the US's geopolitical and 'foreign policy-led' approach to energy security.[29]

Many argued that the internal and external dimensions could be, and were being, pursued in tandem without problem. Diplomats commonly argued that tighter cooperation on the more technocratic aspects of internal energy policy would provide a classic 'spill-over' that would help define the broader values of an external energy policy. Others expressed concern over a potential tension in the EU's emerging balance between these two dimensions. Most notably, the priority attached to reducing external dependencies sat ill with producer state governments, who sought 'energy demand roadmaps' from the EU as the basis for robust interdependence. OPEC Secretary-General Abdalla Salem El-Badri complained that new EU climate-change initiatives 'discriminate[d] against oil'.[30] One expert noted an emerging clash between security and environmental aims in European governments' increasing enthusiasm for substitutes such as tar sands and oil shales: these attractive on strategic grounds by virtue of being available in countries more friendly to the West, but categorized as 'dirty' energy sources.[31]

A number of diplomats and politicians expressed concern that the focus on climate change was having too dominant an impact on overall energy policy. This issue was, they argued, taking the focus away from the short-term challenges of international geopolitics and fomenting the illusion that investment in renewables could obviate the need to take difficult foreign policy choices. In a context of finite resources, some lamented how sizeable new funding of alternative energy sources within Europe was taking priority, while only limited funds were invested in external energy infrastructure links or in stability-enhancing development assistance in energy-rich states, especially in Africa.

Critiques charged Western governments in general with failing to realize that tackling climate change actually *required* a more engaged and geostrategic foreign policy, not just 'internal' renewables targets, as the bargaining dynamics of environmental and security of supply issues would increasingly overlap.[32]

And significantly these trends in EU energy policy represented a familiar replay of analogous developments in other areas of security: the vast majority of EU counter-terrorist measures introduced since 2001, for instance, pertained to internal security matters, with Justice and Home Affairs policy-makers in the lead and CFSP struggling to gain purchase.[33] Only in March 2008 were these shortcomings in the energy field openly recognized as the office of the high representative released what it acknowledged was a first attempt to conceptualize climate change as a 'threat multiplier' that needed to be linked into CFSP strategies. This paper argued that the EU had not yet addressed the foreign-policy dimensions of climate change, as a magnifier of conflict, migration, border disputes and radicalization.[34] The UK Foreign Office created a new post to assess the security-policy implications of climate change. In short, by mid-2008 some signs were emerging of deeper and more probing debate over the linkage between climate change and external security policies.

The internal market as foreign policy

It was routinely asserted that the internal market was the crucial bedrock of the EU's external policies. European commitments, formal documents and rhetoric contained much that approximated closely to the 'markets and institutions' storyline, described in the previous chapter. As an integral part of a general expansion in global markets, the EU's energy security philosophy appeared to be predicated on the spread eastwards and southwards of internal European market rules. The March 2006 Green Paper argued that energy security could best be achieved through a 'pan-European energy community', a 'common regulatory space' around Europe. This required '[r]einforced market-based provisions on energy ... in the EU's existing and future agreements with third countries', such as would 'improv[e] the conditions for European companies seeking access to global resources'.[35] World Trade Organization provisions could also help tie producer states into market-based supply rules. The Green Paper asserted that as a guiding philosophy, 'It would be a mistake to pay too much attention to the geographical or national origin of today's oil imports. In reality, the EU depends ... on a global oil market'.

The Commission subsequently asserted that, 'well-functioning world markets are the best way of ensuring safe and affordable energy supplies'. In this way security 'could be achieved by the EU extending its own energy market to include its neighbours within a common regulatory area with shared trade, transit and environmental rules': 'We need to convince non-EU consumer countries that world energy markets can work for them. If they were to conclude that the only route to security lay in bilateral deals, the risk of disruption of the energy system would grow.'[36] The new energy treaties and agreements with third countries were said to be about 'extending the EU's energy infrastructure' as the main solution to security concerns. It was pointed out that the liberalization of gas markets was particularly necessary; since 1980 gas prices had been linked to oil prices, a situation which now had no logic and merely ensured that European consumers paid unnecessarily high prices for gas.[37]

In a similar vein, the G8 meeting in St Petersburg, July 2006 agreed conclusions stating that energy security was 'best assured by strengthened partnership between energy producing and consuming countries' and that 'open, transparent, efficient and competitive energy markets are the cornerstone for our common energy security strategy'. A St Petersburg Action Plan was adopted to enhance cooperation on market-deepening, transparency and better conditions for energy-related foreign direct investment.[38]

Constant reference was made to the importance of the Energy Charter Treaty for market- and rules-based solutions. This Charter was signed in 1994 and incorporated 51 member states, substituting 1275 highly varied bilateral treaties with a single multilateral regulatory framework, with especially notable provisions in the area of investment protection.[39] The EU's basic philosophy was of extending the principles of the Energy Charter successively to the different areas of the EU's periphery, from Russia, through Central Asia and the South Caucasus, Ukraine, the Balkans and into the southern Mediterranean. In private, a common refrain from European diplomats was: if we approach energy security as power politics, we actually make it more likely that producer states will deploy the 'oil weapon'. European governments eschewed the direct financing and construction of new external pipelines. Proposals that the EU specify that no more than a certain share of its energy supply could come from a single source were rebuffed by the Commission and a majority of member states. (Only Spain operated such an upper limit, in its case of 60 per cent.)

By 2007 debate focused on the Commission's proposal to 'unbundle' the generation and distribution of power. The Commission presented this as key not only to internal efficiency but also to external security: to the extent that large third-country companies, such as Gazprom, would also be required to 'unbundle' within the European market it would protect the EU against these firms gaining a dominant position. Breaking apart national energy champions within Europe would make it harder for large non-European firms, like Gazprom, to negotiate their way into dominant positions simply through a small number of bilateral deals. By 2008 discussions intensified on the need for an EU energy agency to police and regulate the internal market.

The proclamation of this approach was of a piece with the view that the EU's own internal market integration constituted the basis for Europe's external projection. José Manuel Barroso suggested that the internal and external dimensions of energy policy 'must be part of one coherent whole. ... the two must go hand in hand, not walk in separate directions'.[40] It was common for officials confidently to predict that internal market norms would drive external unity. One Commission external-relations (Relex) director asserted, in relation to energy policy: 'The internal market has been the key to our strength in world affairs.' As one diplomat put it, as a result of internal market integration a common EU energy policy 'is a train already in progress; member states will decide when they are ready to board'. Policymakers commonly suggested that the euro was gradually augmenting the EU's energy-related power, as some oil producers switched reserves out of dollars into euros and talk even emerged of OPEC moving to denominate prices in euros rather than dollars. As mentioned, officials were also minded to argue that the EU's leadership in climate change negotiations would serve as an additional basis for convergence on the more strictly strategic external aspects of energy policy.

For some, competition laws would determine much of the substance of foreign-policy positions. One notable impact these had was to oblige the EU to insist with third countries that traditional 'destination clauses' could not be permitted. These clauses enabled producer states to prevent a buyer passing on surplus supplies to other states. Such provisions were vital for producers to protect the exclusivity of bilateral contracts; but the Commission insisted they were incompatible with internal market rules. This issue relating to internal competition law had a significant implied impact on foreign-policy manoeuvrability. As one senior official put it: 'we are good at bureaucratizing the problem', through rules and regulations. Moreover, the more flexible switching of supplies between member states as their respective levels of demand fluctuated was in itself seen as a contribution to better energy security.[41]

Market liberalization was widely perceived to be the EU's most potent negotiating tool in international energy negotiations. The Commission argued in its January 2007 Strategic Energy Review that it was by opening up its own markets that the EU could best hope to gain foreign direct investment (FDI) access to countries such as Russia. As one senior German official opined: while the qualitatively new strand to energy debates was the external dimension, the internal market 'has an incredibly strong bearing on how you organize your foreign policy'; completing that market was a 'precursor', the EU's 'homework' required before an energy-guided foreign-policy approach could be effective. One senior Council official, close to Javier Solana, also cautioned that, 'we can end the bilateralism [national governments undercutting each other in bilateral deals with producer states] only when there is a true internal market'.

A common refrain amongst policy-makers was that completing the internal market in energy was a prerequisite to investing more in the external dimensions of energy security. As one MEP quipped, 'We cannot talk to the world about energy until we have sorted out our internal problems'. The head of the French foreign ministry's energy unit argued that Europe must 'move away from a producers-consumers dichotomy to a logic of market integration'.[42] Spain also proclaimed strong support for this position. Spain's energy sector was already essentially privatized, diplomats' main concern being over the lack of EU backing to overcome France's blocking of interconnections between Spain and the rest of Europe. Spain was also notable for having, in the words of one of its senior officials, made a 'bet on LNGs', in an attempt to inject greater fluidity into gas supplies.

The UK's approach was especially market oriented. UK policy documents placed their highest stress on international energy-market reform and liberalization, and the desirability of more competitive international oil and gas markets. In the 2004 White Paper the Labour government asserted that 'we will not intervene in the market except in extreme circumstances'.[43] Having already liberalized its own markets, the UK had the most to gain from ensuring that market reform was implemented in other EU states and beyond Europe. UK officials claimed that the domestic market responded well to the tight conditions of the 2005–6 winter, with additional supply and storage capacity ready for the winter of 2006–7; indeed, UK gas prices fell in mid-2006 as a result. One UK energy official argued that it was misplaced to think of Europe being in competition for energy supplies with China and India: energy security for the latter would rebound positively on the EU, and should thus be assisted through international frameworks and rules. In 2006 the British government pushed the Commission hard to investigate why other European states had not responded to market signals and moved to cover supply shortfalls in the UK at key moments during the winter of 2005–6. Ironically perhaps, to some extent Britain was one of the keenest advocates of more supranationalized competences in energy policy, extolling the 'dawn raids' of recalcitrant energy firms undertaken by the European Commission.

Sweden placed itself towards the more liberal end of the spectrum, a position influenced by the country's limited use of gas for domestic energy, reducing reliance on politically effected fixed contracts. Hungary also claimed to be more comfortable than many other member states with a liberally oriented external dimension, to the extent that it had already been obliged to undergo structural adjustments in its energy sector as part of its post-Soviet transition. A new Czech strategy argued that deepening the EU internal market was the surest way for it to reduce its national external dependency, while also positing EU measures as the means of prompting internal Czech liberalization.[44] Poland's high dependency on 'non-diversified' sources of natural gas gave it a particular stake in deeper European market integration, as the country made a difficult move away from its heavy use of coal power.[45] The three Baltic states had already agreed to create a fully liberalized Baltic energy market in 1999.[46]

Political realities

In sum, many European convictions appeared strong in their adherence to a 'markets and institutions' storyline. Beneath the surface, however, clarity and unity on this approach were patently more limited. One Council Secretariat diplomat revealed that, notwithstanding the advances of the Green Paper and the Strategic Energy Review, governments were 'only just starting' to consider how the energy security imperative would impact on policy in different geographical areas. Broad principles had been enunciated but the common refrain from policy-makers was that 'the operational side' was poorly developed and that debate was no more than 'embryonic'. Record high oil prices had shocked governments and the different EU institutions into exploring how their differences could be overcome. But a new willingness to debate energy security at the EU level had not translated into definitive resolution of the way in which broad guidelines were to be implemented in different producer states. One official opined that behind all the new initiatives, documents and debate there remained the most basic problem that some of the bigger member states were still not convinced that a truly common European energy policy was in their interests.

Member states' different energy exposures militated against a uniform degree of commitment to strengthening the external dimensions of energy policies. Foreign-policy debates fed into deliberation over the EU's internal 'energy mix', and in particular the issue of nuclear power. While France generated over 40 per cent of its energy from nuclear power, other states had committed themselves to a non-nuclear future. The French investment in nuclear power was referred to frequently by insiders as a major factor limiting the commitment of one of the EU's big foreign-policy actors to a genuinely common energy security strategy. Overall EU energy import dependency increased from 42.8 per cent in 1994 to 52.4 per cent in 2005. But as Tables 3.1–3.3 make clear, this overall figure masked significant differences in member states' import profiles. Seven states – Cyprus, Malta, Luxembourg, Ireland, Portugal, Italy and Spain – registered external dependencies of over 80 per cent; at the other end of the spectrum, dependencies of under 20 per cent were enjoyed by Poland, the UK and Denmark (the latter a net exporter of oil products).

Insiders identified three strands of opinion amongst member states. One strand was still reluctant to cede national independence over external energy security, and saw little alternative to each member state trying to seal the best deals possible with producer states on a bilateral basis. Germany was seen by some as a leading proponent of this view. A second strand argued forcefully that the free market was more or less sufficient to mitigating energy insecurity. The UK was invariably characterized as prime advocate of this philosophy. A third strand argued, against both of these, that geopolitical factors must be heeded, but that precisely because of this stronger European coordination was required. France could be placed in this camp. Diplomats admitted that in an attempt to bridge these three strands of thinking, the EU was 'muddling along' with an uneasy combination of opposed strategic rationales.

Most pertinent were the limits to the EU's internal market liberalization in the energy sector. If the internal market was supposed to set the foundations for a rules-based, market-oriented external energy policy, this logic was undermined by the determination of a number of member states to curtail the liberalization of energy markets within Europe. Liberalization of the EU energy market had proven painstakingly slow and difficult, despite formal

Table 3.1 Energy import dependency (2005)

Country	%
Cyprus	100.7
Malta	100.0
Luxembourg	98.0
Ireland	89.5
Portugal	88.2
Italy	84.4
Spain	81.2
Belgium	79.6
Austria	71.8
Greece	68.5
Slovakia	64.6
Hungary	62.9
Germany	61.6
Lithuania	58.4
Latvia	56.1
Finland	54.7
EU27	**52.4**
Slovenia	52.2
France	51.6
Bulgaria	47.1
Netherlands	37.8
Sweden	37.2
Czech Rep	27.4
Romania	27.4
Estonia	25.8
Poland	18.0
UK	13.8
Denmark	−51.6

Source: European Commission Energy Statistics Pocketbook 2007
Definition: Import dependency=Net Imports of all fuels (solid, oil and gas)/
(Bunkers+Gross Inland Consumption)

opening of the internal gas market in July 2007. In 2006 the Commission stepped up its pressure on member states, issuing critiques of all governments (except the Dutch) for failing to meet market opening commitments they had already signed up to. The Commission increasingly reprimanded the several member states blocking cross-border mergers, especially in the cases of Spain's hindrance of E.ON's bid for Endesa and France's determination to make Enel's purchase of Suez-Gas difficult. Such overt and apparently unabashed preferential protection for national energy champions constituted in many experts' eyes a return to 'economic nationalism' within Europe.[47] In October 2006 the Commission launched another drive to split up big energy giants such as E.ON, RWE and EDF.

While paying lip service to its support for 'completing the internal market', the French government was critical towards proposed new EU

Table 3.2 Oil imports, global rankings (end 2006)

Country	Global ranking
Germany	4
France	6
Italy	8
Spain	9
Netherlands	11
Belgium	15
Poland	16
Greece	17
Sweden	19
Portugal	22
Austria	25
Finland	31
Czech Rep.	32
Ireland	33
UK	40
Hungary	41
Romania	43
Bulgaria	45
Slovakia	52
Luxembourg	55
Cyprus	57
Slovenia	58
Lithuania	64
Latvia	71
Estonia	84
Malta	89

Source: US Energy Information Administration 2007

regulations that would tighten enforcement mechanisms and speed up the implementation of liberalizing reforms.[48] In September 2007, new French President Nicolas Sarkozy pushed through the completion of a merger between Suez and Gaz de France, unashamedly creating a new powerful 'national champion'. French Europe minister Jean-Pierre Jouyet stated that such preferential strategic measures, and not the market-opening proposals of the Commission, represented the 'vision of what could be the energy policy for Europe'.[49] The Dutch government was not afraid to state that the Netherlands' status as the only member state to possess still-sizeable gas reserves meant that it would insist on retaining scope for bilateral policies.[50]

Some member states continued openly to question the kind of market reform enacted in the UK. In continental Europe, the UK's market-based gas policy was widely seen to have led to a rapid depletion of Britain's own reserves and to have left the country dangerously exposed: when British supplies ran dangerously low in early 2006 they (unlike the UK government) judged that market correction mechanisms failed, as other European states declined to react to higher prices as a trigger for increased exports to the

Table 3.3 Gas imports, global rankings (end 2006)

Country	Ranking
Germany	2
Italy	4
France	6
Spain	9
Netherlands	11
Belgium	12
UK	14
Hungary	15
Poland	17
Austria	20
Czech Rep	21
Slovakia	26
Romania	27
Finland	30
Portugal	31
Ireland	32
Bulgaria	34
Lithuania	35
Greece	36
Latvia	42
Estonia	44
Luxembourg	45
Slovenia	52
Sweden	53
Denmark	85

Source: US Energy Information Administration 2007

UK. It was the accusation of such a withholding of supplies that led the Commission to raid a number of European energy companies. The chairman of E.ON concluded that the events of early 2006 proved the failure of the UK's market-based approach and suggested that it was Britain that had to adapt to 'a new reality'.[51]

In its 2007 Strategic Review the Commission admitted that it might be forced to accept a diluted model that would not formally 'unbundle' national energy giants but rather simply contract out their transmission functions to independent operators. Disagreements between member states meant that firm decisions on further internal market liberalization were delayed during the 2007 German presidency, and pushed back to the Commission with a request that the merits of various options be re-examined. By the time the Commission did bring forward its 'unbundling' proposals in September 2007 it won open support only from the UK, Spain, Sweden, the Netherlands and Ireland.[52] Agreement still proved elusive during the Portuguese presidency of the latter half of 2007; by December 2007 a clear blocking majority of France, Germany, Austria, Bulgaria, Cyprus, Greece, Latvia, Luxembourg and Slovakia was firm in opposing the Commission's 'unbundling' liberalization.[53] In June 2008 these states appeared to be on the verge of succeeding in blocking even the diluted option of requiring that distribution networks be run (but not owned) by independent operators. By mid-2008 these states were also seeking to dilute the powers of any EU energy agency, to ensure that such a body could not force liberalization in several key areas of the energy market and was limited to loose coordination between national regulators.

While the debate on the EU's internal market liberalization was fierce and exhaustively covered, the issue in this book is the link between these internal developments and European foreign policy. A common argument here was that resistance to internal market completion sufficed to demonstrate that both its system of energy concessions and its dearth of physical interconnections prevented the EU from responding as a single entity to external energy shocks – thus rendering premature expectations of a coherent foreign policy. The battle-lines drawn in relation to internal market liberalization etched themselves into positions on the external dimensions of energy security. A French memorandum fed into the deliberations over the Commission's 2006 Green Paper emphasized the importance and desirability of politically-negotiated long-term contracts.[54] The French government pushed strongly for the Council to assume lead role from the free-market quarters of the Commission; the French proposal for an energy special representative was openly aimed at the goal of circumventing the market-opening efforts of the Commission.[55] French energy minister François Loos suggested that 'unbundling' would undermine the conditions for external long-term investment.[56] In fact, the Commission itself lobbied strongly for formal positions that recognized the importance of long-term contracts as the basis of the external dimension to European energy security.

A key split within the EU emerged over how far market opening should be used as a conditional, political tool. French, Italian and German positions emphasized the need for any market liberalization to be matched by negotiated reciprocity in producer states. Bilateral deals remained the preferred means of securing such negotiated reciprocity, and a number of governments admitted that if anything their political intervention and backing for such deals was becoming stronger and more overt. If the carrot of downstream access was removed from European governments, they argued, Europeans' prospects would be slimmer of winning upstream access in producer states. The principle of reciprocity was formally included in the Commission's September 2007 package of proposals. The latter threatened restrictions on third-country access to the EU market where European investment was impeded in those markets. This was quickly dubbed the 'Gazprom clause', in honour of its supposed target. Experts suggested that the EU was using its competition policy to deal with its deteriorating geopolitical relations with Russia. One idea raised was that exemptions from 'unbundling' might be allowed where a country exhibited high dependence on one external gas supplier.

A number of member states rejected even the notion of transparency and information-sharing between EU states on the bilateral deals each concluded. For one Italian diplomat, a more political approach was warranted to the extent that it was 'unrealistic' to expect key producer states to sign up to a model based on the extension of the EU's own internal market. Lithuanian president Valdas Adamkus concurred that while Russia in particular insisted on approaching energy in such an overtly geopolitical manner, the EU needed to respond in kind and drop the 'mantra' that the market by itself would provide for Europe's energy security.[57]

German energy diplomats in the Auswärtiges Amt (foreign ministry) sought to wrest influence from the energy minister's unit based in the economy ministry, whose approach was dismissed as 'too technocratic and market focused' and was said to be run by 'people who just know how the pipelines run'. Dutch foreign minister Bernard Bot cautioned that in pursuit of energy security the EU must realize that 'law in itself does not guarantee anything in a world where power is still often the decisive factor'.[58] Even the British Conservative party berated the Blair government for being over-reliant on market solutions and failing to realize the importance of energy geo-politics.[59]

Despite all his pro-market discourse, José Manuel Barroso himself seemed at least obliquely to recognize the need for politically conditioned variation, in suggesting that 'interdependence is mutually beneficial, *so long as* the energy relationship is that of a market, not a geopolitical chessboard'.[60] Market-doubters also tended to stress the differences between oil and gas markets, reiterating scepticism that the latter could approximate in any useful way to the fungibility of international oil flows. They additionally cautioned that market opening would increase price volatility, to the detriment of energy security.

These states in practice continued to conceive of energy security as a state-led responsibility. Energy security, highlighted one member-state energy representative, was a public good whose cost could only be borne and justified to domestic populations by the state. If EU governments sought to direct producer governments to increase production capacity for European security, they could not at the same time claim that within Europe energy was a matter for private actors rather than public authorities. One European diplomat suggested that the EU model was one of 'regulated liberalization'. Another argued that the EU was embarked upon a 'third way ... between markets and geopolitics', predicated upon 'political dialogue and coopera-tion'. One of the EU's particularly senior producer-state interlocutors drew from all this a striking conclusion: the EU was no less 'egotistically geopo-litical' than any other international actor, it just dressed its geopolitics in the finer cloaks of rules-based discourse.

British diplomats lamented that the Commission might be 'making the right noises' on market liberalization but in practice seemed to resign itself to decisions 'that had recourse to power politics'. Relating again to climate change deliberations, UK and other diplomats pointed to a growing tension between internal and external dimensions in the offering of new subsidies to develop energy alternatives domestically, this undercutting the free-market logic that the EU was trying to sell to producers, and which would – in some states' opinion – much better guarantee long-term security than any focus on an illusory low-carbon self-sufficiency.

These states berated as a protectionist pretext the insistence that liberalization be reciprocated, arguing that even where producer states blocked upstream access for European firms it was still in the EU's interest to open its own market – thus locking in more downstream investment and broader interdependence between producers and consumers. They also lamented that EU competition law had not been used to examine bilateral deals between member state 'national champions' and external companies, in particular Gazprom. Again, for all the rhetoric stressing the centrality of internal market rules, in practice the latter were reined back from their potentially full geopolitical impact. Some analysts also observed that the 'Gazprom clause' appeared directly to contravene the EU's own rules against nationality-based discrimination; and, moreover, if member states wished to continue agreeing such bilateral deals with Gazprom the Commission would be unlikely to have the political power to implement this reciprocity clause.[61] Adding further preconditions to market access, in February 2008 the Commission brought forward proposals that would require greater transparency from sovereign wealth funds prior to these being allowed to buy into European energy firms.[62]

Divergence could also be witnessed within the Brussels institutions. The tone and language of Javier Solana's speeches were different from that of his Commission colleagues, and widely interpreted as a diplomatic chide to the latter. The high representative warned that, 'we should avoid thinking that enumerating a list of principles is a substitute for a policy' and that there 'is no such thing as a single solution' to the complex international politics of energy security. Market liberalization, he opined, was 'only part of the answer'.[63] An incipient battle for control over external energy policy between the Commission and Council was described by insiders as one between the competing approaches of 'markets and politics'. One critic pointed out that what was often taken to represent 'the European approach' of extending internal market networks was far from being a rationalized philosophy of energy security, but was simply the area in which the Commission enjoyed energy-related competence and thus the inevitable focus of Brussels proposals hitherto.

The principal division was described by officials as being between the Commission's Energy and Transport directorate (TREN), on the one hand, and Relex and the Council, on the other hand. The latter berated the former's influence as an 'energy technocracy' whose market-based recipes were blind to geopolitical realities. The 'energy technocrats' complained that too much alliance-oriented foreign policy had already infected the coherence of EU strategies. One particular concern in this respect was that increasing talk of the strategic importance of 'diversifying' the sources of Europe's energy contradicted the very premise that energy supplies were fungible and that markets clear at a given price. As pointed out above, producer states picked up on this inconsistency and angrily complained that the EU preached mutually beneficial, market-based solutions but then urged policies that reduced political dependence on these 'partners'.[64] One sweeping assessment was that 'decision-making on energy security in major powers has slipped dangerously from the hands of economic policy-makers to the hands of national security strategists'.[65]

In sum, officials acknowledged that the situation was not one of the 'markets and institutions' storyline having triumphed, but rather of sharply contrasting policy preferences persisting within different institutions and forums. One diplomat likened internal EU deliberation on energy policy to 'walking on eggs'.

Securitization (largely) rejected

Notwithstanding these differences over market principles, European diplomats stressed that adherence to rules-based tenets set the EU apart from the United States' approach to energy security. Most analyses of the 'new geopolitics of energy' indeed focused on what was widely seen as the Bush administration's far-reaching 'securitization' of energy. This represented the latest stage in a long history of US military guarantees being linked to the security of energy supplies. President Roosevelt struck the original deal under which the US committed itself to defending Saudi Arabia in return for a stable oil supply. In 1980 the Carter Doctrine reinforced the commitment to use 'all necessary means' to guarantee US oil supplies. The US showed itself willing to do just this, re-flagging and escorting Kuwaiti tankers under US flags in 1987 and then leading the international reaction to Iraq's invasion of Kuwait.

In 2001, the Bush administration set up the National Energy Policy Development Group, which in May 2001 produced a National Energy Policy whose main conclusion was that access to foreign oil and gas would become the overriding security concern of US foreign policy. On this basis the US military was, in the words of one writer, 'converted into a global-oil protection service'.[66] New military deployments and partnerships were, it was argued, oriented primarily to guarantee oil supplies. Between 2000 and 2003 the Bush administration increased military aid to the US's top 25 oil suppliers by 1800 per cent, with primary increases going to Iraq, Uzbekistan, Kyrgyzstan, Azerbaijan, Colombia, Russia and Oman. While such deployments were justified by the Bush administration in terms of counter-terrorism, in practice they were – it was charged – more reflective of energy security imperatives. The 2001 Defence Review talked explicitly of deploying US armed forces where energy supplies might be impeded.[67] Plans were set in motion for a sizeable relocation of naval forces to protect Nigerian oilfields;

indeed, West African oil was defined as a 'strategic national interest', implying that military force could be mobilized in its protection.[68] In Colombia, US military activities increasingly went beyond counter-narcotics to fighting the guerrilla forces that were threatening key oil pipelines. The US expanded its largest base in the Middle East, in gas-rich Qatar, acknowledging a link to the protection of energy supplies.

All this was characterized by one critic as a new 'brazen energy imperialism', while the US's talk of democratizing the Middle East was likened to 'a drug addict asking his pusher to change his criminal activities'.[69] The 2006 State of the Union address seemed to signal a modest change of tone, with President Bush now suggesting that the US must wean itself off its 'addiction' to oil and declaring the goal of replacing more than 75 per cent of US oil imports from the Middle East by 2025. An Advanced Energy Initiative (AEI) was introduced, following on from the first US National Energy Plan for more than a decade that was signed into law in August 2005. In the opinion of most observers, however, the 'securitization' of energy policy remained a striking feature of US strategy. One writer claimed to have elicited from Bush insiders the assertion that 'US military and energy strategy … were to be one'.[70] One of the most comprehensive studies of US policies lamented that US approaches to energy security exhibited the same military flavour as other dimensions of US foreign policy and were bereft of more holistic, socio-economic understanding.[71]

European politicians and officials rejected such securitization, and insisted that this was where EU energy security policies were and would be clearly distinct from those of the United States. Diplomats were firm in rejecting the deployment of military forces to protect energy security. As one official admonished, 'This is 1945 thinking'. Member states resisted the prospect of formal European Security and Defence Policy (ESDP) involvement in energy security. Following explosions at the Russia–Georgia border in January 2006 there was some internal discussion on the option of deploying EU military assets to protect pipelines coming into European territory and even to assist third countries protect vital sea lanes, such as the Malacca Straits. Such options did not gain widespread support from member states, however.

Germany's energy correspondent categorically rejected the suggestion that there was any hard power dimension to German energy policies. Member-state energy representatives were virtually unanimous in rejecting the notion of 'hard security' instruments being harnessed to energy security concerns. One opined that this would simply provoke producer states into a less cooperative stance on energy. Another, from central and eastern Europe, saw an undue hostility towards Russia as particularly dangerous, arguing that energy policy must be defined 'on an economic not political basis'. One EU diplomat insisted that deploying either naval or ground forces to energy producer states was 'not an option' for the EU, and that the latter was focused more on trying to head off potential crises before they erupted.

Talk about 'security policy' within Brussels was all about the deployment of fledgling ESDP mission capabilities to small-scale local conflicts. One senior advisor suggested that Solana's lack of a clear mandate on broader security challenges, such as energy, in part explained the high representative's focus instead on deploying new ESDP missions, which many diplomats lamented as having diverted CFSP from overarching geo-strategy. ESDP debates were nearly entirely concerned with the conditions for military intervention in civil conflicts. One critic stressed ESDP's failure to broaden its 'strategic culture' out beyond this question.[72] Crucially, no ESDP discussion took place on what reaction would follow if and when energy supplies were reduced to any member state. One senior official revealed, moreover, that 'at 27' (member states) Council meetings had not engaged in an overarching strategizing of energy issues within the context of broader EU security identity. Another reported that Solana's interest in energy security was relatively limited, in particular relative to the high representative's shuttle peace-making diplomacy in the Middle East and Balkans. One expert saw ESDP settling comfortably into a relatively narrow niche of mixed civilian–military crisis management.[73] Another saw the EU's weakness as lying not in a lack of militarization per se but rather in 'ESDP's small do-gooding activities' being used to compensate for a lack of 'securitization of [the EU's] entire identity and image' and a 'continuing evasion of strategic responsibility'.[74]

However, some officials argued that differences with the US were not quite so absolute as it was sometimes claimed. Even as diplomats strenuously rejected the link, some European military cooperation and/or deployments did increase in key producer states – for instance, by Germany in Uzbekistan, France in Algeria and the UK in the Gulf. CFSP diplomats acknowledged that, whatever the criticisms of US policies, even the least Atlanticist of member states sought to retain some degree of (what was deemed) necessary 'coattailing' on US military guarantees in supplier states. Thus far debate on militarization had remained comfortably abstract: unlike the United States the EU had not been asked by producer states to provide military backing. Central and eastern European states, in particular, advocated a more cooperative stance rather than the present (it was judged) competitive energy relationship between the EU and the US.

Some European voices did appear to be toying with a more hard-security approach. In the UK, the Conservative party's defence spokesman argued that '[a]n indivisible energy security and national security policy will inevitably have consequences for the necessary shape and capabilities of the armed forces required to pursue those interests'.[75] Even if not pushing military power as such, many member state governments did support some greater cross-over with ESDP resources. Some lamented that the EU's Military Committee and the Situation Centre should be doing more to monitor potential crisis points specifically pertinent to energy security, at least to have such common analysis fed into CFSP deliberations on a systematic basis. Diplomats from one large member state professed to be 'cautious' over ESDP involvement in energy security, but recognized that the lack of EU consideration of pipeline protection was a worrying lacuna in European planning.

The December 2006 NATO summit in Riga agreed that NATO should be discussing energy security. This proposition was promoted by the US but with support from the British, German and Dutch governments.[76] Poland was the EU state most forcefully supportive of what it called 'the energy NATO', intimating at the need for hard-power protection for those states subject to Russian hardball energy tactics. In general, however, European states kept NATO's putative energy role focused on an extremely limited mandate, assessing no more than where the organization could add value to national efforts in protecting energy infrastructure when a specific threat was identified. One writer suggested that differences within NATO on this dimension of securitization confirmed that the US was focused primarily on the security of energy supplies, the EU on the management of energy demand.[77] Moreover, by the Bucharest summit in 2008 NATO was split over the stationing of US missiles in Poland and the Czech Republic, and little united focus remained on energy challenges. Polish politicians in particular lamented that the EU had eschewed a strategic partnership with the US on energy security.

In short, even if the position on military support was not quite cut and dry, it was still significant that nearly all European policy-makers professed a less directly securitized approach to energy than the US and energy matters did not figure prominently in the geostrategic planning of those tasked with developing the EU's fledgling hard-power capabilities.

Energy and governance

Perhaps unsurprisingly, policy-makers invariably rejected suggestions that their approach to energy security entailed a dilution of concerns over human rights and democracy in producer states. On the contrary, official policy documents and statements most commonly asserted that sustainable energy security required the EU to maintain pressure for governance reforms and better human rights protection around the world. The rise of 'resource nationalism' was widely seen as integrally linked to the non-democratic politics of producer states such as Iran, Nigeria and Venezuela. The Council Secretariat insisted that one of its principal contributions to intra-EU deliberations was to monitor the coherence between energy security strategies and 'overarching European values'. This meant warning that policies towards, say, Russia that obviously contradicted the EU's commitment to normative values would in turn undermine European credibility and effectiveness as a promoter of democracy and human rights in other countries. The argument was made that energy security could not and would not in this sense be pursued in isolation from the broader tenets of the EU's identity and strategic presence.

The internal market's (ostensible) centrality in rooting Europe's international projection was presented as orienting the EU towards energy strategies based on rules-based governance reform. Benita Ferrero-Waldner claimed that the EU's 'added value' to external energy policies would be to ensure that rule of law principles prevailed through 'enhanced legal framework[s]'.[78] The series of new energy partnerships – signed with Ukraine, Azerbaijan and Kazakhstan – represented a familiar EU-style approach of attempting to use contractual agreements to attain adherence to rules-based behaviour on market regulations, transport and safety. Officials laid stress also on the belief that rules-based governance offered the most promising way to approach China's rise as energy consumer: according to one diplomat, an increasingly prominent part of European energy strategy was the effort to convince China 'to trust the market'.

CFSP officials argued that their aim was to introduce into energy debates the notion that security ultimately depended on a broader understanding of 'state stability' in producer states. One official responsible for managing European participation in the Energy Charter insisted that the latter's importance lay in its focus on the rule of law and the role of governments in providing robust frameworks for foreign investment in the energy sector. From within the Commission it was constantly argued that the export of European standards and norms was the key to ensuring both consistency with human rights aims and improving conditions for EU investment in producer states.[79] The Relex director general insisted that good governance had become a key aspect of external-energy polices.[80]

The British Foreign and Commonwealth Office declared that, 'A UK objective is to engage with the international oil and gas companies to help promote good governance, stability and prosperity in ... developing countries'.[81] The JESS report of April 2006 explicitly linked energy security to 'political and economic stability and democratic reform in key producer countries'.[82] A key concern was that many 'producer and transit countries suffer from poor civil, judicial and legislative frameworks, inequality, corruption ... that ... increase the price of oil and gas exploration and extraction'.[83] The UK led the Extractive Industries Transparency Initiative (EITI) that it had launched at the World Summit for Sustainable Development in 2002. This aimed to gain commitments from multinationals to publish details of their payments in producer states, as a means of reducing the scope for bribery. The priority was to extend the EITI into new regions, while Nigeria, Azerbaijan and Kazakhstan were identified as principal country priorities.

A number of member states, especially Nordic governments, claimed they had pushed hard to strengthen the social and governance elements of the South East Europe Energy Community. The Benelux states insisted that they believed 'good governance and human rights [could] contribute to Europe's security of supply'.[84] German foreign minister Frank-Walter Steinmeier argued that the European Neighbourhood Policy's most basic rationale was to bring about 'a binding expansion of the EU legal area' in energy as in other matters.[85] The German energy correspondent suggested that the aspect of current deliberations that was new compared to previous European energy debates was that now prime attention was being paid conceptually to the challenge of 'what is needed politically to make markets work better'. And he claimed that after intense internal struggles the German economy ministry had finally accepted this political dimension and in consequence acknowledged the foreign ministry as a partner in energy policy. Some policy-makers made the argument that political change and integration into the global economy would together ensure diversification within producer states and thus reduce regimes' intensive use of revenues to cover national budgets and lead to more long-term planning and investment.

Subsequent chapters look at how human rights policies evolved in individual producer states; overall there was not an overwhelming diminution of European good governance and human rights initiatives. Funding allocated for human rights and democracy projects continued at a modest level and registered incremental increases in most member states. Political dialogue forums similarly developed in a gradual fashion, while commitments were made to reward democratic reforms in third countries with additional aid and trade provisions. Governments' rhetoric continued to emphasize the centrality of democratic values to the EU's external identity. Overarching European commitments and resources to support democracy and good governance retained their established trajectory – if anything, as indicated, some new initiatives were the result of more acute European concerns over the mismanagement of increasingly scarce and costly energy resources.

At the same time, some diplomats expressed doubts and adhered to a more traditional line of realpolitik. Javier Solana argued that, 'The scramble for territory of the past may be replaced by a scramble for energy ... We have to take our energy from where we find it. ... Thus, our energy needs may well limit our ability to push wider foreign policy objectives, not least in the area of conflict resolution, human rights and good governance ... The scramble for energy risks being pretty unprincipled.'[86] A senior French policy-maker stressed how Paris was concerned to move beyond its image as a 'status quo power' and be more supportive of political reform, with the key *exception* of oil producer states where European interests would suffer from assertive democracy promotion policies and where leverage would in any case be minimal.

One of the top CFSP officials warned that the changing structure of international politics left little scope for issues of democratic governance. EU governments, he argued, thought in terms of the availability of supplies for purchase on the international market, whereas China thought in terms of gaining control over reserves; the EU had not understood the significance of this clash of approaches and its future impact on geopolitics, as fundamentally different concepts prevailed of the basic 'rules of the game' in energy. As a consequence, he highlighted that in practice many in the EU felt: 'The jury is still out on whether global governance is better secured by a single framework or bilateral deals.' Another senior Commission official highlighted that at best only a narrow strand of rule of law issues should be seen as pertinent to energy policy, namely that of reducing the risk of international contracts being repealed.

European policy-makers nearly unanimously rejected the more instrumental link between democratic governance and energy security made by some US neo-conservatives – who argued that high oil prices were the result of autocrats needing to whip up popular resentment against the West and that therefore supporting 'regime change' would be beneficial for Western energy interests. Most European policy-makers admitted that in practice they saw the issue not so much in terms of positive, causal linkages between energy security and support for democratic reforms in producer states, but in an inverse and indirect sense: the more alternative sources of energy were developed the more scope there would be to retain a focus on international human rights. Despite the official EU-level rhetoric on governance standards, in practice much internal European deliberation was couched in terms of how much margin was left by energy imperatives for other foreign-policy objectives, rather than how these other governance-related aims themselves might serve energy interests. One common view was that energy explained why the EU's focus on human rights and democracy was weaker than that of the US, given the latter's lower degree of dependence on the most challenging autocratic producer states.[87]

One clear limitation to European governance policies in the area of energy was that the EITI was conspicuously not Europeanized. By 2007 only four member states – the UK, France, Germany and the Netherlands – had signed up to the EITI – although four further member states did commit during 2008 (Spain, Italy, Belgium and Sweden). By 2007 financial support for the EITI had been forthcoming from only the UK ($5.5 million), Dutch ($1 million) and German ($0.5 million) governments. The Commission declined to support the EITI, unlike a number of other multilateral energy initiatives. While repeating ritually that EITI was a good initiative, most European governments admitted to blocking proposals to exert strong and united EU pressure on states such as Russia, Algeria, Angola, Libya, Qatar or the United Arab Emirates to sign up. The EITI still included states accounting for only 5–10 per cent of world production. There was little pressure from member states to broaden out the EITI from its relatively technical focus on auditing payments made to governments, to cover either expenditure or upstream activities such as procurement irregularities.[88] (If many European governments were not enthusiastic about the EITI, the US also weakened it, undermining a UK proposal that oil companies break down the detail of their payments.)

In fact, the most notable feature of European democracy and human rights policies was that their overarching design continued to be strikingly disconnected from energy policy. The institutional 'turfism' familiar to students of EU foreign policy was especially potent in relation to energy policy. Diplomats working on democracy and governance issues in Brussels and national capitals had negligible locus over or input into energy decisions.

Those working under EU energy commissioner Andris Piebalgs complained at being kept in the dark about – and undermined by – the activities carried out in Africa by the development commissioner, Louis Michel. German energy policy-makers lamented that while in principle more discussion flowed on governance issues in producer states, in practice they still had no influence over those aspects of German foreign policies that related to such states' internal politics; conversely, the Austwärtiges Amt desk officers in charge of democracy and human rights promotion had no link to or knowledge of decisions being taken on energy policy.

In the UK, the FCO and Department for International Development (DfID) were focused on generic reform issues in the developing world, while the trade ministry led on specific energy-related investment concerns, which were most usually bereft of a broader governance focus. The trade ministry's apolitical approach was reiterated in its stressing that the 'sourcing of gas supplies from overseas is a matter for market participants'.[89] The FCO introduced the principle of 'mainstreaming' democracy promotion across all areas of policies, with the idea that all policies would be assessed for their impact on democracy; but those running the democracy unit admitted that this had little tangible impact and they had no input into energy issues. When David Miliband took over as Foreign Secretary in July 2007 he raised climate change to one of three FCO priorities, which did not include the promotion of democratic governance.

Those involved in revising Spain's democracy and governance strategy similarly admitted to having neither engaged with energy security debates nor having had input from diplomats responsible for energy dossiers. Indeed, Spanish diplomats were often critical of the new central European member states for putting energy security in jeopardy by their outspoken focus on democracy and human rights issues. The same situation pertained in Italy, those leading in defining Italy's positions on EU-level energy developments admitting to a lack of any engagement on or even awareness of political issues within producer states. MEPs acknowledged that these disconnects were also replicated in debates within the European Parliament. At a range of levels broad political governance issues – beyond very specific regulatory questions – were absent from energy policy decision-making.

Conclusion

Beginning from 2004–5 a plethora of new energy initiatives was forthcoming both from national governments and at the EU level. Nearly all of these initiatives purported to place energy security systematically at the heart of decision-making on European foreign policies. In practice, it was not clear that absolute priority was attached to doing this. Policy-makers insisted that the internal and external dimensions of energy security were compatible and indeed mutually reinforcing; but there were also significant trade-offs and tensions evident and which acted to the detriment of the foreign-policy dimension. The external dimensions of energy policy received notably less priority than climate change, and the relationship between these two aspects of policy remained strikingly under-assessed.

The notion most strongly espoused was the (familiar) one of the EU's internal market constituting the basis and principles of Europe's external projection and influence. Policy-makers proclaimed a governance-led approach to energy security. The economic (market extending) and political aspects of governance were presented as intertwined, two sides of the same 'rules-based' external energy policy. European governments were largely united in rejecting 'hard-power' approaches to energy security, although some admitted that this was as much by default as by design – moreover, some member states did deploy new security resources to key producer states, while protesting that this had nothing to do with energy.

But the common discourse masked persistent and serious doubts and differences, especially over the extent to which the internal market should be guided by states and deployed in a politically conditioned fashion. It was here that internal European unity appeared distinctly fragile. Many EU – member state and, to a lesser degree, Commission – decisions ran counter to this 'market-governance' philosophy. Those energy initiatives that contained a supposed focus on 'governance' in fact exhibited more of a narrow, technical than political bent. In practice support for democratic reforms continued to be conceived as a trade-off against, rather than a contribution to, energy security. In sum, at an overarching level, some of the basic tenets of external energy strategy remained uncertain as the EU developed a range of new policy initiatives.

4   The Middle East

Three decades before the energy security concerns of the 2000s, events in the Middle East had generated the first attempts at European energy-policy coordination, provoking sharp differences between European governments and with the United States. In the 1970s the US pushed for the creation of a strong consumers' cartel to rival the Organization of Petroleum Exporting Countries (OPEC); France refused and preferred to strengthen links with Arab regimes, through what became the Euro-Arab Dialogue. At the same time France pushed for a common European energy policy; the UK, Germany and the Netherlands agreed only to loose inter-governmental cooperation. The Dutch were affected badly by the lack of European support when Arab states imposed an oil boycott against them, in response to what Middle Eastern regimes criticized as The Netherlands' pro-Israeli foreign policy. Only when the Dutch threatened to cut off gas supplies to other European countries did a European oil-sharing commitment emerge. Differences between European Union (EU) states over broader Middle Eastern issues continued to militate against cooperation on energy security into the early 1990s, until the 1993 Oslo accords appeared to open the way for a more united and engaged EU presence in the Middle East, in particular through the Euro-Mediterranean Partnership (EMP).

This chapter demonstrates that during the 2000s the EU did indeed implement a range of initiatives designed to accord energy security greater priority in its relations with the Middle East. However, these new policies were not commensurate with the region's growing importance to European energy supplies and appeared disconnected from the shifting internal politics of Middle Eastern producer states. The chapter explores the variation in EU policies towards different parts of the region, namely North Africa, the Arabian Peninsula, Iran and Iraq. Other issues are shown to have cut across energy security, while several layers of mismatch could be observed between the rhetoric and the reality of EU energy security commitments. If the Middle East engendered the first efforts at European energy coordination in the 1970s, by the late 2000s it continued to cause much division and uncertainty within EU policy-making.

Middle Eastern challenges

Despite the rise of other energy producers, the Middle East remained pivotal to European energy interests. In 2006 61.5 per cent of the world's proven oil reserves and 40.5 per cent of its proven gas reserves were in the Middle East.[1] As Tables 4.1 and 4.2 demonstrate, in the rankings of global oil reserves the top five places were occupied by Middle Eastern states, while the latter accounted for six of the top ten places in the rankings of global gas reserves. In 2005 31.7 per cent of EU oil imports and 26.8 per cent of EU gas imports came from the Middle East. Spain and Italy were the purchasers of significant gas imports by pipeline from the region. Belgium, France,

Table 4.1 Middle East oil reserves (2006)

Country	Global ranking	Billion barrels
Saudi Arabia	1	264
Iran	2	138
Iraq	3	115
Kuwait	4	102
UAE	5	98
Libya	8	42
Qatar	14	15
Algeria	16	12
Oman	23	6
Egypt	29	4
Syria	31	3
Yemen	32	3
Tunisia	45	1

Source: OPEC Secretariat, *World Oil and Gas Journal*

Table 4.2 Middle East gas reserves (2006)

Country	Global ranking	Trillion cubic metres
Iran	2	28
Qatar	3	25
Saudi Arabia	4	7
UAE	5	6
Algeria	8	5
Iraq	10	3
Egypt	18	2
Libya	24	1
Oman	27	1
Yemen	33	0.5
Syria	44	0.3
Bahrain	49	0.1

Source: OPEC Secretariat, *World Oil and Gas Journal*

Italy, Spain and the UK brought in significant quantities of Liquefied Natural Gas (LNG) from the region.[2] The US imported a far lower share (under 20 per cent) of its oil and gas imports from the Middle East.[3]

The Middle East's share of world oil production was predicted to increase from 30 per cent in 2001 to 49.2 per cent in 2030; its share of gas production from 9 to 23.9 per cent over the same period.[4] Russia's new pre-eminence was based on a relatively high rate of production relative to known reserves; a lower ratio of extraction to reserves in the Middle East suggested that the latter's importance was set to increase over the longer term. Saudi Arabia remained the world's swing producer, the only state with sufficient capacity significantly to temper fluctuations in world oil prices. Much of Saudi territory remained unexplored, also giving it one of the strongest potentials for future new discoveries, industry experts opined.

Moreover, Saudi Arabia and Iraq enjoyed the cheapest oil-production costs in the world. As of 2007, only 22 of Iraq's 87 known oil fields were on stream, with large tracts of the country remaining unexplored. A study released in April 2007 reported Iraqi reserves at almost twice the level previously thought, a level that if confirmed would push the country above Iran into second place on the list of the world's largest reserves.[5] But by mid-2007

Table 4.3 EU oil imports from Middle East (2005)

Origin	% of total imports
Saudi Arabia	9.7
Libya	8.0
Iran	5.6
Algeria	3.6
Iraq	2.0
Syria	1.3
Kuwait	1.2
Tunisia	0.2
United Arab Emirates	0.1
Total MENA	31.7

Source: European Commission, *Energy Statistics Pocketbook 2007*

Table 4.4 EU gas imports from the Middle East (2005)

Origin	% of total imports
Algeria	20.6
Libya	1.9
Egypt	1.8
Qatar	1.8
Oman	0.7
Total MENA	26.8

Source: European Commission, *Energy Statistics Pocketbook 2007*

Iraqi production was still 30 per cent below Saddam-era levels.[6] In 2004 Iraq supplied only 1.4 per cent of EU energy imports, representing Europe's tenth largest supplier; in 2005 this figure rose modestly to 2 per cent.

North African gas offered the cheapest transportation rates into European markets. Algerian gas monopoly Sonatrach itself invested in European energy infrastructure, including LNG terminals in the UK and Spain. Spain established itself as the EU state with the largest LNG regasification capacity based on its increased imports from North Africa. Algerian gas exports doubled between 2004 and 2007. Two new pipelines were commissioned from Algeria to, respectively, Spain and Italy, due for completion around 2009–10. In Egypt significant new reserves of gas were discovered in the Nile Delta. Qatar became the largest LNG exporter in the world, through the South Pars Offshore Field.

In the Middle East, the increased competition facing Europe from Asian markets found acute expression. Analysts predicted that Middle Eastern oil was set to be drawn increasingly towards Asia. In 1980 two-thirds of the region's oil went to Europe and the United States; by 2004 this share had declined to one-third. Saudi Arabia's search for a dominant position in the Chinese market was leading it to offer low prices to China and to divert supplies away from European customers – with China apparently promising in return to sell the kind of military equipment that Europeans had not been prepared to sell.[7] Sinopec reached a $100 billion deal for investment in Iran at the end of 2006. Moreover, as Gulf populations expanded and became increasingly wealthy, there was also rising pressure for more oil to go to domestic energy consumption in the region and for the development of nuclear capacity.

Apparently offsetting the diminution in European leverage, figures showed that in overall terms the states of the Gulf Cooperation Council (GCC) were commercially more dependent on the EU than vice versa. The EU was the GCC's largest source of imports (accounting for 33 per cent of imports in 2004) and its second biggest export market (with 22 per cent of GCC exports going to Europe in 2004). Conversely, the GCC accounted for only 2.5 per cent of the EU's imports, while being the destination for only 4.3 per cent of EU exports.[8] One expert asserted that the Middle East's presumed 'oil weapon' was one of the great myths associated with the region, to the extent that Arab states were strongly and increasingly in need of access to international markets.[9]

Energy and politics in the Middle East

The standard, long-held view was that energy imperatives required Western governments to maintain alliances in the Middle East and that political change would be prejudicial to energy interests. Some analysts argued that the US's pressure for democratization was already too great: as Middle Eastern regimes had begun to liberalize their political systems they had, it was contended, felt more obliged to bend to popular sentiment to prioritize short term revenues and thus move away from support for low oil prices (previously justified in terms of the health and stability of Western economies being in the long-term interest of producer countries themselves).[10] Some observers suggested that Islamists – likely to emerge as the main beneficiaries of democratization – argued even more forcefully that production should be kept at a lower level and be more domestically oriented, rather than any effort made to reduce international prices.

Qatar, one of the most closed political regimes in the Middle East, was its most open to foreign direct investment (FDI) in the energy sector. Similarly, the United Arab Emirates remained highly authoritarian but had an increasingly outward-oriented economy. In contrast, some political liberalization had occurred in Kuwait, that continued to block foreign investment in the energy sector, Islamists in Kuwait's increasingly lively parliament hindering the ruling al Sabah family's proposals to open the oil sector to foreign investment. Where regimes did bend to domestic concerns it often did not augur well for Western interests.

Most crucially, the Saudi royal family played a pivotal role in dampening oil-price fluctuations. After 9/11 Saudi Arabia increased output to bring oil prices down from $28 to $22 a barrel. The Saudi government then promised to temper any upward pressure on oil prices that resulted from the 2003 Iraq invasion. Saudi Arabia helped reduce oil prices from their summer 2006 (momentary) peak of around $75 a barrel down to near $50 a barrel by early 2007. In June 2008 it raised production to a thirty-year high. At the same time, Saudi Aramco launched plans for major increases in productive capacity – arguably, the only National Oil Company (NOC) equipped for such an expansion without external technology. While a proposed opening to foreign investors – through the National Gas Initiative – faltered, limited gas exploration rights were granted to International Oil Companies (IOCs).

In the wake of terrorist attacks in Saudi Arabia in 2003 and 2004 the Saudi regime clamped down harder on radical groups. While not abandoning its historic alliance with Wahabbism, the al Saud family did appear chastened in a way it had not been by 9/11. Security measures on energy installations and foreign workers increased and the feared disruption to oil production did not materialize.[11] An amnesty was offered to radicals to abandon their activities. The regime was seen by many as robustly defending the kingdom and its oil facilities from Islamist terrorists. The government spent well over $1 billion to strengthen security at its production facilities after attacks on the latter in 2003. Saudi Arabia provided 30,000 troops to protect oil infrastructure.

Algeria was often cited as the most notable case of a violent civil conflict and de-democratization leaving energy exports unaffected. This was both because of the regime's ability to isolate energy facilities in security terms and because Islamist groups themselves often recognized that their social-spending plans would require continued revenue from energy sales – during

Algeria's long civil war in the 1990s the main militant groups refrained from attacking oil and gas installations. After revoking elections and taking power in 1992, the Algerian military presided over a regime that prided itself on being a reliable supplier of energy to European markets. The slow move back towards limited political liberalization in Algeria did not have major effects.

Despite such cooperation from autocratic regimes, however, some analysts suggested that the 'oil versus democracy' relationship was more complex than often assumed. They pointed to the ways in which incumbent authoritarian regimes were not serving European interests well and argued that the presumed dangers (for the West) of democratic change were overstated. This was most obviously the case in Iran and Iraq, which are discussed separately below; but it was also a dynamic not entirely absent elsewhere in the Middle East where more cooperative alliances had been established with incumbent regimes.

Questioning the standard line that the rentier states of the Gulf were well protected from democratic dynamics, some analysts suggested that two different dynamics had come into play. First, in some Gulf states resentment grew over government failures to deliver adequate wealth distribution and effective economic policy for long-term growth, as well as over the lack of transparency in the allocation of resources. Second, over time an incipient middle class had become more independent of the state than assumed by state rentier theory. At the same time, it was suggested that, with basic wealth provided, it was probable that political change would be less violent and destabilizing than in many other regions. The combination of wealth and the legitimacy of the region's royal families meant that in the Gulf open politics could be ushered in without complete collapse and discontinuity of the system.[12] In these ways, political opening could be more of a stabilizing force rather than strategic danger. Incipient reform had begun as a means of re-empowering regimes, who now grappled with the question of just how far to enfranchise citizens in the Gulf.[13]

One account argued that the ruling family now resembled a 'headless tribe' comprising several competing circles of power (rather than, as in the standard interpretation, being split simply between reformist and conservative camps). This structure, it was argued, hindered effective policy-making and bred instability as patronage networks around each senior prince constantly shifted in composition, with those 'suddenly excluded ... tend[ing] to switch to extreme hatred'.[14] The result was a growing inconsistency in policy pronouncements and decisions, a sense of drift and a lack of overall control.

A source of popular anger was precisely the fact that oil revenues flowed directly into the royal budget, with no accountability; in some senses, the increase in oil prices after 2002 actually exposed the regime to greater public criticism, even though the budget surplus reached record highs. Oil-related calculations indeed conditioned the modest process of political reform initiated by the Saudi royal family after 2001. This reform process allowed the holding of municipal elections, the creation of a National Organization for

Human Rights, an increased deliberative role for the Shura Council and several rounds of a reform-oriented National Dialogue. While change was carefully modulated by the regime, in particular after the succession of king Abdullah in August 2005 political debate became freer and differing positions within the ruling family itself were debated more openly.[15] Observers suggested that the royal family was concerned to deflect criticism of its management of oil revenues and also that post-2004 oil price increases would be insufficient to correct budget constraints of a more structural nature.[16]

It looked increasingly simplistic to assume that the al-Sauds were entirely beneficial for Western energy interests and that any increased influence for opposition groups risked being entirely prejudicial. With the exception of Al Qa'ida and the London-based Movement for Islamic Reform in Arabia opposition groups sought no radical policy departures but simply a less corrupt politics.[17] The regime scaled back its National Gas Initiative because it feared the political consequences of any significant market opening.[18] Similarly, Saudi Arabia won an exemption for the energy sector when it joined the World Trade Organization in December 2005, because the government realized that its continuing control over this sector was crucial to its political leverage both domestically and internationally. If in many Arab states Islamists stood in opposition to secular governments, in Saudi Arabia the state and Wahhabism were deeply intertwined, and the line blurred between official Salafism and extremist elements.[19] In short, one expert suggested that there were reasons for Western powers to back a controlled process of political liberalization to take the sting out of popular grievances – even if these powers were likely to support the ruling family when they concluded that this process was extending too far.[20]

In Kuwait, higher oil prices were also seen as helping to explain more intense political debate, with the regime coming under greater pressure to explain and justify its use of increased revenues. After the death of Sheikh Jabir in January 2006, both members of the ruling family and the opposition in parliament blocked direct succession of the Crown Prince in favour of Sheikh Sabah, demonstrating that succession was no longer an internal family matter. Elections held in 2006 were freer than on previous occasions, and women were allowed to stand as candidates – although none were elected and Islamists emerged as the biggest gainers from the poll. The Sabah family retained all key posts in government, including energy and foreign affairs, but a new spirit of open debate had taken root. A combination of the post-election opposition majority in parliament and increased cooperation between Islamists and liberals put the ruling family under meaningful pressure for the first time, especially on the profligate and corrupt use of oil revenues. While Islamists continued to oppose opening energy contracts to IOCs, opposition platforms were increasingly organized around pressure for the more transparent and efficient use of oil revenues, as a means of assisting stability and moderation. It was the Kuwaiti parliament, for instance, that put the regime under increasing pressure to release more accurate and transparent information on the state of the country's oil reserves.[21] Circumscribed elections that took place in 2006 in Bahrain and the United Arab Emirates were characterized by similar debates (even if the extremely high per capita wealth of the UAE and Qatar in particular has acted to dampen reform pressure).

In another sign of the status quo not necessarily favouring European interests, in the summer of 2006 the Algerian government reversed a tentative liberalization of the energy sector, as president Bouteflika sought to shore up his domestic support.[22] Sonatrach was henceforth automatically to be given a controlling stake in investment projects involving foreign companies. In 2007 the effective renationalization of the energy sector led Sonatrach to break a flagship 5 billion euro contract signed in 2004 with Repsol and Gas Natural to develop the Gassi Touil gas field in the east of the country. Islamist parties in the governing coalition claimed they sought a deepening rather than reversal of energy sector liberalization. Moreover, as the Salafist Group for Preaching and Combat launched a new campaign of violence in 2007 by attacking foreign oil workers – and as that group later took on the title of Al Qa'ida in the Islamic Maghreb – the illusion was shattered that Algeria's limited process of political liberalization had sufficed definitively to resolve conflict. Parliamentary elections in May 2007 were subject to widespread fraud and attracted a turnout of under 20 per cent, signalling a worrying disenchantment amongst Algerians over the nepotistic, corrupt and inefficient nature of the political system.

Increased gas revenues were similarly a factor in more vibrant oppositional politics in Egypt. Here higher energy prices did not assuage critics – the traditional dynamic expected of the rentier state – so much as increase pressure on the regime and provide a fillip to opposition groups. While Libya was welcomed back into the international fold, Western officials complained that gaining clarity on investment rules remained difficult due to the weakness of institutional structures. In much analysis it was argued that Middle Eastern governments continued to impose restrictions on Western oil investment because they calculated that FDI would be unpopular with their populations. While resource nationalism could not be explained only by the lack of democracy, autocracy had in practice not shielded European energy interests. In short, there were some – albeit modest – signs that changes to oil markets were the harbinger of a new politics. But how, if at all, were these factored into European energy security deliberations?

North Africa

Europe's engagement on energy issues was strongest in North Africa. Under the EMP technical cooperation on energy gradually strengthened after 1995. The EMP provided an institutionalized framework, in which energy issues were nested within an overall strategy that purported to work for both economic and political reform in the southern Mediterranean. A regular Euromed Energy Forum was established. Dialogue on and support for sub-regional integration was a particular focus. From the late 1990s European Commission MEDA (Mesures d'Acompagnement) aid was channelled to southern Mediterranean states to fund infrastructure development; work on the creation of a Euro-Maghreb electricity market; a joint energy office between Israel and Palestine; and various other technical harmonization measures. Loans from the European Investment Bank (EIB) assisted a number of large-scale projects, such as the construction of the Medgaz pipeline between Spain and Algeria.

The most conflictual episode in EU–Algerian relations occurred at the end of the 1990s, when the EU insisted on moving beyond the arrangement where over-priced Algerian gas was bought as part of Europe's support to the country's development process. Negotiations for an association agreement were put on hold, with the Commission pressing Algeria to move its prices towards market levels. Algeria duly complied, and soon was building the new gas pipelines to Italy and Spain. The pipeline being built by Sonatrach and Spanish firm CEPSA between Algeria and Almeria was due for completion in 2009. In November 2007 the Italian government sealed a new gas pipeline deal with Algeria, for the import of 8 billion cubic metres of gas a year into Italy; a larger increase in capacity of the existing pipeline across Tunisia was also completed.

From 2001–6, a relatively modest 14 million euros of MEDA funding was allocated to energy related projects.[23] It was at this sub-regional level, diplomats insisted, that the EU's export of regulatory frameworks for energy market reform functioned with tangible impact. Commitments to enhanced energy cooperation were then stipulated within the new European Neighbourhood Policy (ENP) action plans, based on higher level and more regular energy dialogue; regulatory cooperation; neighbour states' participation in EU energy programmes; the development of common energy networks; and energy cooperation between the different non-EU neighbours themselves.

By the end of 2006, an intensification of energy cooperation could be detected. The Commission proposed the creation of a Euro-Med Common Energy House, and an ENP Energy Treaty. The EU offered a new Strategic Energy Partnership to Algeria, based on commitments to regulatory convergence; resources for the linking of energy infrastructures (possibly including EU support for the trans-Saharan pipeline, from Nigeria); and technological cooperation. The EU also introduced a significantly more ambitious energy chapter into the ENP action plan being negotiated with Egypt, in response to the latter's rapidly increasing production of natural gas; Egypt was then offered the same form of separate energy agreement as that offered to Algeria.

The Euromed ministerial meeting held on 27–28 November 2006 endorsed plans for a 2007–10 Euromed energy partnership strategy and for an energy ministerial summit to be held in 2007.[24] The Commission's new aid programme for 2007–13 identified as priority areas for funding the integration of European and Maghrebi gas markets; support for extension of the Energy Community Treaty to the southern Mediterranean; and integration of Libyan energy markets into the broader regional framework.[25] An Experts Group was established in January 2007 under the Euro-Med Energy Forum to review the structural conditions of national energy sectors. Logistical support for this initiative was to come from the Euro-Med Energy Platform set up in Rome, although insiders noted that by mid-2008 this body had still not in practice started functioning. In November 2007 energy regulators from 23 Mediterranean states – including France, Italy, Spain, Cyprus and Malta from the EU – created a working group to approximate regulatory frameworks with EU energy rules.[26] Also in November 2007 a meeting on energy was held in Egypt with high-level ministerial European and Arab representation with the stated aim of galvanizing energy cooperation.

An EMP energy ministerial was held in December 2007. An action plan was agreed for 2008–13 with commitments to harmonize regulatory frameworks; develop trans-European networks; increase aid to energy projects; work towards Libya's inclusion; and energy-sector reform, especially through southern Mediterranean states creating independent regulatory agencies. Energy commissioner Andris Piebalgs asserted that by 2013 North Africa should be as important to Europe as Russia.[27] A new Commission document on strengthening the ENP at the end of 2007 gave energy a prominent place and made a number of notable commitments, including the aim to negotiate binding provisions on trade in energy with southern partners; to undertake a feasibility study on implementing a common legal framework for the neighbourhood in energy; and to increase the share of the Neighbourhood Investment Facility going to energy projects.[28] A meeting with Mashreq states in May 2008 promised increased EU funding for linking the Trans-Arab pipeline into the Nabucco line and thence onto European markets; support that critics noted was much overdue. Looking further forward, the EU proposed assisting southern Mediterranean states develop renewable energy sources, with the notion that these would increase energy output available for import into Europe.

Despite such developments, southern EU member states expressed frustration. The Spanish government, in particular, lamented what it saw as the relatively limited priority given to energy security issues within the EU's Mediterranean policy. Madrid complained at the extent to which energy security policy was being 'dictated' by Germany's fixation with Russia. This had given the impression that energy security was essentially 'a Russian policy', when for Spain Algeria was much more important as a gas supplier than Russia. Spain claimed that its efforts to deepen commitments on energy cooperation at the EU–Algeria association council in July 2006 had met with relative disinterest from other member states, which could not see beyond their series of meetings due with Vladimir Putin. Despite its energy importance, Algeria was the lowest per capita recipient of MEDA aid.[29] In 2005, France channelled 255 million euros of aid to Algeria; no other member state gave more than 10 million[30] although Spain's aid allocation to Algeria more than doubled in 2006.[31]

Indeed, Spain's priority concern with North Africa led it to prioritize bilateral initiatives outside the scope of the EMP. Sitting uneasily with the supposed region-building philosophy of the Barcelona process, Spain's bilateral negotiations with Algeria for the construction of a new gas pipeline between the two countries provoked critical comments from EU officials that this threatened to exclude Morocco and France, and undermine the essential logic of a regional Euromed energy market. Diplomats acknowledged that behind proposals for enhanced Franco-Spanish cooperation in North Africa, fierce competition on energy issues encouraged both these states to stress bilateral partnerships with Arab regimes.

So strongly did Spanish officials feel that North Africa was being neglected within overall EU energy security planning that they increasingly advocated a prioritization of this sub-region despite this running counter to Spain's own long-standing role as guardian of the EMP's regional philosophy. By 2007 Spain was officially pressing Algeria to show it 'preferential treatment' in energy supplies over other European consumers and proposed a bilateral 'energy partnership'. The French also admitted that the bilateral dimension continued to predominate in relations with Algeria, Paris signing a new energy treaty with Algeria in 2006. Nicolas Sarkozy made his first foreign trip as president to Algeria – breaking the tradition that Rabat was first port of call for new occupants of the Elysée Palace – and offered a deal: firmer guarantees on Algerian gas supplies in the short term, in return for French nuclear-energy cooperation in the longer term. Spain also signed a bilateral cooperation treaty with Egypt in February 2008, strongly focused on energy, with Unión Fenosa developing a large LNG plant in Egypt.[32]

Other states, and in particular the UK, began to take a keener interest as Algeria developed its LNG capacity, spurred by EU gas-market liberalization bringing the prospect of falling prices. The overall level of EU concern and engagement with Algeria increased notably after Gazprom reached a deal with Sonatrach in 2006, in connection with which Russia agreed a new debt relief package with the Algerian government.[33]

France promoted the idea of a new Mediterranean Union, incorporating Mediterranean littoral states and with a denser institutional structure than the EMP, as being in part about locking North African states into a deeper energy interdependence and partnership. Sarkozy identified energy cooperation as one of the top priorities in his vision of the Mediterranean Union – for him this was about both European access to North African supplies and EU/French help to develop nuclear energy capabilities in the southern Mediterranean. In early 2008 the French government proposed that a stand alone Energy Office be set up under the rubric of the Mediterranean Union, even further to upgrade energy cooperation. The Mediterranean Union proposal engendered opposition from northern member states, who were excluded from Sarkozy's plans. In March 2008 a watered-down version of the proposal was agreed that 'EU-ified' the initiative by essentially repackaging the Barcelona process as the 'Union of the Mediterranean'. The commitment remained, however, to use this as a platform to upgrade energy cooperation with North Africa. Sarkozy spoke of a 'common energy policy between the north and south of the Mediterranean'.[34] In June 2008 the Spanish government proposed an EU–Mediterranean energy charter.

Despite such developments it was noted that the EU – including its southern member states – were increasingly driven in their strategic planning towards North Africa by what they took to be a securitized link between migration and counter-terrorism.[35] This contributed to the relatively low profile of energy debates by comparison. It also cut across the EU's supposed commitment to support governance reforms as part of its external energy policies. Such reform efforts and funding were not aimed primarily at the EMP's main energy producers; Morocco and Jordan were the main targets of reform-oriented support, along with the Palestinian Territories. France and Spain, along with other member states, approached human rights issues in North Africa increasingly through relatively 'soft' cultural dialogue, policy driven increasingly by a concern with a supposed 'radicalization' of Muslim minorities within Europe itself.

In 2004 France concluded a military cooperation agreement with Algeria; this military aid was increased in June 2008, despite Bouteflika remaining ambivalent at that moment over the Union of the Mediterranean. The Spanish ministry of defence highlighted that its role was to ensure a basic culture of 'hard security' confidence between Spain and North Africa to permit progress on energy and other issues. If support for the rule of law was frequently heralded as a particular focus and concern of European policies, the lack of EU support for Egypt's increasingly politically active judges was conspicuous. The aim of linking the Trans-Arab and Nabucco pipelines required increased cooperation from highly authoritarian Syria, as a transit state for the former. The French government insisted that a key innovation of the Mediterranean Union would be to exclude the political conditionality of the EMP. Some observers pointed to a discrepancy in EU geostrategic approaches employed in different parts of the European Neighbourhood Policy: if in the East networks and linkages in numerous policy areas had blurred the EU's frontier, in the South a logic of defensive-exclusion and more traditional hegemonic realism prevailed.[36]

Indeed, in the southern Mediterranean the EU expressly sought to circumvent its own conditionality rules. A bilateral energy agreement pursued with Algeria enabled energy cooperation to be deepened outside the scope of a new ENP action plan, without the latter's focus on democracy and human rights – elements that had caused Algeria to stall on concluding the action plan. Indeed, by 2008 Algeria was the only EMP partner resisting the offer of a Neighbourhood action plan, a resistance perceived by policy-makers to reflect the country's more assertive foreign policy that had emerged on the back of increased energy revenues. Adopting positions uncannily similar to those of Vladimir Putin's Russia, Algeria itself proposed a partnership based more specifically on energy, bereft of the 'values' upon which the ENP was nominally predicated and of a sort that recognized Algeria's self-perceived growing strategic pre-eminence. Algeria in fact held out longer than Russia against the EU's demands that 'destination clauses' be dropped from energy contracts. The EU–Algeria Memorandum of Understanding on energy cooperation, formally stressing the centrality of convergence to the EU internal market, was signed just as the Algerian government was reversing its commitment to energy-market liberalization, increasing prices to Spain and, through Sonatrach, signing a strategic partnership with Gazprom. Despite all of which the EU accepted the notion of a bilateral partnership with Algeria that appeared to cut across much of the acquis of its own regional EMP Energy Forum.

Algeria's March 2007 energy price hike against Spain was seen in Madrid as a reflection of this new assertiveness and 'payback' for the Zaptero government's markedly more pro-Moroccan stance on the Western Sahara. During long and complex negotiations between Madrid and Algiers, revolving around the ownership structure of the Medgaz pipeline and Spanish limits on Sonatrach's downstream operations in Spain, Algeria threatened to cut supplies into Spain.[37] And while Sonatrach's decision to revoke its contract with Repsol and Gas Natural did not directly threaten supplies to Spain, it represented a significant blow for the Zapatero government and demonstrated the limited dividends from the attempt to recalibrate relations with Bouteflika. Madrid argued that it also reinforced the need for reciprocity, Spain having finally agreed to open its domestic market (albeit in limited fashion) to Sonatrach before the latter reneged on its contract with Repsol and Gas Natural. Indeed, while the Commission's September 2007 proposal on reciprocity was dubbed the 'Gazprom clause' it additionally engendered a hostile reaction from Algeria, the latter seeing this clause also as a reaction to Sonatrach's increasing downstream activity in Europe.[38] In October 2007 Spain agreed a new deal with Sonatrach expanding the latter's participation in increasing Spanish LNG capacity. However, independent analysts saw Algeria's imposition on Spain of a 20 per cent price increase as a political response to Madrid's refusal to allow Sonatrach to gain the majority share of the Medgaz pipeline.[39]

The re-emergence of terrorist attacks in Algiers in 2007 compounded Spanish and French concerns: even if short-term governance issues did not appear unduly problematic for energy supplies, they mattered, argued one diplomat, insofar as they contributed to a failure definitively to resolve Algeria's internal conflict. Despite all this, president Bouteflika seemed to have won European support for his success in tempering instability, in part achieved through the use of oil and gas windfalls to 'buy off' both Berbers and moderate Islamist groups. The Spanish government complained that, in the midst of its tense negotiations with Bouteflika, Algeria's deal with Gazprom had even been reached with the active support of French and Italian energy firms – an episode which reputedly pushed Madrid into backing Poland's plea for an 'energy solidarity clause' in the new EU treaty.[40]

In short, events in Algeria – a new wave of violence, Algeria's resistance to the ENP and its increasing Russia-like assertiveness flouting liberalization and market integration commitments – left European policy-makers uncertain how to proceed with this vitally important gas supplier and struggling to maintain a 'market-governance' and unified approach. One policy-maker admitted that in North Africa 'we haven't looked at energy from a political perspective as in Russia', the region's politics not having been seen as 'problematic' or even as pertinent as in the Russian case.

This was also increasingly seen in Libya. Libya was a focus of new European initiatives, in the wake of the twin deals on the Lockerbie bombing suspects and Libyan suspension of weapons of mass destruction (WMD) development. Italy – the biggest importer of Libyan oil and gas – in particular pushed the idea of Libya being offered an energy partnership like Algeria, Azerbaijan and Kazakhstan. Rome openly expressed annoyance that this was blocked by Bulgaria over the plight of Bulgarian nurses detained in Libya. Indeed, Italy admitted to circumventing this issue and 'negotiating indirectly' on a bilateral basis to unlock such energy cooperation with Libya. When Tony Blair paid a farewell visit to Colonel Gaddafi in May 2007 he spoke of a 'transformation' in British relations with Libya and presaged the signing of a new $900 million British Petroleum oil contract.

After the Bulgarian nurses were released in July 2007, the EU moved immediately to offer Libya a raft of new cooperation deals. Efforts were made to make Libya eligible for EU funds for the development of energy infrastructure, despite diplomats admitting that democracy commitments were one of the reasons why Libya remained uninterested in joining the Euro-Mediterranean Partnership. Nicolas Sarkozy was the first European leader to Tripoli, offering Gaddafi the same deal as he had proposed in Algiers: oil and gas supplies for France, nuclear technology in return. This provoked open consternation from a number of member states, in particular Germany.

After technical talks commenced with Libya in July 2007 on the possibility of the Commission offering a range of sectoral cooperation, France and the UK were especially active in pushing for a new, formal EU agreement with Libya. President Sarkozy envisaged his proposed Mediterranean Union as an additional means of incorporating Libya – although other member states prevented such an offer from circumventing existing Barcelona process commitments on human rights. In October 2007 ENI concluded a huge $28 billion deal with Libya. During his December 2007 visit to France, Gaddafi signed nearly 15 billion euros in trade contracts. This was followed immediately by a Zapatero–Gaddafi summit, at which an even higher value (17 billion euros) of trade deals was concluded.[41] By 2008 the European rapprochement with Libya was still in its early stages – and indeed overshadowed by a Gazprom–Libya deal in April 2008, which Moscow supplemented with debt relief and arms sales. Moreover, energy was not the only or even primary factor in the EU's rapprochement: after the lifting of the arms ban, member states provided large amounts of equipment to Libya to stem illegal immigration into Europe.[42] European efforts were sufficiently advanced, however, to suggest that this would be a key area of future energy security efforts.

The Arabian Peninsula

Despite its central importance for European energy supplies, the Arabian Peninsula did not witness the same degree of institutionalized EU energy cooperation as the southern Mediterranean. Remarkably no EU–GCC energy dialogue was established during the 1990s; even though differences over market access and investment rules for energy products impeded the conclusion of free trade talks, the benign state of international markets was seen to render separate initiatives on energy unnecessary.[43] In the wake of 9/11 much debate was conditioned by the changing relationship between the United States and Saudi Arabia. Critics argued that oil had become such a predominant issue in US–Saudi relations that the Bush administration was unduly soft on Saudi Arabia's indulgence of radicals, its lack of counter-terrorist cooperation both before and after the attacks on the Twin Towers, and the suspected links between members of the ruling family and militants. In particular, in 2001 the US was hopeful of $25 billion of gas exploration rights being up for grabs in Saudi Arabia under the latter's National Gas Initiative.[44] Despite this, US–Saudi tensions did encourage some in the ruling family to shift towards Europe, as well as China and Japan, at least to the extent that 'contracts were no longer decided reflexively in America's favour' – and indeed Total, ENI, Repsol, Sinopec and Lukoil were awarded contracts under the Gas Initiative.[45]

Energy concerns were a factor behind the EU's new Strategic Partnership with the Mediterranean and Middle East, which purported to deepen European engagement 'east of Jordan' – several of those member states uneasy with the EU's attention being diverted from the EMP area did eventually back this new initiative in large measure because of heightening worries over energy security.[46] The Commission proposed extending its idea for both the ENP Energy Treaty and the Euro-Med Common Energy House to GCC states, as well as offering the latter the kind of energy agreement signed with Ukraine, Azerbaijan and Kazakhstan – Arabian Peninsula states being conscious of their having apparently been relegated even below Central Asian states in the pecking order of formal EU contractual agreements. A small amount of funding was made available for energy cooperation projects in such middle income states under the new 2007–13 EU budget.[47] The Commission advocated support for building pipelines across the Arabian peninsula to reduce the amount of oil that had to pass through the vulnerable Straits of Hormuz.[48]

However, the failure of trade negotiations between the EU and the GCC undercut the prospects for other aspects of policy cooperation. By 2008, EU–GCC free-trade area talks had been running for 19 years. The EU wanted Gulf states to lift restrictions on services investment and raise domestic energy prices to the levels charged to European customers; the Gulf states bemoaned European protectionism in petrochemicals. Indeed GCC representatives asserted that the EU's protectionism negated their enthusiasm for broader energy partnership and exposed the EU's rhetoric of 'extending the internal market' as hypocrisy. The EU proposed a Memorandum of Understanding on energy cooperation; the GCC states rejected the idea, insisting that a free trade agreement (FTA) was the precursor to deepening other areas of cooperation. After some internal debate, the EU decided not to reduce its free-trade demands in order to progress on energy cooperation. Notwithstanding the supposed imperative of energy security, the EU declined to make concessions relating to the openness of its own petrochemicals market that might have unlocked a more systematic energy engagement in the Arabian Peninsula – much to the chagrin of energy officials.[49]

Even after Saudi Arabia's entry into the WTO at the end of 2005, there was still not enough agreement to conclude the FTA, and if anything the political will to do so seemed to ebb.[50] European positions on trade access engendered increasing criticism from some Gulf states that energy relations were being constrained by the 'straitjacket' of the EU insisting on conducting relations on a region-to-region basis. The smaller Gulf states in particular berated the EU for thinking rigidly in terms of exporting its own model of regional integration, without recognizing that the intra-regional dynamics were quite different, and weaker, within the GCC. The insistence on a region-to-region strategy was seen as hindering a deepening of energy cooperation with individual producers and allowing Saudi Arabia to act as a 'big brother' gate-keeper between Europe and the smaller GCC suppliers. Despite acknowledging the increasingly frequent criticisms and negative impact on energy cooperation, Commission officials insisted that by its very nature the EU was drawn to defending the regional approach. External relations commissioner Benita Ferrero-Waldner, on a visit to the Gulf in April 2008, insisted that the importance of energy concerns would lead to the FTA being signed in 2008.[51] At the time of writing, it remained to be seen whether the familiar optimism would this time prove warranted.

GCC states complained also that they were treated by the EU only as sources of energy, when the GCC sought a broader strategic partnership to offset US power, especially in relation to the Arab–Israeli conflict.[52] The Saudi government, in particular, was keen for the EU to buy into its regional agenda, for example on Iran, as quid pro quo for deeper energy cooperation. Saudi officials also suggested that other areas of cooperation had not been helped by the EU's decision not to engage with the Hamas government in Palestine. Some European officials complained, conversely, that dialogue was already far too dominated by efforts to coordinate positions on Palestine and that this issue invariably displaced all debate and cooperation on energy. Indeed, many diplomats suggested that if Europe was showing some, albeit modest, degree of greater commitment to the Gulf this was driven mainly by concerns over broader geopolitical instability in the Middle East, and was especially a reflection of Saudi Arabia's growing leverage in relation to the Arab–Israeli conflict and events in Lebanon, Iran and Iraq – it was in this sense that relations in the Gulf could be differentiated from the more clearly energy-driven focus in EU relations towards Russia. GCC diplomats concurred that it was this broad geo-strategic dialogue that was attractive to Gulf states, rather than the prospect of more formal energy cooperation. If the latter was sought it was less in relation to Europe's import of oil supplies and more on GCC states' desire for European renewables technology.

Senior officials admitted that by 2008 there had been no debate on how the EU's new energy strategy would impact on such high political dimensions of European relations with the Gulf monarchies. One former Commission official described EU–GCC conversation on energy as no more than 'rudimentary'. The EU lacked the degree of leverage it gained in other regions through the combination of development aid and technical cooperation on energy infrastructure links – neither of these policy instruments of strong relevance to the Gulf. Quizzed over experts' predictions of a growing problem of under-investment in productive capacity in the Gulf, European policy-makers acknowledged that smooth and cheap supplies from the region during the 1990s had pushed any such longer-term challenges off the diplomatic radar screen. An absence of transatlantic coordination over Gulf energy challenges was also acknowledged, the relationship with the US being described as competitive rather than cooperative.

Compared to other areas of foreign policy, the degree of Europeanization was limited in the Gulf. One Council official observed that in relation to the Gulf, only the UK and France were interested in political developments and contributed to debates; other states were 'happy to just keep buying the oil'. Remarkably, by 2007 there had been no CFSP discussion on the foreign-policy impact of energy challenges related to the Gulf. One noted Gulf figure lamented that for Javier Solana the Gulf remained a 'black hole'. A number of member states expressed unease with the Commission seeking to fashion a lead role for itself on energy politics on the back of its trade role. Several governments admitted to efforts to rein back the Commission, with the latter lamenting that this hampered the elaboration of a common energy security policy towards the region. GCC representatives acknowledged that they still focused their diplomatic efforts overwhelmingly on the three big member states.

Competitive, national policies prevailed. The UK – that had established a cross-Whitehall Middle East Energy Group – advocated more of a common EU focus 'east of Jordan'. But it also fought to retain its own privileged national links. Indeed, diplomats indicated that as the focus switched from counter-terrorism to energy security this balance in UK policy had tilted back towards a preference for bilateral, national policies. A number of member states complained when the UK reached a bilateral LNG agreement with Qatar in 2006, lamenting that this undermined efforts to conclude a regional free trade agreement. UK officials argued that the EU dimension of policy towards Saudi Arabia was unlikely to play a primary role, the key instead being how Saudi actions related to broader international market structures – Saudi Arabia's importance in a sense took it beyond the standard regional frameworks typically promoted by the EU. In this sense, deepening EU–OPEC dialogue was the key in strengthening engagement with and influence over Saudi Arabia, with progress here compensating for the stagnation of EU–GCC relations. The reliance on Saudi cooperation was thrown into even sharper relief at the international summit called in Saudi Arabia in June 2008 at which the major consumer and producer states debated ways to reduce energy prices.

France's increasing interests and engagement in the Gulf were of particular note.[53] However, while Paris pushed for a more strategic European presence and even raised the prospect of incorporating the Gulf into the EMP, Commission officials complained that the French were increasingly reluctant to entertain the concessions on trade liberalization requisite to concluding the FTA – in particular in the run-up to the closely fought 2007 French elections.

Germany's interest in the region also deepened. The German foreign ministry launched an energy initiative in the United Arab Emirates, designed to boost investment and infrastructure cooperation. When Angela Merkel visited the Gulf, holding the EU presidency in 2007, she declared that part of her aim was to promote a strengthening of Germany's *national* energy ties with the Gulf.[54] Berlin argued that strategic policies should not be made dependent on the FTA and pushed for a directoire (German–French–British) leadership in policy towards the GCC. The latter proposal was blocked by Spain, itself not as convinced as these states that the Gulf merited greater priority from the EU.

However, many efforts were too weak to denote serious intent. A UK–Saudi Arabia Two Kingdoms Dialogue was initiated, but political aid was of little significance in the Gulf. NATO's Istanbul Cooperation Initiative was elaborated as a means of encouraging security-sector reform in the Gulf, but tensions soon arose over its efforts to press for reform of civil–military relations in the region.[55] EU–OPEC meetings were welcomed, it was claimed, in part as 'cover' for addressing political issues mainly in the Gulf, and in particular as a better way to gaining political engagement with Saudi Arabia. Little governance-related leverage resulted from Saudi Arabia's WTO entry. Conditionality was eschewed – although turning geopolitical flexibility artfully on its head, southern member states argued that the lack of democracy in the Gulf was one reason why the EU should not divert its attention from the Mediterranean to the Arabian Peninsula. One high-level Brussels official lamented that the Strategic Partnership's language on political reform was too tough, and that Gulf states' consequently cool response had undermined engagement on energy-related issues. In fact, the EU did not pursue formal dialogue with civil-society organizations in the Gulf. The Commission dropped attempts at 'decentralized', civil society aid programmes in the Gulf after 2002, insisting that these were making no progress and creating tension with regimes. The most the EU was willing to do was to fund World Bank and United Nations Development Programme projects on resource revenue transparency. Brussels officials indeed stressed their belief that this very caution increasingly – and properly, in their mind – distinguished Europe from the United States: a common refrain was, 'we are not the US, we are not in the business of regime change'. By mid-2008 several member states were arguing that the EU should dilute its human rights clause in order to help unblock FTA and energy cooperation talks.

One member-state diplomat captured a common sentiment in suggesting that Gulf states were authoritarian but largely 'well run' and had not presented the kind of energy security difficulties emanating from other producer countries and regions. Despite ubiquitous rhetoric on the desirability of engaging with Islamists and recognizing the latter as legitimate political actors, officials expressed concern over the impact on energy interests of Islamists' rise in GCC states – pointing in particular to their strong showing in Saudi Arabia's first municipal elections. In justification of realist-geopolitics, some policy-makers also pointed to China's increasing influence in the Gulf, as Sinopec signed a number of deals in Saudi Arabia from 2004 and in 2006 King Abdullah promised energy cooperation on a trip to Beijing. Many energy specialists were highly exercised by the lack of transparency in information on Middle Eastern reserves and market rumours that these could actually have been overstated for many years, but policy-makers did not bring this up as being of any concern. One concern that diplomats did mention was not the lack of democracy so much as the opaque nature of internal royal-family politics in states such as Saudi Arabia, especially when more 'radical' wings of these families were able to frustrate relations with European governments.

EU policy approached energy security in a compartmentalized fashion, divorced from both broader Gulf security issues and any understanding of the way in which Gulf states and societies were changing. One diplomat revealed that many in the EU favoured developing relations on an EU–OPEC rather than EU–GCC basis precisely because the former was bereft of 'extraneous' conversations on internal politics. UK diplomats admitted that governments' enthusiasm for pushing Middle Eastern political reform rose and fell in response to other security issues: a commitment to reform took shape in the wake of 9/11 as a perceived means of attacking the political roots of terrorism, and had diminished in response to the 7 July 2005 London bombings, the turmoil in Iraq and the deterioration of the Arab–Israeli conflict. Policy-makers acknowledged that the evolution of political reform policies was completely unrelated to the energy security debate, and indeed noted a persistent lack of linkage between the reform and energy debates. Indeed, CFSP representatives in the Council Secretariat admitted to having little knowledge of the proposed MoU on energy cooperation. By the end of 2007 the Strategic Partnership had in effect been abandoned, having remained devoid of substance and having done little to advance a more comprehensive energy security strategy.

The lack of democracy in the Middle East certainly did not prevent a number of member states from increasing arms sales and deepening military cooperation with Gulf regimes. In 2006 Gulf states benefited from new arms deals totalling 13 billion dollars from the UK and 10 billion dollars from France (along with 11 billion worth of deals from the United States).[56] The credibility of British strictures on good governance was seriously undermined when Tony Blair interrupted an investigation into kickback allegations related to the 1986 UK–Saudi Al Yamama arms-for-oil deal, just as a follow on 40 billion pound deal for British Aerospace was due to commence. The government cited the primacy of national security interests; in line with OECD anti-corruption rules the government would not have been able to cite commercial (that is, energy) interests as reason for dropping the case. A key factor in the government's decision was that France was already lobbying the Saudi royal family – the latter threatening to rescind their contract with the UK if they were pursued on corruption charges – to sign an alternative deal for its Rafale jet. The UK did not inform its EU partners of the new deal. In turn, Nicolas Sarkozy visited the region in January 2008, agreeing a further 12 billion euros of arms sales and nuclear technology transfers, as well as a deal to establish a permanent French military base in the UAE. Spain also agreed military cooperation with the UAE in May 2008.

All this appeared to weaken European governments' claims that their approach to energy policy was governance-led and devoid of hard-security elements. However, the US still predominated in the more direct areas of security provision. In October 2006 US forces moved into the Saudi port of Ras Tanura to ward off possible attacks against the world's biggest oil-export facility – UK troops provided some support, but European forces were not directly involved.[57] When in August 2007 the Saudi regime announced plans further to strengthen the security protection of its oil infrastructure this was to be done in conjunction with US cooperation, on the back of a new $20 billion US arms deal with GCC states. Moreover, by 2008 a number of EU member states were criticizing the new French sales of nuclear technology to Gulf states, arguing that these would diminish rather than enhance security over the longer term.

Iran

In two countries – Iran and Iraq – the issue of energy was clearly eclipsed by other challenges, with the result that efforts to develop contractual, rules-based energy partnerships were either more hesitant or compromised. In Iran the most significant factor was the extent to which the EU pursued an increasingly tough stance towards non-proliferation despite the country's potential importance as energy supplier.

Under the two presidencies of Mohammed Khatami from 1997 to 2005 the EU and Iran had begun to explore cooperation in a number of areas, including energy. From the late 1990s European diplomatic visits increased, as did trade and investment flows. An EU–Iran working group on energy cooperation was created in 1999. Total signed a deal with the National

Iranian Oil Company that had the potential to supply two-thirds of France's domestic gas requirements. During this period oil products accounted for nearly 80 per cent of European imports from Iran.[58] A European Commission communication of February 2001 introduced a package of proposals for closer relations with Iran, in part as a response to reformists' increased representation in the Iranian parliament.

Responding to the terrorist attacks of 9/11, European strategies sought further to reinforce engagement with Iranian reformists. The EU offered a Trade and Cooperation Agreement (TCA) in December 2002. The EU successfully pushed for the creation of a formal Human Rights Dialogue with Iran and the package of incentives offered to Tehran included benchmarks on economic and political reform. However, TCA negotiations soon stalled due to the ambivalence of Iranian conservatives, just as this group reasserted its power after 2003. Throughout this period it was significant that conservatives retained control of the oil ministry, limiting Khatami's efforts to open up oil and gas contracts to foreign companies.[59]

After the discovery of Iran's uranium enrichment activities in 2002, the question of Iran's nuclear programme came to dominate relations with Europe, to the detriment of cooperation in other areas. Under a 2003 agreement, the EU committed itself to supplying low-enriched uranium sufficient to develop civilian nuclear capabilities, while Iran agreed to suspend enrichment and accept a strengthened inspections protocol. After several setbacks, TCA negotiations resumed in January 2005 and the EU agreed to push for Iran's entry into the WTO. A key part of the 'rewards' promised by the EU in return for Iran abandoning its nuclear programme was European assistance to modernize the country's energy infrastructure. Talks soon faltered again, however, as Iran threatened to restart uranium enrichment. When in January 2006 Iran resumed research and development at its Natanz plant, the EU supported a referral to the Security Council, having resisted US pressure for such a move since 2003. Deadlines on a series of ultimatums to Iran came and went, until the EU supported the imposition of a limited range of sanctions in December 2006. These were tightened modestly in March 2007 and again in March 2008.

It thus appeared that the EU opted unequivocally to prioritize the nuclear issue over energy security. Nascent cooperation on energy, investment rules and good governance was sacrificed to exert pressure on Iran demonstrably to limit its nuclear programme to civilian capacity. Indeed, sanctions soon seemed to bite precisely in the energy sector. At the end of 2006 Iran admitted to difficulties in obtaining funding for its oil projects.[60] EU diplomats even openly discouraged European companies from investing in Iran, saying that this was not helpful when Iran was in the 'international dock' over its nuclear activities.[61] Differences emerged here, with the Chirac government offering open support to Total's Iranian plans, but the Blair government warning Shell it was 'walking a tightrope' in the Islamic Republic. Some pointed out that energy security was at odds with the EU's nuclear diplomacy in an even more direct sense: Iranian officials argued that if Iran were to develop a nuclear-energy capability it would have more gas available for export.

It might alternatively be argued that the importance of the energy issue helped explain why the sanctions imposed against Iran were in practice relatively limited and one of the several reasons why European governments were so resolute in their opposition to any military attacks on Iran's nuclear installations. Diplomats' complaints over European oil and gas companies launching new investments in Iran appeared no more than symbolic as the EU was not willing to impose a formal US-style investment ban on its energy companies. If US measures were designed specifically to hinder the development of Iran's energy sector, European measures sought to exert pressure without completely choking off energy ties. Indeed, both Italy and France signed bilateral investment treaties with Iran in 2005. Germany and France remained Iran's second and third largest trade partners, respectively. One EU diplomat insisted that no further sanctions were needed as European oil companies were already dissuaded from entering Iran. Indeed by the summer of 2007, Anglo-French unity tightened against new legislation proposed in the US Congress that would penalize any energy company investing over $20 million in Iran (crucially, without a presidential waiver that had hitherto been used to exempt European companies and temper transatlantic friction).

A common view was that the EU's support for the Nabucco pipeline owed much to an expectation that this would be able to take in a share of Iranian gas, at least in the medium term. The Italian government explicitly supported preparation for energy supply routes from Iran.[62] After the Austrian OMV energy group signed a new energy deal with Iran in May 2007, Austria's foreign minister Ursula Plassnik insisted that any sanctions related to the nuclear issue must not impede the signing of such agreements.[63] UK officials retorted that the EU had no locus to be favouring Nabucco, which was one commercial option amongst several and up to market actors to decide upon, and that doing so merely undercut efforts to put pressure on Iran: an all-too common case of different parts of the EU machinery pulling in opposing directions and cancelling each other out.

An internal EU paper, leaked in February 2007, cautioned against thinking that sanctions would solve the main problems related to Iran and linked this argument to Iran's already growing shortage of FDI to maintain oil and gas production.[64] One senior diplomat reflected the spirit of this 'softer' approach, arguing that the EU's underlying challenge was to make it clear to Iran that the aim was not regime change, but rather to improve governance conditions to help with oil and gas extraction. Another high-level official observed that such caution was reinforced by an 'indirect link' between the energy and nuclear issues, namely that Russia and China would only sign up to sanctions that did not affect their energy interests in Iran.

However, gradually under president Ahmadinejad (who took office in 2005) measures of political deliberalization were implemented – including a gradual frustration of civil-society links with the West – and the relationship within EU strategy between energy calculations, the nuclear dossier and Iranian domestic political developments changed markedly. Iran suffered from an increasing shortfall in energy-sector investment that many saw as related to the nature of its political system. Iran was unable to meet its own OPEC oil-production quotas as prices rose after 2003. Despite sitting on 10 per cent of the world's oil reserves, in March 2007 the Iranian government had to ration domestic petrol use. Even more strikingly, Iran was still a net importer of gas. Under-investment in production capacity was directly linked to the sub-sidization of domestic fuel prices, which choked off revenues for re-investment.[65] This subsidization was in turn seen as a populist measure offered by an embattled regime seeking means to perpetuate its own survival.

Some diplomats acknowledged that part of the pressure against Iran from 2005–6 reflected a desire to undermine a hard-line government that threa-tened a more nationalistic use of energy resources. By this point, the regime had clearly sought to re-establish its legitimacy on the basis of an autarkic, nationalist state-led development model rather than theocracy.[66] Ahmadine-jad routinely called for production cuts to drive up prices; led calls for the creation of a 'gas OPEC'; and spoke assertively of Iran's control over the Straits of Hormuz, through which two-thirds of global oil trade passed. Energy commissioner Andris Piebalgs directly contradicted the musings of some European foreign ministers in arguing that the nuclear issue and energy security could not be traded off against each other: '[U]ntil we have resolved the issue of nuclear enrichment, I doubt that any agreement on gas supplies is possible.'[67]

One senior Iranian dismissed the relevance of the EU's new energy secur-ity strategy with the argument that Iran was interested primarily in selling oil and gas to the east. One northern European diplomat retorted that, 'We can do without Iranian oil for a long time; they need the revenue more than we need their oil', suggesting that in the longer term it was much more impor-tant to invest in supporting political and economic modernization. With Iran being a net importer of gas, the threat to block trade in energy resources was widely judged to be hollow.

If it was the case that energy interests were seen as linked to the desir-ability of a more liberal government in Tehran, it was debatable whether EU policy was coherently aimed at assisting political reform in Iran. Rhetorical criticism of reform reversals increased, but European governments opposed the route taken by the Bush administration of offering funds directly to support Iranian opposition groups. Support for rule of law and governance improvements was a casualty of the breaking of relations. Some officials complained at how soft Javier Solana was on the rigged elections that brought Ahmadiejad to power. Governments opposed taking the People's Mujahedeen Organization of Iran (PMOI, or MKO) off the EU's terrorist list, despite the European Court ruling in 2007 that there was no evidence that this group was engaged in terrorist activity. This ruling sparked protests by the PMOI's sister organization, the National Resistance Council of Iran, the latter accusing EU governments of stalling on legalizing this opposition group as they wished to avoid upsetting the Iranian regime due to ongoing nuclear diplomacy. Doubts remained over whether the PMOI did in fact remain committed to violent tactics, although the UK lifted its national ban on the organization in June 2008.

The question of whether the Iranian government and/or political system were prejudicial to European energy interests attracted different reflections. After losing the December 2006 municipal elections, president Ahmadinejad increased populist promises of expenditure from the oil-investment fund that some European diplomats worried was further drawing resources away from the long-term development of the energy sector. Buy-back terms were toughened, deterring foreign investors quite apart from any geopolitical disincentives. Iran's energy sector remained well below full capacity. The influence of the Revolutionary Guards grew significantly, both over the nuclear programme and energy policy; one reason for the limited opening in the energy sector was the Revolutionary Guards' determination to sew up energy contracts for their own operators.[68] Experienced energy technocrats were replaced by patronage-placed government supporters untrained – and 'completely incompetent' according to one European government official – in energy questions.

On the other hand, in contrast to other producer states' tightening of conditions against foreign investors, Iran introduced a number of steps to court IOCs, mainly with Chinese but also European investors in mind. Iran required such partners for the geostrategic purpose of isolating the US's hard-line stance towards the Islamic Republic. In addition, Iran was increasingly positive towards the Nabucco pipeline: a small number of EU member states admitted to having made some low profile and preliminary steps to exploring possible cooperation with Tehran on this. This position became more pertinent after Turkey signed a deal with Iran in August 2007 jointly to develop an energy corridor for Iranian supplies into European markets. The official EU position was that Iranian gas was not a prerequisite for Nabucco. In April 2008 Andris Piebalgs reiterated his view that the EU would only talk about the prospects of Iran supplying Nabucco if and when a deal was reached on the nuclear issue.[69]

The EU renewed sponsorship of criticism of Iranian human rights abuses in the United Nations (UN). Some smaller EU member states complained that the 'EU3' had drifted towards a position too accommodating of Iranian human rights abuses; other states excluded from the triumvirate criticized the UK, Germany and France for adopting too harsh a position on the nuclear issue, such as would undermine energy security. In the autumn of 2007 debates reopened over the tightening of UN sanctions against Iran. Significantly, the French position, under the new Sarkozy government, now aligned with that of the UK in support of the EU imposing tougher sanctions if necessary outside the scope of UN measures. The UK and France were now pitted against, in particular, Germany and Italy, both of whom resisted pressure for more punitive measures, in part because of energy security concerns. But all member states acknowledged that, despite concerns over political developments within Iran, energy cooperation would be dependent on a nuclear deal and not on human rights improvements.

Chinese companies picked up a number of contracts that European companies had been reluctant to bid for. Shell, Repsol, Total and ENI were all present in some degree in Iran, whereas BP's US operations were a major factor explaining its absence from the Islamic Republic. The French government now adopted a clear position discouraging French multinationals from investing in Iran[70] – although at the same time the EU was united in opposing voices in the US pushing for the extension of extra-territorial US sanctions. Most European companies held off actually signing contracts, to the extent that Iran set a June 2008 deadline for them to decide whether or not they were willing to do so. Angela Merkel criticized the Swiss government for backing the state utility EGL in signing a contract with Iran in March 2008.[71] An exception was the Italian government's backing for its energy companies to progress to sign concrete contracts: in January 2008 Italy and Iran signed a gas deal for Edison to pump Iranian gas to Europe.[72]

The EU was undercut by the report of the American National Intelligence Estimate in December 2007 that concluded that Iran had stopped its weapons programme in 2003 – a judgement several European intelligence services questioned.[73] After a further Internatioanl Atomic Energy Agency report, EU governments united behind support for a tightening of UN sanctions in March 2008 and imposed restrictions on the operations on Iran's largest bank in June 2008. But in general member states – with the exception of France and the UK – insisted that energy concerns were one set of factors discouraging them from contemplating any really significant tightening of sanctions. Iran's 2008 elections suggested that the country's domestic politics were, moreover, at a delicate juncture, with 'establishment' conservatives increasingly angered at Ahmadinejad *inter alia* for undermining foreign investment in the energy sector – these figures consequently pushing for a return to more moderate 'pragmatic conservative' rule.[74] This rendered more complex European calculations over how far to 'deal with' and how hard to press the Iranian regime.

Iraq

In similar fashion, many aspects of European policy towards Iraq could also be read in contrasting ways. The most often posed question in relation to Iraq was, of course, whether the 2003 US-led invasion was 'all about oil'. Doubters suggested that if oil had been the main concern the US and other (European) coalition members would simply have struck a deal with Saddam as they had done with any number of other Arab dictators. Indeed, a common argument was that the West had been complicit in Saddam's circumvention of UN sanctions and oil-for-food corruption as the priority in practice was on maintaining some level of oil supply from Iraq. Those convinced that oil was the primary motive pointed mainly to the now notorious fact that the oil ministry was the only public office protected from looting by US soldiers after the invasion. In terms of European positions, oil certainly seemed to be one factor that pushed member states further apart. Polish officials were cited as apparently admitting that their role in the coalition was driven in part by the desire for access to Iraqi oil.[75] Tony Blair was said to have been influenced by BP's chief executive Lord John Browne warning that, if the US was inevitably going to proceed with an invasion, British oil companies needed to be given a chance of benefiting from the new opportunities that the post-Saddam context might present.[76] Conversely, France's anti-war position was seen by many to reflect its contrasting calculations related to oil contracts: Total gained active backing from the French government to pre-pare the ground for new operations in Iraq, as close as possible to, but without actually starting activities such as would contravene sanctions on the Saddam regime.[77]

Whatever the truth of what lay behind both support for and opposition to the invasion of Iraq, in the wake of occupation it certainly seemed to be the case that the country's deepening and tragic turmoil left little space for the development of a European energy policy in Iraq. In an indirect way, non-coalition members' aim to persuade the US to leave could be seen as moti-vated by the desire to avoid the US securing all Iraq's new oil contracts. British diplomats clashed with US officials on a number of energy-related questions. They insisted that US protection of southern oil fields and efforts to stifle oil smuggling must not contradict efforts to establish the rule of law (this being the issue that prompted the angry and subsequently much-quoted response from Coalition Provisional Authority head Paul Bremer that 'I am the law'). UK diplomats also pushed against the rapid privatization of the oil sector, arguing that any benefit from Western companies winning quick control of the fields would be outweighed by the local antipathy this would engender. Conversely, the UK urged more time and money to be devoted to practical cooperation, such as rebuilding energy infrastructure, rather than what it felt was the US's fixation with the niceties of a new democratic con-stitutional process.[78] There was doubt, however, over how far such positions were shared or promoted from within the upper echelons of the British government.

In general, moreover, diplomats insisted that throughout the post-invasion period European concerns and positions were far more about the immediate, spiralling civil conflict. Equally, while it could be held that those EU states that did participate in the coalition had at least some interest in benefiting from access to Iraqi oil supplies, their policies were dominated by the domestic pressure for troop withdrawals. Most coalition members had withdrawn any significant numbers of troops by 2005–6; in late 2007 the UK signalled sizeable reductions to its troop levels. As of 2008 the UK, Denmark, Latvia,

Estonia, Bulgaria, Romania and the Czech Republic retained small levels of troops in Iraq.

In 2004 the Commission prepared a new EU strategy for Iraq that began by pointing out that European states had a series of strong interests in helping Iraq stabilize. In practice this led to only modest cooperation. The desire not to get too involved remained paramount. Practical cooperation that was offered was related to security, economic and trade issues, together with some civil-society dialogue, rather than any significant engagement in the field of energy. The Commission allocated 720 million euros of aid to Iraq during the period 2003–7. Not much of this was disbursed, except through the World Bank trust fund – to which the Commission was the largest funder, providing just under half its total aid. No EU country strategy was agreed for Iraq to guide aid spending politically. Nearly 80 million euros were spent on the two sets of elections and referendum held in post-Saddam Iraq, but the vast majority of aid went to humanitarian relief. Decisions on aid spending went through the EU Development Committee, so were subject to little political guidance. There was little linkage with energy security. Energy cooperation was identified as a priority for new aid initiatives after 2006, but limited progress was made on the ground – despite a Commission delegation being opened in September 2006.

In November 2006 Iraq opened negotiations for a TCA with the EU. A second round of trade talks was held in June 2007, a third round in December 2007. In the autumn of 2007, the EU rule of law mission was extended through an additional 10 million euros; this offered training courses in the EU itself on how to carry out police and forensic duties, respecting human rights. Germany offered a sizeable aid programme, but still mostly for Stiftungen-organized training courses run outside Iraq. Iraq sought observer status in the EMP, but there was no EU agreement on this, or on the proposal (made by Swedish foreign minister Carl Bildt in 2007) for an EU Special Representative for Iraq. The new French government suggested in 2007 that Iraq should be brought into the EU–Middle East Strategic Partnership, but again this did not occur. Commission aid allocated to Iraq registered a significant drop in 2008, to only 75 million euros.

If the EU's general engagement in Iraq remained circumspect, it was subject to particular problems in the energy sector. Access to energy sources was hampered by Iraq's unsettled political process and efforts to secure a balanced form of power-sharing. Experts argued that development of the energy sector was one of the many problems flowing from the fact that Iraq increasingly showed all the classic symptoms of a failed state, reflected in a range of governance pathologies.[79] The new Iraqi constitution left oil responsibilities highly decentralized, with regions being responsible for the development of new resources. This represented the core problem for Sunnis, while the Kurds soon pressed ahead to develop their own contacts with MNCs and signed a contract with DNO of Norway, the first international oil contract signed in the country since Iraq's 1972 Nationalization Bill. This provoked tension with the Baghdad government, which claimed that the Kurdish government had gone beyond its legitimate powers and threatened to revoke any contracts when a new national hydrocarbon law was agreed. In early 2008 a new 'accountability and justice' law, designed to encourage the reincorporation of former Baathists, succeeded in bringing back the main Sunni party into government. But, at the same time, an assorted group of Shia and Sunni parties formed an alliance to insist that Baghdad retain full control of the oil industry, seemingly making agreement with Kurdish representatives on a hydrocarbons law even more problematic.[80]

On these political issues European influence remained negligible. While the development of the energy sector was impeded by Iraq's failing governance, the EU declined to design the kind of comprehensive 'failed state' strategy implemented elsewhere. Asked whether the EU had sought input into the hydrocarbons law, EU diplomats replied testily that only the UK was engaged and was not minded to Europeanize its involvement on this issue. Insiders on the ground suggested informally that the UK's input into the proposed law had been significant, in conjunction with advisors from Shell, suggesting ways to share oil more fairly with Sunni areas, but that the British government had been unaware of the political blowback the draft law was likely to provoke. As the UK pulled out of Basra, apparently sacrificing its potential leverage over the significant oil reserves that had been under its administration, it did seem to favour more 'Europeanization'. In October 2007 a UK–French–Swedish paper proposed to enhance political dialogue; the Iraqi foreign minister was invited to the general affairs council in November 2007.

The EU supported the process of the 'Ministerial Conference of the Neighbouring Countries', and the creation of energy cooperation under this framework. At the third round of TCA talks an energy chapter was signed, promising EU support for infrastructure development and the transfer of technical know-how. With the Iraqi oil minister visiting Brussels in February 2008, Andris Piebalgs talked of support for Iraq linking into the Arab Gas Pipeline and from there into Nabucco and in turn onto European markets.[81] A Memorandum of Understanding on energy cooperation was agreed between the EU and Iraq in April 2008. However, it remained unclear how Iraq would provide the promised 10 billion cm of gas to Europe; Iraqi ministers argued that the quid pro quo for such supplies must be increased European support for Iraqi reconstruction; and some member states were still cautious about taking forward energy cooperation before a hydrocarbons law was agreed in Iraq, fearing that the EU would otherwise give succour to separatist regions seeking greater control over their own resources. Iraq also committed itself to Extractive Industries Transparency Initiative principles in 2008, but EU officials judged it 'fanciful' that in the prevailing security and political climate this would provide a feasible basis for cooperation.

Disunity appeared between member states on the two crucial issues of Kirkuk and dealings with the Kurdish Regional Government. Kirkuk, holding 5 per cent of global oil reserves, remained sealed off from the rest of the

Kurdish area. Some member states became more willing to support a UN-sponsored autonomy arrangement of some kind, with such energy supplies in mind. As the central government in Baghdad showed itself reluctant to conclude significant international contracts and policy-making deadlock intensified at the national level,[82] some also became more open to direct contact with the Kurdish Regional Government. Hungary's MOL and Austria's OMV were amongst the 15 medium-sized firms that had signed contracts with the Kurdish Regional Government by 2008, despite Iraqi, US and Turkish warnings that they would be 'blacklisted' for doing so.

Conclusion

Gradually during the mid-2000s the EU introduced a plethora of new energy initiatives and projects in the Middle East. However, European energy strategy in this region received less priority than in policy towards Russia. Moreover, other issues often cut-across energy concerns. In the Gulf, a general concern with regional instability and counter-terrorism, along with the EU's protectionist defence of its own markets, complicated energy policy. Iraq's political and security situation, as well as the general diplomatic fall out of the 2003 invasion, militated strongly against this country fitting fully into short-term European energy security strategies. And in Iran the focus on WMD containment increasingly predominated.

Across the Middle East, common EU initiatives co-existed with a significant degree of 'bilateralism', member states prioritizing their own national access to energy supplies. The common EU framework was strongest in North Africa, but even here southern member states were frustrated enough with the limits of such policies to push bilateral efforts. The national policies of the larger member states prevailed more clearly over common EU policies in the Gulf, while in Iran member states were divided over just how far access to energy supplies should be sacrificed for the goal of limiting Iran's nuclear programme. In addition, coordination with the US was limited, the dynamics of competition and counter-balancing stronger than those of transatlantic cooperation.

Despite the formal commitments to extending EU governance structures, approaches to energy security in the Middle East in practice betrayed much logic from the 'geopolitical storyline'. From Algeria to Saudi Arabia, and Libya to Iran, Middle Eastern governments showed little enthusiasm for the EU's offered model of extending its own market-governance norms as a basis for energy cooperation. In Iraq, the EU remained far from situating its incipient energy cooperation within the context of a broader strategy of helping build stronger and more transparent institutions. Some new democracy and governance efforts were implemented in the Middle East. However, diplomats acknowledged that these cautious reform efforts were not driven primarily by deliberations over energy security. Indeed, what was most striking was the disconnect between EU energy policy and the complex 'internal politics of oil' within Middle East producer states outlined in this chapter.

5 Russia

Russia has been the subject of the most high-profile debates over European energy policy. Indeed, it appears often to have completely dominated such deliberations. Russia's increasing assertiveness and the growing tensions within Europe over how to respond have attracted much analytical attention. In chronicling European Union (EU) energy-related positions towards Russia through the 2000s, this chapter seeks to dissect the fluctuating EU–Russia relationship in light of the questions guiding this book's overarching assessment of European energy security strategies. It finds that Russia's prominence within EU energy debates has exceeded its actual importance for many member states' supply dependency. From the early 2000s the EU sought to deepen technical cooperation on energy matters with Moscow, even while high politics tensions intensified. Paying particular attention to the relationship between European energy interests and the evolution of Russian domestic politics, the chapter points to the particularly striking uncertainty and division amongst European governments on such governance-related questions. When president Vladimir Putin concluded his second term as president in 2008 the EU appeared more – if belatedly – aware of the pertinence of Russia's democratic reversal to its own energy concerns. How this would affect policy during the Medvedev presidency remained unclear, particularly as the EU embarked on fashioning a response to Russia's invasion of Georgia.

Russia as energy superpower?

Russia accounted for 40 per cent of the growth in world oil production between 2000–2007. While routinely discussed as the most important third-country supplier, however, Russia's importance as a supplier varied enormously between EU member states. Three groups could be identified. First, those states with low dependence on Russia, which included Spain, Sweden, the UK, the Netherlands, Portugal, Belgium and Ireland; in total ten member states imported under 5 per cent of their gas from Russia. Second, a group exhibiting medium dependence, including France, Italy and Germany. Third, a group of countries with high dependence on Russian energy, including Austria, the Czech Republic, Greece, Hungary, Poland, Romania, Slovenia,

Finland, Latvia, Lithuania and Slovakia (the last four of these obtaining 100 per cent of their imported energy from Russia).[1] In absolute terms the largest importers of Russian gas were Germany, Italy, Turkey and France. Only 1 per cent of the United States' oil imports came from Russia.[2]

During his two-term presidency Vladimir Putin regularly intimated that more Russian gas would begin to go eastwards, towards Asian markets. Experts agreed Russia needed the West less than in the 1990s, as economic growth was strong, debts were repaid and indeed reserves accumulated. As a source of energy power, an increasingly central issue was Gazprom's ability to use its windfalls to acquire assets, including in energy (and other) companies in the EU. While countries such as the UK and Spain continued to receive no significant amounts of energy directly from Russia, the latter affected them indirectly as it impacted upon international prices and the broader climate of international energy. In 2006 the first Russian Liquefied Natural Gas shipments commenced to the UK.

On the other hand, several factors tempered Russia's energy-based power. Russian production was relatively mature, and estimated to peak by 2010. Overall Russia was more reliant on the EU than vice versa. In 2006, the EU25 accounted for 65 per cent of Russian gas exports, while the EU obtained 50 per cent of its gas imports (amounting to 25 per cent of its gas consumption) and 30 per cent of its oil imports from Russia. In terms of overall trade, the EU was Russia's biggest trading partner; Russia was only the third biggest trading partner of the EU. Experts noted that in practice it would be costly and difficult for Russia to switch supplies away from the EU to the East, this requiring a costly and lengthy reconfiguration of its transportation infrastructure. In 2006 Russia decided that new gas from the Shtokman field would go into the European pipeline system and not to the US as LNG. The possibility of new pipelines circumventing Russia's transit monopoly was explored with increasing intent. Russia also still required the advanced energy technology of Western companies. And many argued that Russia was not a rising power in the same sense as China, but one on a long-term path of decline enjoying new influence thanks to a moment of rising energy prices; Russia's underlying fundamentals, they highlighted, were not those suggesting a long-term trajectory of greater power.

European engagement

The overarching European aim was to entice Russia into a common energy space based on market-based rules and clear governance structures. Key to this was the Energy Charter Treaty (ECT), which would place Russia's pipeline network under multilateral regulations and challenge Gazprom's monopoly. Russia signed this in 1994, but then backtracked and refused to ratify the treaty. The EU complained that this demonstrated that Russia was unwilling to abide by market principles and relinquish its monopoly over Caspian supplies. Russia pointed to double standards in both European governments blocking Gazprom from buying EU energy companies and the fact that the ECT's crucial transit protocol would not apply between European countries themselves (the EU defining itself as a single economic space). Moscow also pointed out that other suppliers like Norway and Algeria had declined to sign the ECT without negative consequences for their relations with the EU.

The EU sought alternative avenues to persuade Russia to adhere to at least some ECT principles. The EU–Russia energy dialogue commenced in 2000. This aimed at enhancing infrastructure connections, general consumer-producer cooperation, business-to-business links and the facilitation of foreign investment. Funding was offered under the Commission's Tacis (Technical Assistance to the Commonwealth of Independent States) programme for increasing productive capacity in Russia. In 2002 an EU–Russia Technology Centre was created in Moscow, bringing together industry representatives. From 2003 the formal aim was enunciated of extending the internal European energy market to Russia. The EU linked its support for Russian World Trade Organization (WTO) accession to its aim to 'favour the growing integration of the continent's energy markets'.[3] Cooperation was held back by Russia's (erroneous) charge that the EU imposed on member states a requirement that no more than 30 per cent of their imports of fossil fuels should come from any single source – only Spain operated any such upper limit and several member states already relied on Russia for well over 30 per cent of their imported gas.[4] The Northern Dimension – incorporating the Nordic and Baltic states, Germany and Russia – attempted an alternative route to practical energy cooperation, this forum excluding controversial political issues such as those related to human rights or democracy.

Under the rubric of the EU–Russia energy dialogue a first Permanent Partnership Council dedicated to energy issues took place in October 2005. The declared objective was to work for the development of an attractive, stable and predictable investment climate in Russia that foresaw an active role for foreign investors. European officials spoke of increased pressure on Moscow for 'a level playing field'. Russia's double pricing of gas was a particular point of tension. Four bilateral Thematic Groups were inaugurated, on investment, infrastructure, trade and energy efficiency, respectively. A scheme was introduced through the European Investment Fund for mitigating commercial risks in Russia, while in 2004 a further 3 million euros was allocated from Tacis for improving Russian oil and gas infrastructure. As outlined in Chapter 3, the EU pushed to overturn the inclusion of restrictive 'destination clauses' in Russian contracts (through which Moscow sought to prevent excess supply in one European country being sold onto another).[5]

The focus on practical cooperation was reinforced by the agreement in 2003 to reorganize EU–Russia relations around four 'common spaces' – economics and trade, internal security, foreign-policy issues, and science and culture. In practice cooperation proceeded slowly within these four spaces, diplomats on both sides expressing disappointment in the limited degree of progress. Even at the technical level, the bodies supposed to be set up to make progress under the common spaces failed to materialize.

Moreover, at the political level, relations with Russia were dominated by growing division between member states. The Commission's February 2004 communication on EU–Russia relations was openly critical of the lack of coherence within European policies. This came after Italy's presidency, during which Prime Minister Silvio Berlusconi promised Putin that he was pushing for Russia's entry into the EU.[6] The common lament amongst diplomats was over how easily Putin was now playing member states off against each other, successfully adopting divide and rule tactics to neutralize criticism from the EU. It took the EU three weeks to agree to a common response to Russia's shut-down of gas supplies through Ukraine in January 2006. Many member states insisted on diluting the reaction. Many officials cautioned that the harder-line states such as Poland could hardly complain that Russia was moving prices towards market rates, when this was what the EU had been demanding of Moscow for many years. If Russian communism had pulled Europe together, Russian energy power was pushing the continent apart.

In particular, a raft of new bilateral deals was struck with Russia. Most notably, anger arose within the EU at Germany's North European Gas Pipeline (NEGP) deal, under which energy supplies would flow direct from Russia to Germany, by-passing other states such as Poland. Many admonished this deal as reflecting blatant geopolitics, the pipeline not being efficient economically in the medium term. But other states' energy champions were soon following suit, sewing up their own bilateral deals. By the end of 2006 Gazprom had negotiated deals with energy companies in nearly all EU member states, with particularly notable deals signed in Belgium, France, Italy, Hungary and Austria, along with further deals with German companies. Under these deals Gazprom gained greater market access in return for agreement to maintain supplies on a bilateral basis to each of these countries. A number of member states competed against each other fiercely to become the key 'hub', lucratively managing incoming Russian gas for the EU market: Latvia sought this status through the NEGP, Hungary through support for the southern Blue Stream pipeline. Far from the Russian government opening up to European companies in return, shock-waves went through the industry when first Shell and then BP were forced to sell their controlling stakes in key energy projects (at the Sakhalin II and Kovykta fields, respectively) in a move that was tantamount to de facto re-nationalization.

By autumn 2006, debate focused on preparations for negotiations over a new Partnership and Cooperation Agreement (PCA), the existing agreement due for renewal in 2007. Draft negotiating directives for a new EU–Russia agreement were agreed by the Commission in July 2006. The priority was defined as the 'fair and open development of the energy relationship between the EU and Russia'. External-relations commissioner Benita Ferrero-Waldner stated that 'it is of great importance that the mutual interest we have in energy cooperation should be expressed in concrete terms in the new Agreement'.[7]

With Russia categorically opposed to being included in the European Neighbourhood Policy, the Commission sought to replicate as much as possible of the structure of ENP action plans within the format of a new PCA. Energy cooperation was to be strengthened, focusing again on access to markets; a level playing field on investment; and support for upgrading transport infrastructure. Now accepting that Russia was unlikely to ratify the ECT the Commission proposed incorporating the latter's basic principles within the new PCA, as part of an EU–Russia 'common economic space'. The EU was now clearly looking for a trade-off, holding out the prospect of access to the EU internal market for Gazprom as a bargaining chip to push Russia to sign up to Energy Charter principles. Still diplomats described the general approach to energy security with Russia as being focused on market structures and interdependence, one claiming (perhaps with feigned innocence): 'we don't want to start playing geopolitical games'.

This strategy engendered significant debate. Some analysts argued that a new PCA-type, comprehensive agreement would be too cumbersome and that the EU should rather adopt 'the China model' of a broadly defined political strategic partnership accompanied by sector specific agreements.[8] Some diplomats also argued for a more pragmatic approach. Officials commonly pointed to a fundamental change in dynamics, with Russia now feeling dominant and seeing little need to court the EU for a new agreement. The EU appeared to have little leverage in the current climate; as Russia had paid off its debts, conditionality was less feasible and European aid was seen as having become largely irrelevant. Above all else, Russia sought strategic status, built on the back of rising energy prices. Hence, argued many diplomats, the EU had to play a long game with Russia, waiting for the current wave of high prices to subside and for Russia once again to feel the need for cooperation with Europe, for example in boosting productive capacity.

At an informal EU summit in Lahti, in October 2006, the Finnish presidency tried to clamp down on internal EU disunity, sending a letter to member states warning them not to break ranks. To some degree, the new German government did seem to heed this. France ended up adopting the softest line, at some odds with Berlin. Just prior to the summit new German Chancellor Angela Merkel rejected Putin's offer to supply Germany with gas from the Shtokman field, insisting that the focus must be on the principles of the Energy Charter, not bilateral deals. Putin's offer was condemned as a clumsy attempt to prize Germany away from its EU partners. The Italian and Spanish premiers, Romano Prodi and José Luis Rodriguez Zapatero, spoke at the summit of the need for the EU to diversify supplies away from Russia; President Chirac undercut them, opining that EU energy security 'depends mainly on Russia'.[9]

Differences emerged between member states on whether the EU should adopt a more flexible position on Russia's accession to the Energy Charter. Fudging these differences, an October 2006 Commission communication suggested that a new agreement with Russia 'confirming both market principles and the relevant principles of the Energy Charter Treaty, could also remove many of the obstacles to Russia's eventual ratification of the Energy Charter Treaty'. Russia declared itself already alive to the Commission's attempt to smuggle parts of the Charter into the new PCA mandate. A German spokesman expressed sympathy with Russian objections to the ECT, dismissing the latter as too naively market-based. Italian diplomats also insisted that the ECT was 'not important' and that the EU should deal with Russia bilaterally rather than through depoliticized multilateral frameworks. These positions were starkly in contrast to those of the UK, Nordic and central and eastern European states.

Quashing thoughts that Merkel's line would depart radically from that of her predecessor, Gerhard Schröder, in the autumn of 2006 a new German strategy was unveiled of 'rapprochement through inter-linkage' with Russia. Merkel had criticized the Nordstream deal in opposition but refused now to revoke it; her Russia policy was influenced strongly by her foreign minister, Frank-Walter Steinmeier, a notable 'Russia dove' of the Schröder administration.

Differences magnified in November 2006 when Poland vetoed the opening of negotiations for the new agreement. The veto was wielded ostensibly in response to Russia's ban on Polish meat imports; but Polish diplomats acknowledged that it was as much about energy and Warsaw's argument that Putin should be confronted more vigorously by European governments. Russia should, it was also argued, implement existing commitments under the PCA before being offered a new agreement. The combative Kaczynski government remained particularly angered by the Northern Pipeline deal, that it complained left the country exposed to Russian political pressure. Germany had undermined Poland by agreeing to a direct pipeline without the originally touted link to Poland. This lay behind Poland's push for an energy-solidarity clause. Lithuania's president Valdas Adamkus routinely reiterated his determination to stop Nordstream, including through the use of environmental standards. In contrast, the Commission supported the project as potentially beneficial to overall European supplies.[10]

Indeed, Poland did not gain support from many of its EU partners. Most member states opposed the veto. The German foreign ministry warned Poland that it was isolating itself.[11] In December, Italian foreign minister Massimo D'Alema made a trip to Moscow to agree a bilateral energy cooperation initiative with Russia. Conversely, diplomats from other member states admitted to 'hiding behind' Poland and quietly sharing its 'taking a stand' against Russia. Some professed a reassessment of strategy in light of Russia's 'bullying' tactics against Ukraine early in 2006, when Moscow not only abruptly closed off gas supplies but then insisted on greater control over the Ukrainian energy monopoly as part of the deal subsequently struck with Kiev. One argued: 'we cannot ignore this, as in the past'. One official acknowledged that, whatever the EU's formal language on cooperation and market integration, it was in the need to curtail Russia's power over its neighbours that 'geopolitics comes in'. Another justified the need for a more politicized approach with the defence that it was 'the Russian leadership [that was] securitizing the energy issue'. The Russian response was that Poland had, in the words of one of its diplomats, 'politicized a technical problem ... that [was] now harder to resolve'.

Policy thus progressed at two levels. At one level was the slowly accumulating technical and regulatory cooperation between Europe and Russia. The report of the seventh annual round of the EU–Russia energy dialogue, held in November 2006, talked of advances on technical issues, surreally not mentioning any of the high politics contretemps occurring at the very same moment.[12] The dialogue's four working groups were reduced to three – energy efficiency, market developments and energy strategies – supposedly signalling a concentration of practical cooperative activities. Detailed work on the integration of Russian and European electricity markets was said to be advancing. The main results claimed for the energy dialogue were reiterated as the agreements that no quantitative restrictions were to be placed on EU imports of fossil fuels; that Russian long-term gas supply contracts were to be made more compatible with EU internal market rules, in particular through the elimination of 'destination clauses'; and that the concerns of European investors were to be resolved.

At a second, high-politics level talk emerged of redefining a new agreement as a Strategic Partnership Treaty to accord Russia the strategic symbolism and political influence it coveted. At this level, not only were stark differences between member states on view; in addition these were underlain by divergence on just how important Russia really was in both geopolitical and energy terms. Officials revealed that in Council debates active participation came mainly from the big three member states, the new central and eastern European states, Finland and Sweden.

Geopolitical reality-check?

The geopolitical dimension was increasingly the stronger element of EU policy. By now the EU had more high-level political dialogue with Russia than with any other third country except the United States, and more than existed with any of the EU's partner states in the Neighbourhood Policy. Conversely, the depth of 'network' inter-linkages and integration was less than elsewhere in the East. Relative to the ENP action plans the four common spaces made less mention of the incorporation of EU governance rules and standards. The EU even acquiesced to an exemption for the energy sector in the terms for Russia's accession to the WTO. One expert parodied that the common spaces were 'as empty as the word "space" implies'.[13]

A greater degree of EU unity was apparent in response to the energy dispute between Russia and Belarus in January 2007. This erupted when Russia increased prices to Belarus; in retaliation Belarus imposed a tariff on the transit of Russian oil supplies; Russia refused to pay; Belarus started siphoning off oil as payment in kind; so Russia cut its supplies to Belarus. It did so without consulting the EU. European reactions were angry. Angela Merkel criticized Russia's decision as 'unacceptable'. After three days Belarus (largely) caved in. Just prior to the dispute Russia had also gained 50 per cent control over Belarus's gas pipelines.

Apparently sensitive to another dent having been made to Russia's reputation as a reliable energy supplier to Western Europe, Putin declared that he would start to reduce dependence on transit states, through direct pipeline links to the EU. He also claimed that Russia had accepted a 'bad deal' with Belarus because European governments had become so jittery about Russian reliability. Merkel drew a different lesson, suggesting that any reworked agreement with Russia should contain a new coordination mechanism on energy, to avoid a repeat of the Ukraine and Belarus episodes. As a result a new 'early warning mechanism' was agreed within the context of EU–Russia dialogue. The impact of the crisis filtered into the EU's January 2007 Strategic Energy Review, which included a phrase aimed obliquely at Russia and Gazprom, committing the EU to 'assess the impact of vertically integrated energy companies from third countries on the internal market and how to implement the principle of reciprocity'.[14] Belarusian president Alexander Lukashenko traced the roots of the crisis back to the EU's timidity in the post-Soviet space, arguing that, 'If Western energy companies had stakes in the Belarusian energy transport network, Russia would never have acted so brutally.'[15]

If there appeared to have been a degree of unified admonishment of Russian tactics in Belarus, bilateralism soon reared its head once more. In March 2007 Hungary signed a bilateral deal with Gazprom's Blue Stream project to guarantee its medium-term national supplies. This had the effect of undercutting the rival Nabucco pipeline project, only two days after the EU had confirmed the latter as a priority. Subjected to angry criticism from other member states, Hungarian officials retorted that these other governments had shown little solidarity or serious intent to devise a genuinely common energy security policy and that Hungary consequently had to secure its own immediate interests. It would be difficult to imagine more direct corroboration of Russia's success in playing 'divide and rule'. Four days later Greece and Bulgaria reached similar deals with Russia, guaranteeing their supplies through a Trans-Balkan pipeline running from the Russian Black Sea, as a continuation of the Caspian Pipeline Consortium line from Kazakhstan to Novorossiysk, and the first line to be controlled by Russia on EU soil.[16]

In the same week, Putin visited Italy and signed ten new bilateral cooperation agreements with Prime Minister Romano Prodi, including on energy. The energy agreement included a deepening of the 2006 partnership deal reached between ENI and Gazprom, under which the latter was granted downstream access to the Italian market in return for guaranteeing supplies to Italy until 2035. Both ENI and Enel even helped Gazprom to acquire additional Yukos assets in return for a foothold in Russia's gas field development and a seat on Gazprom's board.[17] Gazprom was then offered assets in the merged Gaz de France–Suez energy giant in return, it was widely acknowledged, for Total being granted the key Shtokman gas field contract. This was followed by Gazprom and Gaz de France signing a new agreement in January 2008 committing themselves to upgraded cooperation, including on the development of LNGs.[18] And rumours continued of a possible deal with the UK: Gazprom participation in Centrica in return for an eventual extension of the NEGP to Britain and a long-term contract to supply 10 per cent of the UK's gas demand.[19]

All this sat uneasily with the Commission's efforts to implement single-market commitments that would nominally militate against such bilateral deals with Gazprom. Russian diplomats complained that criticisms of these deals revealed the double standards of a number of EU member states: long-term contracts were signed with other suppliers, such as Qatar, without the 'demonization' that prevailed against Gazprom. They also insisted that in these bilateral contracts Russia had agreed to sell at below-market rates, and that the Commission had within the Energy Dialogue already accepted the case for long-term contracts.

Early in 2007 Lithuania joined Poland with a second veto against talks for a new EU–Russia agreement. Lithuania's complaint was that Russia's inter-ruption of oil supplies through the Druzhba pipeline to its Mazeikiu refinery ostensibly for technical reasons was in fact a political gesture, after the refinery had been sold to the Polish firm PKN Orlen rather than a Russian rival bid.[20] Lithuania criticized other member states for a lack of solidarity and accused the Commission for failing to keep its promise to tackle Russia on the supply cut. Poland also hardened its position, now pushing for a clause in the new EU treaty to permit suspension of third-country partnerships in the event of an energy dispute. It also threatened to extend its veto to anti-competitive positions on *internal* energy policy too, seeing this as integrally tied to the bilateralism besetting external policy towards Russia.[21] In the autumn of 2007 Estonia blocked a feasibility study due to be carried out in respect of the Nordstream project's effect on Estonian coastal waters.[22]

The May 2007 EU–Russia summit in Samara was frosty and soured by a range of public disagreements, on energy, human rights, Kosovo and market-access issues. In the wake of the BP and Shell contretemps, the EU tried but failed to win guarantees against politically motivated arbitrary measures targeted at European investments. The summit finished without a formal declaration. It was noted that the EU was becoming less flexible on the terms for Russia's entry into the WTO. EU unity was more notable and assertive than for a long time. Barroso commented after the summit: 'The solidarity system will prevail … there is no satellite system in Europe.'[23] Commitments were repeated to work on improving investment conditions and on information sharing and notification in the energy sector. In return, Putin pushed again for greater clarity from the EU over future demand.[24] Against this background, low-profile technocratic rapprochement was said still to be progressing under the Energy Dialogue.

Tensions deepened further as Russia cut oil supplies through Estonian ports in response to the removal of a Soviet memorial in Tallinn. European diplomats talked of the 'post-Samara' context being fundamentally different. Indeed, relations were soon dominated by the UK's application of diplomatic sanctions against Russia for the latter's refusal to extradite the chief suspect in the murder of Alexander Litvenenko, an outspoken critic of Putin based in London. Apparent change in French policy emerged under Nicolas Sarkozy, who commented shortly after taking office that Russia was 'playing its trump cards, notably oil and gas, with a certain brutality'.[25] In the autumn of 2007, in negotiations over the EU's new reform treaty Poland insisted that the latter include a clause stipulating that decisions on European Investment Bank loans be taken by unanimity and not QMV expressly so as to have greater leverage to block loans to Russia.[26] The European Parliament called for the EU to block Russia's accession to the WTO until it signed the ECT. Sweden posed new environmental obstacles to Nordstream, whose commencement was now estimated to be delayed until 2009. Russia for its part threatened retaliation against what commentators had dubbed the 'Gazprom clause' proposed by the Commission in September 2007 (that is, the reciprocity clause outlined in Chapter 3). In August 2007 Russia cut oil supplies to Germany to pressure the German intermediary of a Bulgarian gas contract to renegotiate terms.[27] Few now believed a new EU–Russia agreement to be on the cards.

But again, tension had its opposing and matching force in efforts at retaining cooperation. Spanish premier José Luis Rodriguez Zapatero visited Russia in the autumn of 2007, quite openly focusing on bilateral energy concerns and avoiding EU 'difficulties', with the aim of securing a new LNG contract for Iberdrola for exports through St Petersburg. After the apparently more critical tone from Sarkozy, when the latter met Putin in Moscow on 10 October the atmosphere was cordial and a new Franco-Russian cooperation agreement signed. At the EU–Russia summit in October 2007 leaders stressed the need further to develop an effective early warning mechanism.[28]

At this summit Putin suggested that the 'Gazprom clause' was misconceived given that European investment in Russia was ten times that of Russian investment in the EU, 'so who should be concerned?' (One view was that Gazprom would anyway be able to carry on reaching bilateral deals sought by member states themselves.)[29] The Energy Dialogue held just before the summit made progress on electricity interconnections between Russian and European markets.[30] Beyond the latest phase of diplomacy, additional new deals continued to set the terms of the energy relationship. In November 2007 Dutch gas company Gasunie took a 9 per cent stake in Nordstream, a deal pushed by the Dutch government that was eager to establish the Netherlands as a new gas hub for Europe.[31] Gazprom in consequence gained an option to buy a stake in the former's pipeline into the UK for the first time.[32] And in the same month, at a meeting between Putin and Romano Prodi,

Gazprom and ENI signed a new deal to develop a South Stream pipeline from Russia into Europe under the Black Sea. By spring 2008, Bulgaria, Hungary, Serbia and Greece had all signed up to cooperate on South Stream.

By March 2008, in response to Dimitry Medvedev assuming the presidency, the EU talked of re-opening negotiations for a new EU–Russian agreement. Poland's new government dropped its veto, as Moscow lifted the embargo on Polish food imports. Lithuania held out against dropping its veto until slightly firmer language was agreed in the mandate for the new agreement on energy governance issues and Russian actions in Georgia. On 27 May 2008 a new negotiating mandate was agreed. Negotiations were launched at the EU–Russia summit at the end of June 2008. In principle both sides agreed that an energy agreement would be concluded under the new treaty, around the notion of mutual-investment guarantees.[33] However, fundamental differences remained not only between Europe and Russia, but between those EU member states wanting a quickly agreed treaty without heavy political conditions and those insisting the EU adopt a tougher stance during the negotiating process.

Just as relations appeared to be on the brink of making progress, Russia's August 2008 invasion of South Ossetia raised even more far-reaching challenges for the European Union. At this writing, the EU was just beginning to debate its response to Russia's military action. On the one hand, Moscow's aggression in the South Caucasus suggested that the EU's relatively soft approach towards Russia had not secured far-reaching cooperation in return. Quite apart from Russia's apparent challenge to European norms, issues of energy self-interest presented themselves to EU policy-makers: by the end of the conflict a number of the pipelines running across Georgian territory had been shut down. And indeed, the EU's ability to reach a common decision to suspend the recently-opened negotiations with Russia was widely interpreted as a reflection of new resolve. European statements took on a different tone, with more stress on the need for greater independence from Russia rather than the virtues of mutual interdependence. On the other hand, signs of Europe's perception of its own weakness vis-á-vis Russia remained evident: the EU insisted only on a withdrawal of Russian troops from South Ossetia not a restoration of Georgian territorial integrity and the scope of a prospective ESDP mission was drastically diluted.

While EU energy engagement evolved thus, concerns over Russian energy supplies were also integrally tied to the evolution of European policy towards Ukraine. Eighty per cent of Russian gas into the EU crossed through Ukraine. Member states read the implication of this in different ways. Some states saw it as making it more important to get Ukraine into the EU to help lock-in Russian supplies to European markets and provide backing to any further possible shutdowns of supplies to Ukraine, to lessen the prospect of Moscow 'bullying' Kiev. Others saw the offer of accession now as more likely to be prejudicial to the extent that it would sour the relationship with Russia. As a result of the Ukraine–Russia gas deal from January 2006 the Ukrainian state monopoly NaftoGaz Ukrainy lost control over the distribution and export of natural gas to UkrGazEnergo, a joint venture between NaftoGaz Ukrainy and RosUkrEnergo, a Gazprom offshoot. Stakes in regional energy-distribution companies were transferred to Gazprom.[34] Ukraine became an important battleground over the control of transit routes between Russia and the West. Amidst Ukraine's political crisis of 2007, the EU called for an inclusive political process that kept the country's pro-Russia camp 'on board'.

When the September 2007 Ukrainian elections raised the prospect of the Orange coalition being reformed under the prime ministership of Yulia Tymoshenko, Russia leant heavily on Ukraine for the repayment of further energy-related debts, raising again the spectre of gas-supply interruptions. The EU reaction – a compromise between member states – was to offer to bring Ukraine fully and formally inside the Energy Community South East Europe, with the aim of undercutting Russian influence by integrating Ukraine into EU market rules. As this new Russia–Ukraine dispute deepened, leading to a brief halt in Russian gas supplies in January 2008, the EU activated its network of Energy Security Correspondents to monitor Russian moves.[35] The Commission welcomed, as potential competition to Russia's South Stream project, Tymoshenko's (rather audacious) proposal for a 'White Stream' pipeline passing from Turkmenistan, Azerbaijan, Georgia and then into Ukraine and through to EU markets.[36] Gazprom's vice chairman Alexander Medvedev argued that despite Ukraine owing Russia over $1 billion the company had made concessions so as to reassure EU governments, and asserted that 'Gazprom needs Europe as much as Europe needs Gazprom'.[37]

Energy and Russian politics

Under the rule of Vladimir Putin Russia suffered a well-chronicled deterioration in democratic rights. Independent television stations were taken over, civil-society activity was restricted and regional governors moved from being elected to being appointed by the president. While Russia was chairman-in-office of the Council of Europe, the government issued instructions to schools to report on Georgian children attending school in Moscow. Murders and attacks on critics became increasingly common. In addition to Litvinenko's murder, investigative journalist Anna Politkovskaya and the vice president of the Central Bank were killed. The concept of 'sovereign democracy' – of which little was democratic – gained currency amongst the Russian elite, as an ideological challenge to the norms of Western liberal democracy.

Russia's drift into authoritarianism was integrally linked to developments of profound significance for European energy interests. Putin's centralization of power at home was of a piece with his attempt to re-establish Russian influence abroad. One expert argued that Russia's assertive energy diplomacy could not be delinked from the abuse of good governance and market principles internally.[38]

The relationship between political and economic power was profoundly reconfigured under Putin. Most dramatically Yukos, formerly the country's largest oil firm, was specifically targeted due to the outspoken opposition to Putin of its owner, Mikhail Khodorkovsky. Rosneft, the state oil company, acquired Yukos assets in a rigged auction in 2004. Far from breaking up Gazprom, as he originally promised, Putin came increasingly to rely on and support the latter as a vehicle for projecting Russian influence. The political backing for Gazprom certainly sufficed to give the latter a striking international self-confidence. In April 2006, the Gazprom chief executive warned European ambassadors that 'attempts to limit Gazprom's activity in the European market will lead to no good results'.[39] Gazprom's deal with Algerian gas monopoly Sonatrach was widely interpreted as a politically backed putsch to head off avenues of possible European diversification (although Sonatrach was reported subsequently to be questioning its commitment to this deal). The intermeshing of political and economic power was most colourfully suggested by the frequent rumours that Putin would take over as head of Gazprom after he left office.

The impact of this politicization of economic power on European interests was contested. Some European officials pointed out that despite the Yukos affair and the dismantling of democracy, several respected indices of business confidence continued to rate Russia highly.[40] Despite increasingly arbitrary rule, noted one expert, Western businessmen did not seem concerned about sudden and unexpected changes in government policy, but were rather 'flocking to invest in Russia'. In the 1990s FDI just to Hungary was greater than to Russia; now Russia received more than the whole of central and eastern Europe.[41] Some opined that Western investment in the energy sector during the 1990s had if anything been more problematic, with chaotic and unpredictable government regulations limiting multinationals' interest.[42] Political difficulties did not seem to hinder general commercial interaction too seriously. In 2006 overall trade between the EU and Russia increased by a third, and the EU consolidated its position as the largest investor in Russia. Putin regularly pointed out that Russia was significantly more open to energy investments than Gulf producers. Insiders pointed out that Putin was ambivalent over the notion of a 'gas OPEC' precisely because this would limit his political room for manoeuvre in striking bilateral deals with European states, in which Gazprom committed itself to increasing supplies in return for downstream access.

Other views and indicators were less sanguine. Overall trade with the EU grew exponentially and FDI in most sectors progressed smoothly, but the energy sector was increasingly managed by the Kremlin 'as a strategic asset which it can use to assert itself on the world stage'.[43] KGB veterans moved in to take senior positions in Gazprom and key *siloviki* became generally influential in the energy sphere; one of its number, for example, assumed the chairmanship of Rosneft, the largest state oil company.[44] Gazprom revenues were used to buy up other sectors of the economy rather than being invested to develop gas production. Some commercial openings were negotiated, but then placed in doubt. After the Shell and BP episodes, in July 2007 Total was awarded a limited participation in the Shtokman field along the same lines as the Shell and BP deals: helping provide Gazprom with select technical services but without ownership rights of the field. In December 2006 a new law was introduced requiring a minimum 50 per cent Russian ownership of gas pipelines and 75 per cent for oil pipelines, and placing additional restrictions on foreign ownership.[45]

Many observers linked the strengthening of the Kremlin's political control to decreases in oil and gas production. Prior to the Yukos affair in 2003 growth in oil output was 9 per cent a year; by the end of 2007 it was running at 1 per cent per annum;[46] and in April 2008 production registered its first drop for over a decade. An increasing lack of transparency meant that it was not clear even what levels Russian reserves and production actually stood at. A key element of uncertainty flowed from the difficulty of ascertaining the precise nature of the relationship between Gazprom and the Kremlin. Foreign investors may in general have retained interest through the Yukos and Sakhalin affairs but with serious concerns over the rule of law and sanctity of contracts and property rights. Mafia-style violence subsided, but bureaucratic-level corruption became more firmly rooted. Anti-corruption purges were aimed at settling scores, not strengthening the rule of law, and thus were often of unpredictable course.[47] Many Western executives and investors linked to Yukos were forced out of Russia. By 2008 Russia occupied bottom position in the Forbes 'Best for Business' rankings.[48]

One argument increasingly made was that the threat to European energy security derived not so much from Russia's strength in playing power politics as from its weakness in modernizing and increasing domestic productive capacity. One former UK ambassador observed that Russia's naked use of energy-based power politics was in this sense sign more of its long-term decline than its revival.[49] A lack of investment in energy infrastructure was in turn related to the changing nature of the political system. By 2008 the government had set aside nearly $150 billion in an oil-investment fund, but this was used as a political slush fund and not primarily for structural investment. Russia seemed to be suffering an acute form of Dutch disease, as manufacturing and hi-tech developments atrophied. Here lay a crucial difference between Russia and the Gulf states, namely that Russia was itself a significant consumer of energy resources, and thus the politically-caused inefficiencies in the management of its energy sector were more of a cause of domestic frustration and instability.

British ministries openly complained that foreign investment was being discouraged by Russia holding domestic energy prices artificially low; this central part of Putin's strategy for winning popular support was seen as a major cause of the shortfalls of investment in new production capacity.[50] These shortfalls also pointed to sharp divisions within Russia, with a sector of Europeanized diplomats looking for reform-oriented engagement and, often in league with small Russian producers, pushing strongly for an opening-up of the pipeline network, precisely because the political nature in which oil monopoly Transneft was managed was holding back production and exports.

However, the extent to which Russia needed cooperation from the West to rectify these problems was not clear. In 2006 IPOs for Gazprom and Rosneft won huge capital investment from Western financial markets. On the one hand, some governments were expressing a geopolitical approach to dealing with Russia's energy diplomacy; on the other hand, European stock markets invested heavily in Rosneft's flotation and Gazprom's capitalization.[51] With Putin apparently restricting the scope for Western MNCs to invest in Russian oil and gas, he seemed confidently to be concluding that Russia did not have a great need for FDI, but could rather raise capital for Russian companies on global financial markets.

Demonizing or pandering Putin?

The EU's 1999 Russia Common Strategy defined support for democratic consolidation as its main goal – this, of course, prior to Putin's assault on democratic values and when democracy programmes could be seen as largely running with the grain of Russian state policies. Crucially, the largest element of European democracy support efforts during the mid-to-late 1990s were aimed at 'state building', that is at strengthening the policy-making capacities of centralized public administration institutions – and in this sense were consistent with one of the main elements of Vladimir Putin's manifesto when he assumed the presidency. Indeed, initially EU programmes offered assistance to Putin in his policy of recentralizing state capacities, seen as necessary to correct the fragility and instability of the post-Yeltsin Russian polity.[52] European diplomats later admitted that they had missed a moment of opportunity in the early stages of Putin's presidency, when a group of technocrats committed to governance and market reforms still held some sway and could have been supported more vigorously, before Putin consolidated his hold on power.

As Putin gradually adopted a more clearly authoritarian path, European governments struggled to delineate a common response. As Russia came more strongly to object to European language on democracy, as already mentioned, northern European states devised the Northern Dimension, as a framework for practical cooperation with Russia without mention of political conditions or issues – apparently circumventing the supposedly baseline values of EU external relations. European criticism of Russian actions in Chechnya was not entirely absent, but became less audible. In the late 1990s the French government had adopted one of the toughest lines against Moscow's policies in Chechnya, but by the early 2000s was less outspoken. Western forbearance of Russian control over Chechnya was widely seen as support for the kind of centrally controlled stability needed to maximize exploitation of the province's significant oil reserves. Italy's 2003 presidency was generally regarded as being the most egregiously uncritical towards Putin.

The Commission allocated 392 million euros of aid to Russia for the period 2004–6. Of this, 30 million was targeted at administration reform, supporting in particular president Putin's Civil Service Reform programme, judged to be making headway on reducing corruption; 32 million at legal reform, similarly seen by the Commission as having 'gained momentum'; and 20 million at civil society, for projects on legal, social and media rights. Under the previous programme, covering 2000–2003, a similar overall amount of 366 million euros had been awarded to Russia, with 97 million for administrative and legal reform, but with a smaller civil-society component of under 10 million euros. A 2 million euro 'Promoting Democracy through social NGOs' project was aimed at partnerships and mutual confidence-building between NGOs and local administrations. Throughout this period, the Commission was the largest provider of humanitarian assistance in Chechnya.

In formal terms, within the new four 'spaces' the Economic Space included a commitment to cooperate on good governance standards, while the Common Space of Freedom, Security and Justice mentioned democracy, rule of law and human rights. More practically, EU–Russia Human Rights Consultations were acknowledged to have been ineffectual. This dialogue did not include Russian NGOs. Some European officials in Moscow defended this exclusion on the grounds that these NGOs were 'too pushy' in their advocacy of democratic rights. These officials also admitted to being relatively unconcerned about the controversial new NGO law, which they saw as having allowed a reasonably generous round of licensing – a view contrary to most interpretations of this law as more restrictive of civil-society activities.

At a Russian–German energy and political summit in April 2006, that involved significant business representation from both sides, the German economics minister said diplomatic criticism of Putin's human rights record would only 'spoil the atmosphere'.[53] Leading Austria's EU presidency, Wolfgang Schüssel clarified his view at an EU–Russia summit in May 2006 that 'buying and selling oil and gas is a purely commercial activity; it is not politics'.[54] French, German and other member state representatives declined the offer of attending a meeting of Russian NGOs and opposition figures during the St Petersburg G8 summit; the British ambassador did attend and spoke against the undermining of democratic rights – and for his pains was subsequently tailed by the security services and targeted by regime-orchestrated protests. This came on top of the acutely embarrassing episode of the FSB uncovering British security services' electronic pick-up devices connected to UK contacts with civil-society organizations.

Some of the member states adopting the toughest line towards Moscow were those with the highest rates of gas dependency on Russia – this including the Baltic states, Poland and Slovakia.[55] France held one of the 'softest' positions, despite obtaining a more limited amount of its energy from Russia. Overall, the relationship between countries' energy dependency and the nature of their foreign-policy positions towards Russia was variable. The Czech Republic's imported gas came almost entirely from Russia, but

Czech diplomats suggested that it was their country's search for greater energy independence based on nuclear power that accorded them more room to be 'tough on Putin'. One Finnish policy-maker admitted that Finland's positions had to take into account the country's extreme vulnerability, noting that, 'we import gas from one country, through one pipeline'.

Internal strains over Russia's domestic politics were vibrantly on display at the Lahti summit in October 2006. José Manuel Barroso argued publicly that the EU should adopt a tough response to the murder that month of investigate journalist Anna Politovskaya and not forget human rights in its pursuit of energy security. France, Greece and Luxembourg, in contrast, used the summit to dilute criticism of Russia's imposition of sanctions against Georgia. Putin argued that the EU lacked credibility to give lessons on good governance, pointing out that corruption was rife in Spain and Italy. Northern member-state diplomats in Moscow admitted privately that Putin's tactics had now reached the point where it would be better not to attempt a new agreement with him and rather await his exit from office in 2008. Diplomats from another, large member state disagreed fundamentally, arguing that the situation regarding democracy and human rights in Russia was not as bad as these countries insisted. One Nordic diplomat claimed in November 2006 that there was 'more sympathy for Poland now than when this veto dispute began',[56] while another European energy official argued that some in the EU were politicizing relations with Putin too much, and that Europe should not let any lingering cold war legacy make it 'afraid of buying gas from Russia'. German and French officials argued it was Poland that was isolated in being so critical of Putin's dismantling of democratic checks and balances. Poland openly criticized chancellor Merkel's inability to confront Putin. President Chirac set himself up to mediate between Russia and Poland, rather than backing the latter.

One member-state diplomat arguing against the feasibility or wisdom of any European focus on Russia's democratic pushback saw as a strong point of his government's strategy the fact that it did not react critically to specific cases of democratic reversals as much as the US, and admitted that 'for us it is about tangible, immediate interests'. Several officials even argued that if any form of diplomatic pressure was key for energy security it was the need for European governments to join with Russia to push the United States to reduce carbon emissions, this judged to be more important than the EU joining the US to press Russia on democratic abuses. Several European policy-makers with a specific energy, rather than external-relations, remit opined that the EU's foreign policy-making machinery was guilty of an over-zealous demonization of Putin and Gazprom. Both of these, they suggested, were hard-headed but not unreasonable and were not the source of Europe's problems, which were far more the result of internationally set energy prices. Europe looked self-servingly unconvincing in bemoaning Russian nationalism now when the latter had gone unremarked during the period of low energy prices up to 2002.

The Kaczynski government itself was, its practitioners admitted, driven more by a post-Soviet concern over identity and independence from Moscow than by any carefully weighted approach to energy security and Russian internal policies. Despite the hard-line position against Russia, the 2001–5 Polish government had actually ceased development of alternative pipeline routes, especially from Norway. The tougher stance adopted by the Kaczynski government after 2005 did engender some attempts at diversification, but policy was increasingly about making a point to both Moscow and Berlin. Poland's hard-line stance on Russian authoritarianism was criticized by many older member states as more anti-Russian than pro-democracy. Poland's tendency still to be 'fighting the cold war' was said by one report to differ from the 'frosty pragmatism' of states such as the UK, Sweden, Denmark, the Czech Republic, the Netherlands, Ireland and others who sought to balance governance concerns and strategic interests.[57]

Against this background, Nordic states observed that biltateralism could cut both ways, and did not only lessen the focus on democracy and human rights: the scope for distinctive national policies allowed them to keep a focus on reform challenges through small-scale bilateral activities. They claimed to be revisiting the case for a single EU policy, to the extent that such policy might presently tend towards a 'German realpolitik writ large'. One analyst argued that, contrary to much commentary, what was really significant was that many European governments had retained a critical focus on issues of democracy and human rights despite the obvious importance of energy relations.[58] A common critique was that EU had actually become far tougher on Putin than on Boris Yeltsin as under the latter's rein the main opposition had been communist. At the October 2007 EU–Russia summit Putin cheekily proposed a Russia–Europe Institute for Freedom and Democracy, to enable Russia to fund democracy projects in the EU as the EU did in Russia! Putin frequently argued that it was not Russia seeking to 'divide and rule', but rather member states queuing up to solicit bilateral deals with Gazprom.

The problems that arose in the autumn of 2006 with European contracts and bids in relation to the Sakhalin and Shtokman fields did elicit some firmer reactions. After the episodes with Shell and BP, British ministers chorused admonishment of Russia for not adhering to the rule of law. Tony Blair urged Russia to 'play by the rules'.[59] EU energy commissioner Andris Piebalgs expressed concern over the need for a more 'secure and predictable investment climate' in Russia.[60] There was pressure from the European Parliament, especially from the Liberal group, for the EU not to offer Russia a new agreement.[61] Swedish foreign minister Carl Bildt argued that developments were such that for the EU the 'hard nosed and realistic' position was now precisely to 'stand up for our values' vis-à-vis Russia.[62] Lithuanian prime minister Gediminas Kirkilas opined that Putin's authoritarianism was the source of unpredictability over energy: 'During the cold war, Russia was a more reliable partner than it is today.'[63] One Russian civil-society group criticized Germany for leading the EU into the mistaken belief that a trade-off existed between energy security and human rights: 'Speaking out on human rights in Russia won't threaten Europe's energy security, but it would really help to curb the government's crackdown.'[64]

This related to arguably the crux question for European energy interests: what was the impact on external actors of the intertwining of political and economic power in Russia, at the heart of the country's de-democratization? President Putin rejected accusations that the actions taken to the detriment of European firms represented his anti-Western political manipulation of the energy sector, arguing these reflected Gazprom's legitimate insistence on fairer production-sharing arrangements. More broadly, however, officials argued that while Putin had addressed some issues of concern to European investors (such as taxation reform) general political uncertainty meant that still few really big investments had been forthcoming from European oil giants.

By early 2007 many were already predicting how Putin would stage-manage a 'succession', placing his candidate as president and himself taking over as prime minister. And yet officials lamented a dearth of debate within the EU on how to approach such an eventuality. Few thought the prospect of a new EU–Russia agreement offered much leverage. It was now clear to many in the EU that any new agreement formally based on 'shared values' would ring extremely hollow.[65] At the Samara summit the EU's line was tougher and more united in criticism of Putin's treatment of political opponents. And Italy was slightly more critical after two Italian members of parliament were detained in a march in Moscow in May 2007. Britain linked its diplomatic sanctions to the broad concept of the rule of law not being accepted by the Putin government. The UK's visa bans were said to be hurting members of the Russian elite.[66] Russia's response was to close offices of the British Council; a move which elicited no tangible solidarity from the UK's European partners.

At the end of 2007 a number of member states were relatively critical of the conditions surrounding Russia's parliamentary elections, that secured a comfortable majority for Putin's United Russia party – although these concerns were undermined by Nicolas Sarkozy calling Putin to congratulate him. In the run-up to the presidential elections, in February 2008 Javier Solana was unusually forthright in admonishing Russia for investing in 'future leverages' rather than increased energy output.[67] Russia refused to accept an OSCE observers' mission to the elections. After the elections, however, a majority of member states supported a more positive position, including the offer to resume talks for an EU–Russia agreement – this despite Putin retaining de facto power behind Medvedev. The agreement on a negotiating mandate for a new agreement was reached relatively quickly while most observers agreed that Putin retained de facto power.

Conclusion

Russia cast the longest shadow over EU energy security policy, even though only a minority of member states had high dependency on Russia energy supplies. Russia was the one place where energy clearly dominated the EU's foreign-policy agenda and where energy security was the pre-eminent issue at the level of high politics. As one writer put it: a 'hyper-realist Russia' had forced a realist response from the European Union.[68] This reflected not only events related to Russia's own energy production but also the fact that Moscow continued to control supplies coming from Central Asia. One view was that EU efforts too instrumentally reflected a power politics approach and that when Russia had sought to be a largely cooperative partner European concerns looked like 'thinly-veiled Russophobia'.[69] The most common view, however, was that the EU was weak and divided in the face of an increasingly powerful Russia, looking in vain for cooperative and market-based solutions rejected by Moscow.

Russia's argument was that it desired cooperation but objected to the EU dictating all the reforms it must undertake simply in order to allow European companies access to supply contracts, without engaging in a broader strategic partnership that treated Russia as an equal. A contradiction appeared in the EU's approach: one of the main policy incentives was to guide Russia into the WTO, but when Russia moved towards market prices in former Soviet republics, the EU accused it of 'power politics'. Despite formal stipulations to the contrary, the EU in practice seemed disinclined to recognize that a balance was needed in the way forward: if the EU wanted upstream access in Russia, Russia asked why it was blocked from much downstream access in Europe. The EU's focus on primarily technical cooperation produced meagre results, unable significantly to counter-balance the more political obstacles to EU–Russian energy-market integration.

Clear uncertainty and difference persisted on the question of whether energy security required more assertive pressure on Russia to re-establish democratic norms or conversely acceptance that any effort to encourage the Russian government away from its authoritarian drift had to be sacrificed. European policy hovered uneasily between these two positions. Not only was there obvious divergence between member states, but also the balance of opinion and what was presented as the common European line veered between the two positions over time. There was little correlation between member states' respective degree of dependency on Russian energy supplies and the robustness of their criticism of Russia's declining human rights and governance standards. A combination of the dispute with Ukraine in 2006 and the Sakhalin 're-nationalization' on balance triggered the beginning of tougher European criticism of President Putin's rule.

In the 1999 Common Strategy support for democracy was declared a priority goal, when democracy did not appear to be under threat; but when Putin's authoritarianism took hold this aspect of policy lost prominence at the behest of a number of member states. The Commission's judgement that rule of law and administrative reform projects were running with the grain of Putin's policies looked, at best, highly charitable. Conversely, the fact that some member states were (at least temporarily) willing to sacrifice a new strategic partnership on the altar of democratic values suggested either principled behaviour or that they had concluded that unlike many other autocrats Putin was not good for European energy security. Certainly, as the presidency became so strong, to the detriment of institutional strength and predictability, state interference with basic market mechanisms increased. The end of the Putin presidency engendered optimism that such impediments might diminish, but even as the EU moved to unblock its offer of a new strategic partnership most observers predicted that the basic constellation of autocratic power in Russia was set to persist.

6 The Caucasus and Central Asia

Energy-security debates helped propel the southern Caucasus and Central Asia to greater international prominence. The region included significant energy producers in Kazakhstan, Turkmenistan, Uzbekistan and Azerbaijan. After the states of the former Soviet Union gained independence they attracted little attention from European governments and were not significant sources of European Union (EU) external energy supplies. As the search for energy diversification intensified the EU committed itself to correcting this neglect. This chapter outlines how the EU invested new hope in the energy potential of Central Asia and the Caucasus, introducing several energy-related programmes and initiatives after 2002. Central Asia undoubtedly came to claim a place on the EU's 'energy map' in a way that it had previously not done. However, the chapter also highlights how and why Europe's engagement in the region remained circumspect. Russia's influence in the region, the challenge of transporting supplies into European markets, a range of other security issues that cut across energy interests and the opaque nature of Central Asian regimes all militated against a more concerted European focus on energy security. As of 2008, several member states claimed firm commitment to strengthening policy towards Central Asia, but it remained unclear whether the region would in practice cease to be something of a 'poor relation' within the overall hierarchy of Common Foreign and Security Policy (CFSP) priorities.

Caspian challenges

After collapsing in the 1990s, supplies from the countries of the former Soviet Union began to figure prominently in international energy politics after 2000. While low oil prices had discouraged the development of Central Asian fields in the 1990s, this situation changed dramatically as markets tightened. The region was estimated to hold around 5 per cent of global reserves. It was an area of increasing European interest related to energy supply and one where Europe's interests seemed to imbue greater urgency than those of the US, the latter not concerned with purchasing energy supplies from the region. The region was largely about future potential. It had hitherto not accounted for significant shares of EU energy imports. The Commission's list of EU energy sources for 2005 showed only Kazakhstan and Azerbaijan amongst the suppliers of oil (accounting for 4.2 and 1.1 per cent of EU imports respectively) and no Caspian or Central Asian state amongst the top suppliers of gas to the Union.[1]

Kazakhstan was the most enticing of the Central Asian states. Its Kashagan field represented the largest oil find for over 30 years, and one that promised to make Kazakhstan one of the world's largest oil exporters. The country was set to become one of the world's biggest gas producers too. The Kazakh government committed itself to tripling output by 2015, with modest domestic demand ensuring that most of this was earmarked for export. Turkmenistan was also positioned in the top 15 of world gas reserves. This remained the region's most closed market, in which the state oil company accounted for over 90 per cent of total output. The Turkmen government claimed discovery of a huge new gas field in March 2007, dwarfing even Russia's largest fields – although many doubted the veracity of this claim.[2]

Azerbaijan became a prime target for European oil companies from the mid-1990s, as the country opened up to Western investments in the hope of securing Western backing for Azeri independence. The country's geostrategic importance increased amid drawn-out negotiations over the construction of an oil pipeline from Baku to Tiblisi and then onto the Turkish port of Ceyhan, the Baku–Tblisi–Ceyhan (BTC) pipeline. Built by a consortium led by BP and Azeri state company Socar, the BTC pipeline finally opened in 2006. This highly geopolitical pipeline offered the first significant supply route into Europe that by-passed Russia; its route was additionally chosen to avoid conflict hotspots in Armenia and Nagorno–Karabakh. An

Table 6.1 Caspian and Central Asia oil reserves (2006)

Country	Global ranking	Billion barrels
Kazakhstan	9	40
Azerbaijan	20	7
Uzbekistan	46	1
Turkmenistan	47	1

Source: OPEC Secretariat, *World Oil and Gas Journal*

Table 6.2 Caspian and Central Asia gas reserves (2006)

Country	Global ranking	Trillion cubic metres
Kazakhstan	11	3
Turkmenistan	13	3
Uzbekistan	19	2
Azerbaijan	22	1

Source: OPEC Secretariat, *World Oil and Gas Journal*

accompanying BTE (Baku–Tblisi–Erzurum) gas pipeline became operational in 2007.

There were downsides to Caspian and Central Asian resources that continued to cast doubt on how important the region would be for European energy supplies. Production costs were high. Several oil majors revised downwards initial estimates of reserves in the area. Rates of profit retention from international investment were high.[3] Azeri production was predicted by some to peak as early as 2010. One respected organization concluded that Central Asia was not highly promising for EU energy security, due to the combination of expensive transport; Gazprom's monopsony position that had locked countries in the region into long-term deals with Russia; delays and over-runs to the much-vaunted Kashagan field; the prospect of international involvement in Turkmenistan existing only in off-shore sites; and a general tendency towards exaggerated reserve estimates.[4]

The transport of supplies into Europe certainly presented a set of searching geopolitical challenges. The region's dependence on pipeline networks routed through Russia enabled the latter to exert political influence and charge mark-ups that significantly increased the cost of Central Asian supplies to European consumers. A host of pipeline projects were mooted aimed at circumventing Russia. In addition to the BTC and Nabucco projects, in June 2006 Kazakhstan and Azerbaijan signed a deal to build a pipeline under the Caspian to link into the line flowing out of Baku. But the dents in Russia's dominant position were small. The most economical route for many Central Asian supplies across Iran was hindered by geopolitical factors. The Caspian Pipeline Consortium – which commenced in 2001, led by Agip, and including British Gas, BP, Shell, Chevron, ExxonMobil, plus the Russian and Kazakh governments – continued to use a route via the Russian Black Sea port of Novorossiysk. The Russia–Ukraine 2006 dispute ended when Kiev agreed to abandon attempts to circumvent the Russian monopoly over the transport and marketing of Central Asian gas to Europe.[5] In May 2007 Russia secured a deal with Turkmenistan, under which the latter agreed that its supplies to Europe would go through Russian pipelines. Some observers argued that this undermined the viability of the Nabucco pipeline – although others noted that Nabucco still held a potentially key advantage of not facing the same acute challenges of deep-water construction as Russia's North and South Stream projects.

European engagement

European foreign policy struggled to gain a meaningful foothold in Central Asia after the break-up of the Soviet Union. During the 1990s Partnership and Cooperation Agreements (PCAs) were signed with Kazakhstan, Kyrgyzstan, Uzbekistan and Turkmenistan; a Trade and Cooperation Agreement (TCA) was agreed with Tajikistan. Trade benefits were limited to non-preferential (most favoured nation, MFN) status, and then with additional restrictions in

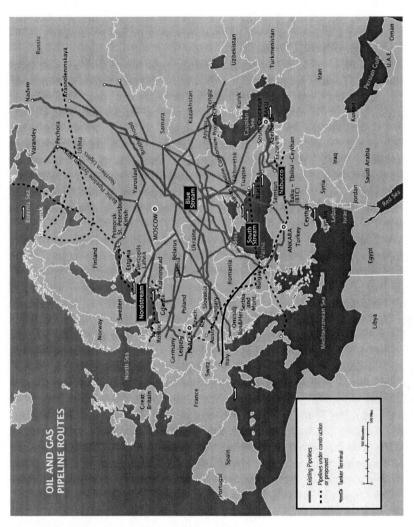

Map 6.1 Oil and Gas Pipeline Routes

relation to certain products. From the early 1990s to 2002, EU aid averaged 100 million euros a year to the region. For 2002–4 the Commission allocated the region 150 million euros of assistance. These amounts were negligible compared with, for example, the magnitude of MEDA aid.[6] European aid was mainly humanitarian, complemented by a gradually increased focus on cross-border infrastructure, and later on support for the technical implementation of the PCAs. The Traceca – Transport Corridor to Connect Europe via the Caucasus to Asia – initiative was launched in the early 1990s but was not significantly funded.[7]

European diplomatic presence in the region remained limited. Germany was the only EU state with embassies in all Central Asian states. Commission diplomatic presence remained negligible, for instance with one small office in Almaty dealing with Kazakhstan, Kyrgyzstan and Tajikistan. The EU did appoint special envoys, one to Central Asia, one to the Southern Caucasus, in 2005 and 2003 respectively. However, the first special representative to Central Asia, Jan Kubis, failed to complete a new strategy for the area, to the disappointment of many EU diplomats and delaying efforts to strengthen European presence. When then external relations commissioner, Chris Patten made a trip round the region in 2004, it was the first by a commissioner in ten years.[8]

While the EU was the region's largest aid donor, compared with other developing regions aid amounts were limited relative to private-sector foreign direct investment (which itself was modest, especially outside the energy sector). At the end of the 1990s aid to Kazakhstan amounted to only 4 per cent of British Gas's investment in that country.[9] Germany was the biggest national donor, followed by the UK, France and the Netherlands, all with much smaller aid programmes. Central Asian states were identified formally as partner countries for German development assistance, but even German aid was relatively modest, reaching just over 100 million euros from 1993 to 1996.

In 2002 the German government introduced a new 50 million euro Central Asia Strategy. The UK increased aid flows after 2002, from a low base to 14 million euros for 2004–5. British aid was poverty-focused and not energy-related, limited to Tajikistan and Kyrgyzstan; funds were taken out of Kazakhstan as this moved into the middle-income bracket. The UK agreed a bilateral agreement on energy cooperation with Kazakhstan in 2005, related to sharing experience on regulatory reform of energy markets, and also appointed an energy advisor for the Caspian and Central Asian region.

One of the earliest marks made by the new member states of central and eastern Europe on EU foreign policy was their push for the Southern Caucasus to be included in the European Neighbourhood Policy (ENP), with a primary focus on energy.[10] When Azerbaijan was indeed included in the ENP, Commissioner Benita Ferrero-Waldner declared that this offer reflected the country's 'geo-strategic location and energy resources. For this reason' (she claimed) it was included in the ENP.[11] In 2004, the EU launched the Baku Initiative, which incorporated the Commission, the Caspian littoral states and their neighbours, with the declared aim of developing regional energy markets and network interconnections. The EU's stated objective was to drive energy-sector reform in the region, around EU regulatory standards – once again using Europe's internal market as a template to be exported into the foreign-policy domain. The Baku Initiative was, ostensibly, based on a trade-off: European funding and investment for infrastructure development in return for a guarantee of supplies to European markets.[12] New European Bank for Reconstruction and Development funds were due to be offered, along with an increased 500 million euros of European Investment Bank lending. From 2008 these organizations committed themselves to prioritizing energy-related infrastructure projects.

Indeed, while overall aid was modest, it increasingly exhibited an energy security orientation. Commission aid priorities for 2002–6 were identified as technical assistance for reform of energy policies; improving the investment climate in the energy sector; and support for pipeline monitoring and other technical energy services. Two formal funding programmes, Traceca and Inogate (Interstate Oil and Gas Transport to Europe), increased funding for infrastructure and pipeline development, respectively.[13] The second Baku Initiative ministerial meeting was held in November 2006. This meeting agreed a new Energy Road Map, with commitments to enhance energy cooperation on both infrastructure and regulatory convergence. The underlying EU approach was to nudge countries in the region to create a regional oil market, which would be powerful and well organized enough to link directly into the EU. One European diplomat identified as the main energy-related priority the need to lead Central Asian states towards membership of the World Trade Organization (WTO).

Commission officials claimed that the series of new energy papers compiled after 2005 would have a particularly big impact in terms of beefing up engagement with Central Asia, now seen by some as a top priority for energy security. It was recognized that the region had attracted a modest increase in attention after 2001, by virtue of its proximity to Afghanistan and counter-terrorist concerns, but that now energy security was driving a more fundamental reassessment of EU policy. In late 2006 the Commission proposed plans to move towards 'sub-regional energy markets' in the Caspian Basin, Caucasus and Central Asia, through a new EU–Black Sea Synergy initiative. Policy would be based on prompting and supporting the convergence of these energy markets with that of the EU, with the ambitious aim of having this whole broader region 'functioning on the basis of the EU internal energy market'.[14] In February 2007 the Commission proposed that this initiative have its own secretariat and be funded from the European Neighbourhood Partnership Instrument (ENPI). The overlaying of a Black Sea regional dimension on the array of existing EU agreements in the area was recognized to reflect the growing importance of energy considerations. The first ministerial meeting between EU and Black Sea states took place in February 2008.

As outlined in Chapter 3, new bilateral energy-partnership agreements were signed with Azerbaijan and Kazakhstan. Energy commissioner Andris Piebalgs emphasized how concerned the EU now was over China's encroachment into Kazakhstan and how this had been a key factor spurring the EU to focus more assertively on the region and to stress the need for open and transparent markets and the extension of EU regulations.[15] The EU special representative began to incorporate energy issues into his brief on a more formal and systematic basis. It was recognized that a more political approach and presence was required as the importance of gas increased relative to oil – the former being linked to long-term contracts over fixed pipeline routes, very different to the dynamics of oil supplies to international markets.

Germany declared Central Asia a top priority for its stewardship of the EU during the first six months of 2007 and at the end of its presidency a new EU–Central Asia Strategy paper was agreed. This promised a doubling of European aid; more Commission delegations in the region; strategies more tailored to individual Central Asian states on a bilateral basis; regular foreign ministers' dialogue; an EU rule of law initiative to establish clearer rules in relation to foreign investment; a new formal energy dialogue that would work towards a new 'transport corridor' and the extension of EU internal energy-market principles; and support for public–private partnerships to strengthen energy infrastructure links.[16] In March 2007 an EU delegation met with Central Asian leaders in Astana. This meeting was significant for including representation from Turkmenistan. Even Spain declared Central Asia a priority and opened an embassy in Kazakhstan in 2007.

Notwithstanding such initiatives and new commitments, most diplomats attested to a persistent lack of political will to become seriously engaged in Central Asia. Unlike other regions, and despite Germany's emerging role, Central Asia had no member state consistently championing its cause in the EU. It was argued that the EU remained no more than 'a bit player' in the region.[17] One EU diplomat admitted that political considerations in Central Asia were still not getting 'the attention they deserve'. Contrary to its rhetoric, the EU in practice did little to convince policy-makers in the region that Central Asia was in fact seen as a priority for energy security. Policy-makers and observers, within both Europe and Central Asia, most frequently bemoaned the extent to which the EU continued to approach the region as a 'by-product' of policy towards Russia.

Diplomats from a number of member states implicitly corroborated this view in suggesting that it was unrealistic for the EU to seek to rival Russia in the region and that overly ambitious new policies could prove counterproductive and highly damaging. The EU declined to entertain two innovations that, according to officials and experts in the region, might have provided some leverage: first, European support, against the United States, for more economical pipeline routes through Iran; second, a more systematic incorporation into EU policy-making of Turkey, as both a weightier diplomatic player in Central Asia and a potentially vital transit hub for the region's energy exports.

While in terms of potential supply shares Central Asia 'mattered' more to Europe than the United States, the latter's geostrategic engagement in the region became far stronger. As US politicians travelled to Central Asia to announce new initiatives and deployments, they reiterated how important the region was for energy supplies into Europe and almost seemed to be engaging on behalf of a still-more-cautious Europe. For example, the US pushed far harder than EU states (with the partial exception of the UK) in favour of the BTC pipeline, a project that secured European support only very late in the day. Central Asia seemed to be a case of the US seeing itself as acting on behalf of a broad Western market-oriented supply *system*, as opposed to its own narrow national energy interests. However, as the US restructured its approach to the region, conceiving Central Asia as a secondary part of its Afghanistan strategy, the unease this invoked in Central Asian capitals led some European diplomats to feel an opportunity had again opened for a greater EU role.

A number of European diplomats themselves doubted how significant Central Asia and the Caucasus were for energy interests, both in terms of the size of the region's reserves and the practicality of transport options. Doubts were strong, for example, over the Nabucco pipeline – doubts raised to justify the decisions taken by some member states to opt instead for bilateral deals with Gazprom. One energy representative argued that the EU should not let a desire to 'take on Russia' lead it to distorted judgement on Central Asia's real energy fundamentals.

Scepticism prevailed in the region over the impact of EU energy-related projects.[18] Moreover, one critic argued that while the EU formally had a policy of supporting regionalism in the area in practice its policies prioritized bilateral relations and drove wedges between different Caspian and Central Asian states.[19] Indeed, from 2007 Central Asian states were split under the EU's new budgetary structures, the Caucasus placed under the rubric of the European Neighbourhood Partnership Instrument, the five Central Asian countries under the Development Cooperation and Economic Cooperation Instrument – a division that diplomats acknowledged would complicate the nominally regional approach to energy. Kazakhstan reacted badly to being excluded from the Neighbourhood Policy, souring political relations.[20] One diplomat noted that Central Asian regimes were increasingly asking Europe for direct and concrete contracts, underpinned by geo-strategic preference, while the EU was asking them 'to buy into the more abstract notion of a market distribution system'.

The Russia–Ukraine gas dispute revived EU interest in direct links to Central Asian supplies, through a Trans-Caspian pipeline. The proposal for such a pipeline had been forwarded by the US in the 1990s, but was not taken up with interest. In the summer of 2006, the Kazakh government asked the European Commission to undertake a new feasibility study for this pipeline; it made this request after US Vice President Dick Cheney had visited president Nazarbayev and urged the pipeline dossier to be reactivated.[21]

In late 2006 feasibility studies commenced also for a Georgia–Ukraine–EU gas pipeline, to link up to Azerbaijan's Shah Deniz offshore field. This added to ongoing work in relation to the Nabucco and Baku–Tbilisi–Erzurum pipelines – these latter promising the prospect of bypassing a Ukrainian network over which Russia was gaining greater control. The Commission supported studies into the Nabucco project, but there were political differences as it remained unclear where such a pipeline would eventually terminate – some member states stressed that the commercial viability of Nabucco remained to be demonstrated.

Despite this movement in relation to new pipeline links to the region, one official admitted that the EU was 'keeping quiet' on this issue, so as not to cause problems with Russian President Vladimir Putin. Internal debate ensued amongst European governments over how far to condition the new 2006 energy partnership agreement with Kazakhstan on a clear commitment to develop a direct (Russia-bypassing) pipeline link to Europe. In light of this, it was significant that the new EU agreement ultimately did not make such an unequivocal commitment. Indeed, in reaction to these tentative efforts, Putin courted Nazarbayev with increasing assiduity, and won from the latter more positive statements on Kazakhstan preferring the Russian route for its oil and gas. At the very least, the Kazakh government was unwilling to support any EU-backed initiatives that did not win Russian and Iranian acquiescence, and without broader agreement on Caspian Sea status issues.

One authoritative source detected a significant transatlantic difference: while the US wanted to 'tighten the screws' on Russia and push hard for new routes for Central Asian–Caspian energy supplies that broke Russian control over the region, the EU sought to work in partnership with Moscow in negotiating access to Central Asian energy.[22] Commission officials saw Russia's May 2007 deal with Turkmenistan as 'unproblematic' for Europe, as Russia was anyway committed to transporting Central Asian supplies to the European market; in this sense, the new focus on targeting Central Asia as a competitor supplier to Russia represented an 'hysterical' over-reaction on the part of some member states. Indeed, Andris Piebalgs himself observed that these deals would increase supplies into the EU and were 'no bad thing.'[23] Another Commission official suggested that the EU should withdraw its support from the Trans-Caspian pipeline project, as this was a 'political bomb' for EU–Russia relations.[24]

Crucially, underlying all these limitations to EU policy were sharp differences between European governments over how much attention the Caspian and Central Asia really merited and over the importance of the region to energy security. As said, some policy-makers shared doubts over the region's energy potential. Diplomats from some member states questioned the viability of attaining direct supply routes from Central Asia into European markets. Some thought German hopes in Uzbek gas to be particularly over-stated. Southern EU member states admitted to a lack of significant engagement in the region and a primary concern with ensuring that any new Central Asia strategy did not draw attention or resources away from North Africa. A common refrain from European diplomats on the ground in Kazakhstan was that the country's energy potential was in danger of being exaggerated.

There was increasing divergence over how far the EU should seek to confront Russia in Central Asia – an area where Russian cultural and linguist influence remained primary. Some central and eastern European states admitted to a highly geopolitical perspective of wanting to strengthen preferential ties with Central Asian states primarily as a way of squeezing Russia. Others questioned the feasibility and wisdom of such an aim; with Russia engaged in a new rapprochement with both Kazakhstan and Uzbekistan, and with China continuing to move into Kazakhstan and Turkmenistan, they warned that a sense of 'realism' was required. With Gazprom offering increased prices for Central Asian gas and new infrastructure investments, the incentives diminished for Central Asians to accord more priority to their relations with Europe. One expert judged that as a geopolitical battle took shape in the region between Russia/Iran and US/Turkey in overall terms the EU had adopted a 'neutral stance'.[25]

Hungary's Blue Stream deal with Russia seemed momentarily to kill off the Nabucco project. Russia's May 2007 agreement with Turkmenistan and Kazakhstan was widely attributed in part to this ambivalence of Western powers in backing direct energy links with Central Asia. In the shadow of this agreement, the Azeri, Georgian and Ukrainian presidents met with their Polish and Lithuanian counterparts in an attempt to resurrect cooperation for such links; although the European Commission and other EU member states declined to attend the meeting.[26] Poland pushed for EU funding to help develop the Odessa–Brody pipeline extension to Gdansk, this pipeline (or its reversal of direction) stalled due to insufficient commitments of Caspian oil. And, as so often during his rule, President Nazarbayev counter-balanced his deal with Moscow by signing an agreement with the Azeri president to link Kazakh supplies into the BTC pipeline.

Then in September 2007 the Nabucco project appeared to be given a new lease of life, when Hungary declared that it would after all support the pipeline as its first priority. Hungarian diplomats argued that they had simply wanted to give a 'nudge' to Nabucco, and were keen for the latter to bring crucial 'hub' business into Hungary. They suggested that the Hungarian position was as a crucial pivotal player between the extremes of, on the one hand, indifference towards the Caucasus and Central Asia in many European governments and, on other hand, the desire to 'out-compete' Russia in the region. The EU needed to develop its own policy and prioritize more energy supplies from Central Asia, they argued, but also do this in a way that avoided simply making Russia 'more aggressive'. As the EU appointed former Dutch foreign minister, Jazias Van Aartsen, to coordinate work on the pipeline, Andris Piebalgs ruminated that, 'Nabucco is more than just a pipeline; it is the embodiment of the existence of a common European energy policy'.[27]

But prospects for the line still fluctuated. A Greek–Turkey deal on a parallel link line for Caspian supplies raised expectations further. Conversely, new doubts were engendered by the fact that – as outlined in the previous chapter – by summer 2008 Italy, Bulgaria, Hungary, Austria and Greece had all signed up to the Russia-led Nabucco-competitor, South Stream project. Austria also offered Gazprom the possibility of using Nabucco for Russian gas – a position explicitly opposed by the United States.[28] In early 2008 Russia offered a sizeable increase in the price it offered for Turkmen gas, aiming to head-off any possibility of Turkmenistan committing supplies to the Nabucco line.[29] Commission officials insisted that gas suppliers had by early 2008 been identified for Nabucco to commence operations around 2013–14.[30] German energy company RWE became the sixth partner within the Nabucco consortium in February 2008, giving the project a boost. However, the consortium still lacked a major producer company, with gas of its own to supply (meaning that firm contracts could still not be awarded to producer states), and Azerbaijan was the only producer state to have committed. The Turkish partner rejected Gaz de France's entry into the consortium because of the French government's sceptical position on Turkish EU accession; the Gaz de France bid had been explicitly promoted by the Commission in order to give Nabucco a more European identity.[31] Concern was expressed over Turkey increasingly using its putative role in Nabucco as leverage in its accession negotiations with the Union.

Others still argued that if Central Asia was important it was from a broader security perspective. As noted, the EU's interest in the region in fact began to deepen after the attacks of 9/11, for counter-terrorist and Afghanistan-related reasons (in particular in response to US operations in Afghanistan) and before energy security hit the headlines. The stationing of a German military base in Uzbekistan was (albeit unconvincingly to some observers) justified by the need to service troops in Afghanistan. When the UK participated in US-led military exercises in Central Asia, its energy specialists revealed that they had not been consulted on this involvement, suggesting less of a link up with energy concerns than in US policy. Kazakhstan gained support from a number of EU member states for an intensified partnership with NATO.

For some diplomats the EU's interests were mainly related to concerns over weak governance and the lack of development fostering drug trafficking, criminal networks and Islamist radicalism in the Fergana Valley, a combination of factors destabilizing the whole region. They cautioned that addressing such broader security concerns did not necessarily require the same set of policies that energy interests might invite. If security was recognized as the priority, then the focus of new funding should be on Tajikistan and Kyrgyzstan, not the region's big energy players. For energy interests, the liberalization of regional markets might be key; for security, the focus might better be placed on strengthening border controls. Indeed, in this light it was significant that from 2006 the EU launched one programme on Border Management in

Central Asia and one on combating drug trafficking (Central Asia Drug Assistance Programme). Within the EU, security policy-makers saw the region through the prism of the Afghan conflict, while energy experts saw it through a Caspian/Wider Black Sea Area regional lens.

Energy and politics in the Southern Caucasus and Central Asia

As in other regions, in the Caspian and Central Asia the EU made a formal commitment to supporting democratic reform, good governance and human rights standards. The need to press the region's autocrats for improvements in the rule of law was rhetorically presented as a vital element of energy security policy. The EU special representatives for the Southern Caucasus and Central Asia were charged with promoting democratic change as a formal and priority element of their respective mandates. Outlining the new regional plans drawn up in late 2006 by the Commission and the Council, Benita Ferrero-Waldner claimed that, 'the first and most important strand ... [of this new policy] ... is the need to promote good governance, human rights and democratization' and committed the European Union to 'support [ing] local democratization efforts'.[32] The new Central Asia Strategy agreed in 2007 was replete with commitments to encourage the region's democratization, establish a rule of law initiative and deepen human rights dialogues with each country on a bilateral basis.

Central Asia received funds from the Commission's new Institution Building programme. Both Germany and the UK funded rule of law, governance and administrative reform projects. As the biggest European investor in the region, a key priority for the UK was to press Azerbaijan and Kazakhstan to sign up to the Extractive Industries Transparency Initiative (EITI). Some reasoned that democratization would serve to delink the region from China and Russia: normative values would in this sense serve instrumental geopolitical purpose. Indeed, Central Asian leaders increasingly mimicked the Putin regime, creaming off oil rents to boost political power. One view from the region was that, while this at one level made regimes comfortable in prioritizing partnership with Moscow, it also gave the EU influence as a standard bearer of democratic norms – as many elites in the region also felt nervous about being completely 'left to the mercy of Russia and China'.[33]

In practice, however, European policies did little to challenge regimes. Democracy and governance funding was modest in magnitude. In 2005 only 2 million, and in 2006 4 million, euros under the European Initiative on Democracy and Human Rights (EIDHR) was made available for the whole of Central Asia, while funding rules prevented the EU from supporting opposition forces in the region. Reform oriented dialogue was thin. The fact that senior officials on the European side rarely attended meetings with Central Asian governments undermined any prospect of EU policy unleashing prodemocratic 'socialization'. Implicitly the EU seemed to agree that the OSCE should deal with reform and human rights issues in Central Asia. Commission aid itself listed virtually nothing as being done to support democracy proper in its regional strategy. The head of the OSCE's democratization office (OIDHR) warned that the EU was indeed relying *too* much on the OSCE to engage with Central Asian reform issues, which it was increasingly prevented from doing by Russia. The EU's role in the one positive breakthrough, Kyrgyzstan's 2005 'Tulip revolution', was conspicuously limited; indeed the EU had supported president Akayev's cosmetic 'reform' commitments as a way of heading off any destabilizing democratic rupture.[34]

One Commission official admitted that in Central Asia the EU had not been able to 'reconcile energy and democracy'. Political reform and governance initiatives that were supported had been determined and pursued on a 'separate track' from deliberations over energy policy. Germany's new bilateral Central Asia Strategy formally included a focus on democracy and rule of law funding, but energy specialists complained precisely because they had not had any input into these issues.

One member state diplomat explained internal debates in the following terms: all member states were keen to have good relations with Central Asian regimes, but there was a clear and growing difference between those focused on 'the conditions needed for investments to succeed' and those focused more narrowly on 'how to guarantee given quantities [of oil and gas] through bilateral deals'. The fact that political and economic power were linked more directly in Central Asia than in Russia (the oligarch phenomenon not so prevalent in the region) encouraged some to believe that secure deals could be more easily sewn up through engagement at the highest level. One factor pulling governments in the latter direction was the fact that the Shanghai Cooperation Organization created a Business Council that brought Chinese investment into energy infrastructure projects that European investors had declined for a range of governance and security concerns.[35]

Jan Kubis was judged clearly to have prioritized the strengthening of diplomatic engagement to the detriment of any focus on democracy and human rights.[36] His successor, Pierre Morel, expressed a desire to integrate energy into his political mandate and use this to prompt a stronger focus on governance reforms, but a number of member states and Brussels officials resisted such a move. Indeed, when the EU's new regional strategy was presented, Morel changed position to argue that aims to boost the EU's political presence should be delinked from democracy and human rights conditions; that the use of democratic conditionality had been tried and failed; and that now the EU needed to gain geostrategic influence vis-à-vis Russia and China in the region. It was on these grounds that the draft strategy provoked strong criticism in the European Parliament in February 2007. It was noted by critics that the new aid package proposed would be channelled to governments. Crucially, and in the vein of Morel's reasoning, the bilateral energy partnerships offered to Azerbaijan and Kazakhstan did indeed serve to delink energy from democracy and human rights strictures.

A key German politician argued that the EU should have an (even) less 'heavy handed insistence on democracy and human rights'.[37] Defending the geopolitical realism of the EU's new strategy one official argued that, 'Energy embargoes on Central Asian states will do nothing for human rights'. The comparison with a (perceived) US coercive attempt to impose democracy was routinely made. EU officials insisted that the US had erred in treating Central Asia only as an energy market, failing to understand its regional geopolitics and having gone out of its way to antagonize Russia; the EU approach was said to be different, working with rather than against the grain of Russia's influence in the region.

If political will was one factor, another was the complexity of the reform challenge in Central Asia. Diplomats recognized that European knowledge was limited of domestic dynamics and developments within civil societies in Central Asia. One official observed that the obstacles to democratic reform in Central Asia were significant enough that any concerted EU democracy support would 'have to use tools we are not used to using'. Many 'liberal reformists' in Central Asia themselves complained that Europe was underplaying the danger of radical Islam in its talk of democracy and showing undue leniency to radical groups headquartered in London. The complexity of steering stable democratic change was highlighted by the model of Kyrgyzstan, whose transition bred instability, criminality and a rise of anti-Western Islamic opinion.

The complex interplay of politics and energy varied, moreover, across different producer states.

Azerbaijan

As said, the extension of the European Neighbourhood Policy to the Southern Caucasus owed much to Azerbaijan's importance to EU energy interests – although other factors also played a role: the difficulty of refusing Azerbaijan if Georgia were offered a place in the ENP and the desire to bring Azerbaijan and Armenia together in the same framework in the hope of making progress on the frozen conflict on Nagorno–Karabakh. These factors meant that the EU turned a blind eye in 2003 when, shortly before his death, long-time ruler Heydar Aliyev rigged elections to pass the presidency to his son, Ilham. The late president had pushed forward the BTC pipeline, promising to fund the project even when European governments themselves were less than fully committed.[38] After 2003 modest judicial reform was undertaken, but no political opening entertained. Elections in November 2005 were declared as not free or fair by the OSCE and the Council of Europe. While Azerbaijan stagnated politically, in 2005–6 it recorded the world's fastest rate of economic growth and the government confidently announced that the country would free itself from external aid within five years. In practice, the increased revenue flowing into the Azeri State Oil Fund was used for political patronage, leaving large pockets of extreme poverty in Azerbaijan.

The ENP offer represented a notable gear-change in the EU's relations with Azerbaijan. The EU–Azerbaijan Partnership and Cooperation Agreement entered into force in 1999, but this offered little in the way of concrete substance and fell well down the pecking order of EU external agreements. Tacis aid amounted to only 7 million euros a year up to 2004. This modest amount of aid was spread between humanitarian assistance, food aid, budgetary relief and rehabilitation projects in Nagorno–Karabakh. For the three year period from 2004–6 a slightly increased 30 million euros was allocated, with some civil-society support included.[39] Until February 2008, when a small delegation opened, the Commission still lacked a permanent office in Baku (unlike in Tbilisi and Yerevan). Only France and Germany offered any significant bilateral aid, 15 million and 19 million euros respectively in 2005. These amounts were extremely limited relative to both Azerbaijan's energy revenues and the aid provided to other EU partner countries (including Armenia and Georgia).

While engagement with the Aliyev regime strengthened, governance reforms were apparently seen as important for European energy security. The state oil company, Socar, and decisions affecting anything related to oil remained firmly under the control of the Aliyev family, with often unpredictable consequences for European investors. Despite strong economic growth, the country remained heavily reliant on the oil and gas sector, which accounted for over half government revenues and 90 per cent of exports. Diplomats complained at an increasing lack of transparency, for example when a hefty energy price rise in February 2007 was announced out of the blue and without consultation, including with the EU. Oil revenues were also being used for a significant rearmament programme.

European officials insisted that energy interests warranted a priority focus on governance reforms. Out of the 30 million euro Commission aid commitment for 2004–6, 17 million was allocated for 'institutional, legal and administrative reform'. The Commission aid programme concluded under the Neighbourhood strategy listed democratic and energy reforms as two priority areas of support.[40] At the same moment they endorsed an ENP action plan, in November 2006 the EU and Azerbaijan signed a strategic partnership on energy that was predicated on the aim of Azeri convergence with EU internal market and transit provisions – and in respect of the latter also mentioned the prospect of European protection for the BTC pipeline. With Aliyev standing next to him, José Manuel Barroso declared that, 'This [agreement] is not just about energy ... what we are doing is exactly the way to promote democracy and the rule of law.'[41] Plans agreed under the memorandum of understanding signed with Azerbaijan proposed the integration of energy markets and a host of concrete institutional reform commitments on Azerbaijan's part, under which the latter would adopt, for example, an independent energy regulatory authority and independent transmission system operators along the lines of European models.[42] Officials insisted that the most crucial challenge was to press Azerbaijan through this agreement towards 'a more democratic way of doing things'.

However genuine the conviction may have been in the espousal of EU-based governance-regulatory reforms, there was no willingness to sacrifice engagement. Before the 2005 Azerbaijani elections Benita Ferrero-Waldner asserted that the poll would be a 'litmus test' and that the state of democracy would 'be duly taken into account' by the EU in negotiating the terms of the action plan.[43] It was not. The EU declared itself unwilling to 'interfere' when Azeri authorities arrested a number of opposition figures – indeed it chided the latter that political rights must be exercised 'in a moderate fashion'. Even Poland was cautious, admitting that it was not minded to assume the same 'forward-leaning' role in Azerbaijan that it had adopted in Ukraine, Belarus and Georgia. Member states increased arms sales, even as they were warned that these could help reignite the Nagorno–Karabakh conflict, as oil-primed Azerbaijan felt newly emboldened vis-à-vis Armenia. Aliyev won additional credit from the EU as Azerbaijan was the one state in the region to oppose outright efforts to form a 'gas OPEC'. He was also supported as a bulwark against opposition voices in Azerbaijan who increasingly pushed for a rene-gotiation of contracts with Western oil companies.[44] In 2007 European offi-cials insisted that Azeri energy companies were adopting internal EU procedures and regulations, this moving Azerbaijan towards integration into EU energy markets.

Only six European governments had bilateral aid programmes, and none of these allocated more than the negligible sum of 3 million euros a year, while only the UK and Sweden funded any programme defined as being pursuant to democratic reform.[45] Moreover, some of these donors were scaling down support in response to Azerbaijan's strikingly strong economic growth. ENP aid was delayed – the agreeing of a national indicative programme hampered by the lack of an EU delegation in Baku – and anyway EU yearly budget support amounted to only one afternoon's income from BTC fees.[46] Of the 92 million euros allocated to Azerbaijan from the ENPI for 2007–10 one third was set to be used for transport, the environment and energy cooperation, one third for democracy and good governance.

Azeri civil-society actors mobilized against the ENP action plan, criticiz-ing the EU for diluting democracy concerns because of energy interests – even if the plan included formal language on the need for free elections and other political reforms. European representatives in Baku pointed out that they were attacked from both sides, from the government for supporting civil society, from the latter for prioritizing energy interests. Crucially, in nego-tiations over the ENP action plan Azerbaijan only accepted a non-specific and diluted commitment on joining the WTO, its government seeing market liberalization as unnecessary due to the country's energy resources – this position resisting a central pillar of the EU's energy security philosophy. The plan heaped praise, however, on the Azeri record within the EITI. Negotiations were overshadowed by the Nagorno–Karabakh issue: the Azeris insisted on mention of the primacy of 'territorial integrity', while in its action plan Armenia demanded language on 'self-determination', with the EU allowing each of these apparently irreconcilable positions.[47] Significantly, as one of the three 'mediators' on Nagorno–Karabakh, France (together with Russia and the United States) was considered to be strongly pro-Armenian – this despite Azerbaijan's importance for energy supplies and reflecting again Paris' desire to keep on good terms with Moscow.

Progress under the ENP was slow. The Commission's review in March 2008 admitted that in Azerbaijan no progress had been made on democracy and human rights; corruption had worsened; the 'non-oil sector' had shrunk; and inflation had risen.[48] Frustrated with the limits to EU commitments, Greece reached a bilateral energy deal with Azerbaijan in March 2008.[49]

Additionally great power rivalry provided a backdrop to the EU's evolving policies. Presidents Bush and Putin had both begun to court Aliyev. Bush gained a waiver from the Freedom Support Act, that prohibited aid funding to Azerbaijan due to the conflict with Armenia, to fund the Azeri security services for 'counter-terrorism' support – this was in practice directed especially at protection of the Caspian Sea and BTC pipeline. The Azerbaijan–US Chambers of Commerce, full of notable US former politicians, was used to negotiate new deals with Aliyev. Putin sent Aliyev warm congratulations after the fraudulent 2005 elections, and progressed with plans for a Russian-led Caspian Rapid Reaction Force and a new trade deal with Baku.[50] European influence in Azerbaijan was greater than in Central Asia, due to the BTC and BTE pipelines; but the Commission representative lamented that the EU risked being 'too late' to play a major energy-related role in the country.

Kazakhstan

In December 2006 Kazakhstan followed on the heels of Azerbaijan in signing an energy partnership with the EU, also based on cooperation around the adoption of European regulatory and market norms. Significantly, the EU–Kazakhstan memorandum of understanding was very much less oriented to cooperation on institution-building and broader governance convergence than was the equivalent agreement signed with Azerbaijan.[51]

Like Azerbaijan, Kazakhstan seemed to represent a clear case of the West supporting what it judged to be a benign form of autocracy in the pursuit of energy interests. Kazakhstan was generally regarded as both the most lucrative energy market and the most stable and European-oriented state in Central Asia. President Nazarbayev introduced a significant measure of economic reform, Kazakh GDP was set to double between 2004–8 and the country recorded one of the world's highest foreign direct invesetment/GDP ratios. A programme of administrative reform commenced; oil revenues went increasingly into social projects and an oil fund; and a number of human rights improvements were introduced, such as a moratorium on the death penalty. But Nazarbayev did not pilot Kazakhstan towards meaningful political opening. Presidential powers were strengthened and restrictions tightened on NGO activities. Successive crackdowns against opposition groups followed, as in

2005 when the Democratic Choice of Kazakhstan was banned. Presidential elections in December 2005 saw Nazarbayev win a clearly manipulated 90 per cent of the vote; the OSCE was highly critical of the poll. A leading opposition figure was murdered in February 2006.

The EU's most senior foreign-policy figures defined Kazakhstan as the main target for European energy security concerns in Central Asia, the potentially most significant energy prize in the region. Other policy-makers cautioned that the country's potential was still relatively modest. Commissioners issued instructions that here the EU must 'do energy first', then think about political and economic reform. The official strategy for Kazakhstan praised Nazarbayev as a 'reliable partner'.[52] On the ground, diplomats most commonly opined optimistically that the regime was not as repressive as it was often said to be.

New efforts were launched to strengthen Europe's hitherto limited engagement. In 2002 France reopened the diplomatic mission it had closed in 1999, in part due to operations in Afghanistan.[53] Talks were opened for a new EU–Kazakhstan agreement, to replace the limited, non-preferential PCA in force since 1999. Kazakhstan pushed for a place in the ENP, with a tailored action plan and access to Neighbourhood Policy funding instruments. While such a possibility was entertained by some member states in reflection of Kazakhstan's energy-supply potential,[54] there was no agreement that Kazakhstan should be offered the ENP carrot. A small number of northern member states wanted at least not definitively to close the door; southern member states were firmly against a further eastwards stretching of the 'neighbourhood'. Policy-makers acknowledged that this undermined EU influence over Kazakhstan.

From 2002, the EU overtook the US as the biggest source of FDI into Kazakhstan, this surge coming from oil-related investments from the UK, Italy and the Netherlands.[55] It was recognized that the tight control exerted by the presidential family over energy contracts – Nazarbayev's son-in-law was chairman of state gas monopoly, Kazmunaigaz – had directly facilitated many new investment projects. Nazarbayev's team had, for example, helped set up the Caspian Pipeline Consortium, using their centralized control over government institutions to overcome resistance.[56] The president was also judged to be pushing forward Liquefied Natural Gas (LNG) plans in opposition to significant parts of the political elite. One diplomat summarized: Nazarbayev might be corrupt, vainglorious and unpredictable, but he was surrounded by good, pro-market advisors. Policy-makers spoke positively about the appointment to government of economic reformers in 2007. And meanwhile, the US very openly ceded its talk of democratizing Central Asia to a raft of new visits to Nazarbayev and his team to strengthen cooperation.[57] Indeed, as vice president Cheney spoke of his 'good friend' Nazarbayev and political aid efforts in Kazakhstan diminished, this was cited as one of the most dramatic examples of Bush's 'democracy vision' going into reverse.[58]

European pressure on governance and the rule of law was not completely absent, however. The EU referred (whether genuinely or not) to the lack of progress on democratic reform as the reason why Kazakhstan could not be offered a place in the ENP, its politics falling short of – in the words of one diplomat – core 'ENP values'. This appeared to represent a degree of prior conditionality and firmness not applied, for instance, in the Middle East. Nazarbayev was said to have retorted angrily that he would not be interested in signing a lesser agreement. Kazakh civil-society groups won new EIDHR funding from 2002, albeit on a relatively small scale (2 million euros for 2002–5, a further 2 million in 2006). The UK funded a legal-reform project designed to strengthen protection for foreign investment; Spain funded a project to develop the post of ombudsman. The governance rules-based approach was again seen as the EU's route to a distinctive presence and influence: diplomats argued that it was only by focusing on such norms that the EU could carve out a role for itself between Russia, China and the US, selling itself to Nazarbayev as a useful 'balancer' for Kazakhstan. One diplomat argued that the EU in this sense offered an alternative framework 'between the US and Russia' – before lamenting, 'but Nazarbayev is not listening'. Within the scope of a finely balanced 'multi-vector' foreign policy, Nazarbayev both coveted European partnership and conversely Russia and China as counter-weights to the West.[59]

Other officials and analysts concluded more optimistically that Kazakhstan's desire for foreign investment and relatively advanced degree of market reform gave the EU a greater potential to engage on rule of law issues than elsewhere in the region.[60] Awash with increased oil revenue, Kazakhstan was less in need of European aid. But it did covet international recognition and often a more central place within Western institutions as a means of diversifying its own regional dependencies. The leverage this provided was seen most clearly when Nazarbayev pushed for Kazakhstan to be offered a term as OSCE chair in 2009. The president journeyed to several European capitals to press his case. The EU did not respond with unity, however. European ambassadors in Kazakhstan signed a letter opposing the OSCE chair being offered to Nazarbayev; many were ignored by their own capitals. At the December 2006 European Council summit Germany, France, Netherlands and Poland supported the bid, while the UK, the Czech Republic, Slovakia, Slovenia and Hungary insisted that democratic reforms be implemented first (this being similar to the US's position); a decision was put back until the end of 2007.[61]

This outcome was characterized as 'half way' to keeping democracy and human rights issues alive: no state wanted categorically to reject the bid, debate taking place on the question of how much conditionality to exert as a means of leveraging human rights improvements. When Nazarbayev visited Tony Blair in London in November 2006 for the first time he sought to sell Kazakhstan as central to regional solutions, involving Iran, Iraq and counter-terrorism challenges, recognizing that energy alone had not sufficed completely to neutralize European criticism over corruption.[62]

European reform efforts also reflected the fact that Nazarbayev was not seen by all as the entirely benign autocrat. Corruption was increasingly rampant and the president was known to have requested extravagant personal kick-backs (a personal jet, presents for his daughters) in return for concessions to multinational corporations (MNCs). Mobil in particular was subject to a US investigation in relation to its operations in Kazakhstan. In 2002 Nazar-bayev admitted to having transferred $1 billion from Mobil to a Swiss bank account. When opposition figures criticized this corruption, he launched another clampdown.[63] Although foreign investment increased, from 2003 access conditions were toughened to allow FDI only in Kazakh-controlled joint ventures.[64] The fact that the oil fund was run by Nazarbayev cronies and used as a patronage fund was increasingly the source of public discontent. Some EU officials expressed concern that Nazarbayev was increasingly set on emulating Vladimir Putin, using high energy prices as the basis for assertive foreign policy, while attempting to drive wedges between member states. Commission officials in Kazakhstan lamented that the effective implementa-tion of laws was increasingly rare, rendering the whole business and economic climate unpredictable. Notably, local NGO pressure for greater transparency in the management of oil revenue emerged as the foundation for stronger political opposition to Nazarbayev.

Europe's policies certainly laboured in the shadow of great power rivalry. Where Nazarbayev did introduce modest human rights improvements he tended to do so in response to US criticisms, just before a trip to the White House or when Washington threatened to support the exiled opposition in London. US military exercises in Kazakhstan were seen as sending a mes-sage that Washington was willing and able to intervene even at this distance in the event of interruptions to Central Asian energy supplies.[65] Some writers argued that favourable terms had been granted to US energy companies on the back of this military presence.[66] In September 2006, the UK also ran counter-terrorist military exercises with Kazakh forces, but these actually engendered consternation on the part of energy-policy diplomats.

Kazakh officials insisted that their preference was to prioritize pipeline routes and exports to the faster growing East rather than to the West. A joint venture was signed between KazMunaiGaz and the China National Petro-leum Corporation in 2005; this deal was backed up by Chinese development aid, including a large programme to train Kazakh civil servants.[67] A sub-sequent 2006 deal with the China International Trust and Investment Corp (CITIC) hit problems when the Kazakh energy minister obliged the Chinese company to sell back a significant part of the assets in a declared attempt to preserve energy sovereignty.[68] A new deal was signed with China for pipeline development in the summer of 2007, while Kazakhstan joined Russia, China and other Central Asia states for a high-profile military training exercise. In 2007 Poland failed to entice Nazarbayev into an alliance of ex-Soviet states to counteract Russian power, and when President Lech Kaczynski visited Kazakhstan Nazarbayev reportedly told him that he was not interested in excluding Russia from new pipeline routes.[69] Again, balance was a factor of Kazakh aspirations, the government planning eventually to transport 20 million tons of oil through the BTC pipeline and another 20 million tons eastwards to China.[70]

In 2007 Nazarbayev implemented political reforms, granting a slight increase in parliamentary powers in return for dropping term limits to his presidency. There was little EU reaction to highly flawed parliamentary elections held in August 2007, in which Nazarbayev's party won all 98 contested parliamentary seats. Indeed, a compromise deal was reached at the OSCE ministerial meeting in December 2007 to award Kazakhstan the OSCE chair in 2010. The decision not to grant the chair in 2009 was presented as a modest 'punishment' for the nature of the elections; diplomats revealed that they were keen to exert even this limited degree of pressure through the OSCE rather than the EU, to leave the latter free for security- and energy-related engagement.

The elections were followed by Kazakhstan mimicking Gazprom and taking back greater control over the Kashagan field from the foreign consortium led by Eni. In response to Kazakhstan reopening the Kashagan contract, Andris Piebalgs criticized the lack of 'mutual respect, transparency and predictability'.[71] While there was still much talk of Kazakhstan being the most European of Central Asian states in its values and aspirations, by 2008 its government's actions were doing little to substantiate such assertions or provide much reassurance for European energy security.

Uzbekistan

An even clearer reversal in respect for human rights and democratic standards was witnessed in Uzbekistan and here appeared to have a detrimental effect on European energy engagement. The Karimov regime had gradually restricted political space, justifying such moves as necessary protection against the rise of radical Islam, in the form of the Islamic Movement of Uzbekistan (IMU). It had also kept the energy sector relatively closed to foreign investment as part of its strategy of self-survival. European investment was negligible, foreign companies often targeted by the regime's arbitrary rules and restriction of private sector activity. Only small independents, such as UK firm Trinity Energy, seemed willing to risk much involvement in Uzbekistan. For all the West's kowtowing, Karimov drifted towards preferential partnership with Gazprom.

The EU admitted to having done little to seek to reverse these negative trends in the wake of 9/11.[72] The UK government had removed its ambassador to Tashkent, Craig Murray, after the latter's high-profile human rights campaigning and criticism of growing British counter-terrorist cooperation with the Karimov regime. This prioritization of security cooperation had been supported by Joschka Fischer and other notable EU politicians.[73] European donors had funded a small number of rule of law projects, but these had not attempted meaningfully to challenge Karimov's blatant manipulation of the judicial system to imprison large numbers of 'Islamist extremists'. Likewise the EU paid for consultants to draw up rules of parliamentary procedure, which did little to prevent Karimov reinforcing the merely rubber-stamping role of the legislature in the name of 'the war on terror'. Significantly, European relations with the Karimov regime were seen through the prism of counter-terrorism and, as a secondary concern, cooperation on stemming the flow of narcotics in particular from Afghanistan. Energy security received far less attention.[74]

When in November 2005 government forces opened fire on demonstrators in Andijan the EU implemented a partial suspension of its Partnership and Cooperation Agreement. Cooperation projects were halted, but political dialogue was kept open. An arms embargo was imposed, along with a visa ban on a number of Uzbek officials. Plans to open a Commission delegation were dropped. Uzbekistan was not offered an EU energy partnership agreement like Azerbaijan and Kazakhstan. European governments also withdrew their bilateral aid cooperation. European NGOs were hassled out of the country and the EU special representative was denied a visa to visit.

However, the overall European response to the Andijan killings was actually half-hearted. The Uzbek official at the top of the visa-ban list was allowed medical treatment in Germany. France, Germany and Spain voted against a UN resolution critical of the human rights situation in Uzbekistan. While the EU appeared to react in a principled fashion, member states were careful to structure their response in a way that did not threaten future energy supplies. The US reaction was less equivocal. When Karimov threatened to eject the US from its base in Uzbekistan if Washington did not soften its human rights criticisms, the US preferred to withdraw its troops and wind down the military support that had flowed to Uzbek forces after 9/11. In contrast, Germany chose to adopt a softer line in order to retain its military base in the country. In 2005 Germany provided a 17 million euro bilateral aid package; no other member state offered meaningful amounts of assistance.

One year on from the Andijan massacre in November 2006 the EU diluted its sanctions, leaving in place only an arms embargo and a visa ban on 12 officials. The EU argued that this move was justified as European pressure had already succeeded in pushing the Uzbek government to agree to an EU experts meeting on the Andijan events and to start a human rights dialogue. Germany led the push to relax sanctions. The UK, Sweden, Denmark and the Baltic states initially resisted.[75] The dilution of sanctions was strongly condemned by human rights organizations, who judged the move to be clearly explained by the safeguarding of energy interests.

Germany's position was linked to its new 'ENP plus' concept, within which Tashkent would be offered a place and strengthened engagement. This proposal was strongly criticized by activists in Uzbekistan. Berlin continued to push for a complete lifting of sanctions during its 2007 presidency. In October 2007 the EU renewed for one year its arms embargo and visa restrictions of certain officials, but with the latter restrictions not applying for six months, after which they would be lifted if progress were made on the

Andijan investigations. This represented a compromise, Sweden backing the German presidency only on the condition that sanctions would be re-imposed if no human rights improvement were forthcoming. In fact – this time with the Dutch holding out longest – the suspension of the visa ban was extended in April 2008 and all sanctions were due to lapse in October 2008 if a unanimous decision were not taken to re-impose them. Pierre Morel argued that continued sanctions would endanger over-flight rights necessary for NATO operations on Afghanistan.

Germany, and others, argued that even if many had criticized the European response to Andijan as feeble it had already proved strong enough to push the Karimov regime appreciably closer to Russia, including on energy matters. In the same month that US troops left, Tashkent and Moscow signed a mutual security pact. Gazprom and Lukoil moved to increase their investments in Uzbekistan, directly assisted by Karimov's daughter – evidence to many that Karimov was increasingly distributing energy contracts and revenues to shore up his regime rather than investing in long-term capacity increases.[76] The year of 2006 saw record levels of FDI from Russia, China, Malaysia and South Korea, marking a clear change in the country's foreign-policy orientation. Moscow pushed to get its Gazprom-linked man in Uzbekistan shoed in as successor to Karimov. It seemed that the EU had declined to impose tough sanctions but had not in return succeeded in gaining any notable influence in Uzbekistan.

Turkmenistan

Turkmenistan presented a very different set of policy challenges from those facing the EU in states such as Azerbaijan and Kazakhstan. If presidents Aliyev and Nazarbayev at least proclaimed a desire to cooperate with the West on energy matters, apparently presenting European governments with the standard dilemma of whether this justified ignoring an absence of democracy, President Saparmurat Niyazov revelled in his isolation from the West. While frequently criticizing Russia, he depended on Gazprom for gas sales and was susceptible to constant pressure from Moscow not to develop direct energy-supply links with Europe. Niyazov's clear preference was for a trans-Afghan pipeline, more than European links. He was increasingly uncooperative on the development of a Trans-Caspian pipeline, wanting to retain his cosy deal and mark-up with Gazprom, for all he railed against Moscow. This proved sobering to European diplomats who had hoped that Niyazov's constant promises to break Turkmenistan's dependence on Russia might open the door to Western engagement.

In April 2006 Niyazov also struck a deal to supply energy to China – a move described by one commentator as the 'consequence of the chronic lack of a Western policy' in Central Asia.[77] EU investment in Turkmenistan was negligible and fell even further. The sheer opacity of the regime made engagement difficult. Even the size of energy reserves was not known, qualified as a state secret. Niyazov's rule was arbitrary; the public administration regularly purged; and the most basic of rules governing investment absent.

Despite having one of the world's most closed and totalitarian regimes, Turkmenistan was not completely ostracized by the European Union. No trade or investment sanctions were imposed on the Niyazov regime. The EU was the largest source of imports into Turkmenistan, and these imports increased by 15 per cent from 2000–2005. Turkmenistan received nearly 50 million euros from the EU in the second half of the 1990s for 'institutional reform' – reform that clearly failed to materialize. Due to 'serious implementation difficulties' an aid programme for the early 2000s was not drawn up.[78] A small amount of aid was allocated thereafter, totalling 2 million euros per year for 2002–4 and 4 million per year for 2005–6, mainly for rural development, education and economic reform.[79] Bilateral European donors did withdraw, the French after being accused by Niyazov of spying against him. Significant support for democratic reform was not forthcoming. Exiled opposition groups, such as the Democratic Forces of Turkmenistan, did not attract EU backing. In contrast, in 2002 the US implemented $50 million worth of democracy programmes.

Debate centred on the offer of a new EU–Turkmenistan agreement. A Partnership and Cooperation Agreement was signed in 1998, but was not ratified by a number of member states and the European Parliament. The Commission proposed separating out those elements related to human rights and democracy so that Turkmenistan could agree to a new, purely commercial and economic agreement. A majority of member states supported this proposal, but the EP blocked the option of dropping the EU's supposedly universal democracy clause. The German foreign minister, Frank-Walter Steinmeier, visited Ashgabat in November 2006 to explore options for unlocking cooperation.

Niyazov's sudden death in December 2006 unexpectedly opened the prospect of a policy reorientation. The transition to a new government was tightly controlled by the elite that had been close to the late president; indeed it was so smoothly stage managed that many suspected foul play in Niyazov's death. New elections were choreographed in February 2007, with all independent, opposition candidates excluded. European leaders were silent about the undemocratic nature of the transition, openly hoping that the new regime would be more amenable to cooperating with the EU on energy. A series of European ministers and officials travelled to Ashgabat, and Turkmen officials made return visits.

The new regime adopted a slightly more rational style of government, ending the Turkmenbashi 'personality cult'; talked of a better distribution of gas revenues to disaffected areas; created a new state agency for the management of hydrocarbon resources; and at least formally recognized the need to improve technical capacity on oil and gas issues within state institutions.[80] It opened talks with Georgia and Azerbaijan, implying at least a little distancing from Russia.

In return, the Commission suggested immediately unblocking the PCA. Many in Council felt this would be too hasty, and reined the Commission back. They were particularly unhappy with promises and commitments that Benita Ferrero-Waldner made during her trip to Turkmenistan in late 2007. In April 2008, however, a deal was announced under which Turkmenistan would provide the EU with 10 billion cm of gas per year from 2009 – although there were doubts over how this gas would be transported and whether it represented additional supply or simply a share of the gas Turkmenistan had already agreed to sell to Russia that would be sold onto European states. The EU also offered the country a Memorandum of Understanding on energy cooperation that would circumvent the EP's continuing block on the PCA. Poland opened an embassy and said its ambassador was charged with working on 'energy, not democracy'. Lithuanian president Valdas Adamkus took a lead role also in pushing for new EU cooperation and engagement with Turkmenistan.[81] New Commission aid programmes started work on improving FDI rules, and in June 2008 the first EU–Turkmenistan human rights dialogue was held. Turkey also deepened relations with Turkmenistan, offering to transport its gas into the EU.

The US made parallel efforts during 2007 with a battery of high-level visits. Washington sought to bring Turkmenistan into the Caspian Guard (the air and maritime defence provisions covering Kazakhstan and Uzbekistan). However, in some ways Turkmenistan tilted even more towards Russia after the new government took office. The new leaders appeared even more cautious about upsetting Russia and did not offer positive signals on supporting the Trans-Caspian pipeline.[82] As already indicated, in November 2007 Russian increased by 30 per cent the price it was willing to pay for Turkmen gas, in a deal ensuring Gazprom monopoly for the foreseeable future, along with a deal for a Caspian littoral pipeline through Russia (undercutting prospects of a line through the Caspian to BTC).[83] As the country suffered new capacity shortfalls it maintained supplies to Russia at the cost of temporarily halting supplies to Iran – with knock-on effects for Turkey and Greece. In early 2008 Turkmenistan rejected the Ukrainian proposal for (a Russia bypassing) 'White Stream' pipeline. While Europe sought new forms of engagement with post-Niyazov Turkmenistan, it appeared that the dictator's death had unleashed a far broader and fierce struggle for geopolitical influence in the country.

Conclusion

As part of its commitment to strengthen the external dimensions of energy strategy, the EU went some way to mitigating its erstwhile neglect of Central Asia. As policy-makers registered the region's energy potential a range of new funds and strategies were introduced. The new EU–Central Asia strategy agreed in 2007 and Azerbaijan's entry into the ENP signalled a potentially significant upgrading to European policy. At the same time fundamental differences remained between member states – and indeed within the Commission – over just how great Central Asia's energy potential really was and how much effort it was worth investing in the region. For many European diplomats the region still presented overwhelmingly difficult challenges, from the complications of its energy transport options to the political structures of its autocratic regimes. The prospects of supplies from the region entering Europe other than through Russia seemed slim in the short term. The overall level of European funds dedicated to Central Asia remained limited, while many member states were still strikingly disengaged diplomatically and fearful that new efforts in the region were simply a diversion from more established EU policy frameworks.

The attempt to incorporate the southern Caucasus and Central Asia within EU internal market and governance structures looked highly ambitious. The 'market-governance' approach made little headway against Russia's – and increasingly, China's – more overt power politics. The EU was tepid in 'taking on' Russia's dominant influence in Central Asia; the region was still approached as an off-shoot of Russia policy. Member states used Central Asia to stake-out positions – either confrontational or appeasing – towards Russia, rather than reaching judgements based on the region in its own right. The EU also lagged behind US engagement, despite the latter's negligible dependence on Central Asian energy supplies. US interest reflected the fact that other security issues increasingly conditioned approaches towards energy security in this region.

Uncertainty once again reigned on the relationship between governance reform and energy interests. The EU sent mixed messages – different lines emerging often even from within the same institutions. Many diplomats were clear that the EU's priority was energy-related engagement and that there was no interest in pushing political reforms in Central Asia. Many EU positions in practice seemed to mimic Russian power politics more than they offered an alternative model of energy security. Others asserted that the EU's only possible advantage in this region was its democratic, educational and cultural values, and that the latter were a vital source of – rather than trade-off against – strategic presence. Reformers in Central Asia sent the same mixed messages over the extent to which EU values-based influence was indeed sought as a counter-balance to Moscow and Beijing. In short, by 2008 both the depth and nature of the EU's putative engagement in Central Asia remained difficult to determine – and hard to judge in highly positive terms.

7 Sub-Saharan Africa

In similar fashion to Central Asia, Africa's energy potential was overlooked by European governments during the 1990s. Of course, Europe's colonial past had given it a powerful and formative role in the politics of African oil, invariably with highly prejudicial effects for Africa itself. However, during the 1990s Africa had slipped down the list of European foreign-policy priorities, with high-level political dialogue atrophying. By the early 2000s analysts were extolling Africa's growing importance as an energy producer. This encouraged the European Union (EU) to reassess its commitments, but even at this stage European governments reacted slowly and their influence was gradually overtaken by more concerted US and Chinese efforts in Africa.

This chapter explains how from the mid-2000s the EU sought to rectify its waning presence in Africa and assesses the extent to which Africa became part of Europe's external energy policy. It finds that, despite increasing diplomatic activity, the EU's high-level political engagement remained relatively limited and that new energy-related policies emerged more from development policy initiatives. In Africa this development focus was more prominent than EU efforts to base energy policy on extending internal market structures, which were still highly incipient. This also meant that Africa did not attract the kind of high politics divisions within the EU itself that Russia or the Middle East occasioned. The fact that the EU introduced new energy initiatives primarily through a development angle gave its presence a number of strong points, including a relatively tighter link between energy interests and on-the-ground governance reform efforts than that seen in other producer regions. It also left doubts, however, over how attuned EU policies were to Europe's own strategic energy concerns. A disconnect also existed between new EU conflict-resolution efforts and energy security deliberations. By 2008 there were some signs that the EU was developing a more geo-strategic purchase on energy questions in Africa, but it remained unclear what degree of balance could be attained between such a more political approach and the existing development-oriented focus on energy poverty.

African energy challenges

By the mid-2000s, Africa enjoyed the highest rate of new oil and gas discoveries in the world. It also registered faster growing production than any other region, up a third since the mid-1990s. Nigeria and Angola were the continent's two major producers. Nigeria was the tenth largest producer in the world. Estimates of Angola's total reserves quadrupled between the early 1990s and mid-2000s, and the country was set to rival Nigerian levels of production. New offshore drilling technology and the rise in oil prices rendered more feasible and profitable exploration of sites in the Gulf of Guinea. The long-standing second-order producers of Gabon, Congo-Brazzaville and Equatorial Guinea were increasingly matched by Sudan and Somalia. Chad began production in 2003, all for export. Equatorial Guinea commenced Liquefied Natural Gas (LNG) exports in 2007. A large number of African states claimed small new discoveries. Africa was still the least explored continent, with greatest potential for new discoveries as yet unidentified on geological maps.

Moreover, most African oil was of high quality, with low sulphur content. Shipping routes were easy, unlike in Central Asia or parts of the Middle East. Much production was off-shore, so could be exported straight out to Western markets. Most African governments still offered Western investors relatively generous production-sharing agreements (PSAs). By 2006, the biggest recipients of overall foreign direct investment (FDI) in Sub-Saharan Africa were Nigeria, Sudan, Equatorial Guinea, Chad and Ghana – reflecting the growing share taken by oil and gas related investments.[1] Some observers cautioned that many in the energy industry were starting to *over*play Africa's potential. The Commission forecast that Africa's share of world oil production would increase modestly from 10.8 per cent in 2001 to 11.6 per cent in 2030, and its share of global gas production from 5.6 to 12.5 per cent over the same period.[2] Even doubling output by 2025 would leave the continent accounting for no more than 14 per cent of world production. Notwithstanding this, few questioned the assumption that Africa looked set to become more important for international energy security deliberations.

Nigeria proclaimed plans to increase production counter to Organization of Petroleum Exporting Countries (OPEC) targets, this increasing the West's enthusiasm for Nigerian supplies. Nigerian gas reserves were even more significant than its well-established oil production, greater than those of Algeria, for example. Nigeria's forecast development of LNGs was set to make it the

Table 7.1 Africa oil reserves (2006)

Country	Global ranking	Billion barrels
Nigeria	10	36
Angola	18	9
Sudan	21	6
Gabon	33	2
Congo	35	2
Equatorial Guinea	36	2
Chad	42	1

Source: OPEC Secretariat, *World Oil and Gas Journal*

Table 7.2 Africa gas reserves (2006)

Country	Global ranking	Trillion cubic metres
Nigeria	7	5

Source: OPEC Secretariat, *World Oil and Gas Journal*

world's second largest LNG exporter, after Qatar. Demonstrating the new significance of African oil, violence in the Niger Delta was responsible for some of the most notable hikes in the international oil price in the mid- and late 2000s, the deepening conflict associated with intermittent supply reductions. The year 2006 saw 20 per cent of Nigeria's supply interrupted, causing a far bigger impact on international markets than, for example, parallel developments in policy towards Iran.

Europe had traditionally been the primary player in Africa's energy, and long associated with the pathologies of the continent's politics. Gabon's president Omar Bongo was the closest French ally in Africa, the nerve-centre of *la Francafrique*, the original base for Elf, archetype of the French deal of offering military protection in return for favourable terms on energy investments. In Congo, France/Elf was accused of plotting a coup in 1992 to oust a government that had come to question the terms of oil contracts. Then when the replacement prime minister invited UK and US firms in for talks (Chevron won a license in 1995), Elf and the French government were seen to be behind the chain of events that in 1997 installed Denis Sassou-Nguesso as president, who supported a move back to preferential relations with France and Elf. In Angola, the oil industry had been a classic 'enclave' sector since independence, cordoned off from the country's conflict and replete with Portuguese advisors. Angola occasioned some of the most emblematic absurdities of the Cold War: the US moved in to embark on oil business with the Marxist government, its oil facilities enjoying protection from Cuban security forces there propping up the regime against Western-backed UNITA (National Union for the Total Independence of Angola) rebels. The French energy giant Elf was notoriously found to have been helping equip both the government and UNITA and acting directly in concert with the French state mediated a series of arms-for-oil deals during the 1990s.[3]

Even though companies such as Shell, Agip and Total remained significant players in Africa, by the 2000s Europe's historically primary role was fast disappearing. Amidst the talk of Africa's energy potential, European shares of the market were modest. As Table 7.3 shows, the continent accounted for under 5 per cent of EU oil imports. The Commission's list of main energy sources for 2005 showed only Nigeria in the list of top gas suppliers (accounting for 4 per cent of EU gas imports, the fourth largest supplier).[4] In 2007 Spain, France and Portugal were the three largest importers of Nigerian gas.[5] Nigeria was Spain's second largest gas supplier in 2006 (supplying 21 per cent of the Spanish market, behind only Algeria, with

Table 7.3 European imports of African oil (2005)

Supplier	% of total imports
Nigeria	3.0
Angola	1.1
Cameroon	0.5
Gabon	0.1
Congo	0.1
DRC	0.01
Total Sub-Saharan Africa	*4.81*

Source: Eurostat, 2007

Russia absent); a slowly growing UK interest in Nigerian supplies was also detected.[6]

The European presence had increasingly fallen behind that of the US and China. The US announced that it would aim to source 25 per cent of its oil imports from West Africa by 2015. By 2005 the United States was already importing more oil from Africa than from the Middle East and Nigeria accounted for nearly 10 per cent of US gas imports.[7] China invested $8bn in Sudan, and concluded big new deals in Nigeria and Angola. By the mid-2000s Africa was providing a quarter of China's oil imports. Angola became the largest source of Chinese oil imports, Sudan the second largest. (Some experts argued that China's strategy was unsustainable in so far as it had been pumping in far higher rates of FDI for each barrel of oil obtained than either European or US investors).[8] In addition, Russia eyed Africa's markets more closely; in early 2008 Gazprom made a major move into Nigeria. In terms of key investments, European firms looked increasingly marginal. ExxonMobil became the main player in Equatorial Guinea, and also in Angola together with Chevron. Even Omar Bongo – the doyen of *la Francafrique* – made new entreaties to the Chinese. As well as the Chinese and Americans, Indian, Brazilian, Korean, Malaysian and Arab investors all seemed to be making inroads. There were still exceptions – Total remained responsible for three-quarters of Congo-Brazzaville's production – but the trends increasingly ran to Europe's disadvantage.

Energy partnership, through development?

The EU's focus on energy within its Africa policies indeed lagged far behind the attention it received in other producer regions. Energy was not a prominent topic in EU–Africa relations until the late 2000s. At the level of high politics, European attention to African energy resources appeared scant. Energy security was not a prominent issue at the first EU–Africa summit held in 2000. Moreover, the holding of a second such summit was then delayed – for reasons related primarily to Zimbabwe – until 2007. Energy was not a sector funded from the European Development Fund (EDF).

Javier Solana admitted the obvious, 'We have not paid enough attention to Africa's energy potential and its needs'.[9] Commentators observed a new 'scramble for African oil'; but European governments did not appear to be doing very much scrambling at all.

The overriding impression was of the EU being squeezed out of Africa. Relative to other powers its energy engagement in Africa was strikingly limited. In Washington, in the wake of 9/11 there was a frenzy of briefing and advocacy activity around the notion of augmenting US access to African energy specifically as a means of decreasing reliance on Arab states. Nothing of remotely the same intensity was seen in Europe. Indeed the plethora of new analyses of the 'new scramble for Africa oil' conspicuously excluded much mention of European powers, rather comparing US with Chinese engagement and the efforts of secondary players such as Malaysia, India, South Korea and Brazil.[10]

In Abuja in 2005 the Pentagon ran a seminar on energy and security in the Gulf of Guinea.[11] In February 2007, President Bush authorized the creation of a new Combatant Command for Africa in the Pentagon, that observers saw as reflecting the intensified US interest in energy, as well as counter-terrorist cooperation. It was then agreed that a new US military command for Africa (Africom) would become operational during 2008 (albeit still operating from Stuttgart). At the end of 2007 the US launched a new initiative to train the security forces of states in the Gulf of Guinea in the protection of oil and gas facilities, while US naval patrols increased dramatically from 2006.[12] It was significant that it was the Pentagon leading the US interest, where European defence establishments undertook no such engagement. In 2005 the UK bilaterally joined the US in establishing the Gulf of Guinea Energy Security Strategy; and the French and Dutch governments subsequently joined a number of monitoring missions under this initiative designed to crack down on illegal bunkering. But the European Commission and most other member states were highly critical of this Strategy, arguing it was 'too strategic' and insufficiently development-oriented, eschewing deeper coordination with the United States.

The 2006 China–Africa summit in Beijing attracted a far higher turnout of African leaders than any European gathering in many years. Across Africa China engaged at the highest political level, with energy the specific priority of this new assertive diplomacy. China made 2006 the 'Year of Africa' and released its first ever Africa Policy White Paper. In 2007, China offered $5.5bn in development packages and $10 billion of debt relief in return for being granted oil contracts, while also becoming the second largest supplier of arms to Africa.[13] This even led to the curiosity of China building new parliament buildings for a number of Africa autocrats. Contracts for construction projects were reserved for Chinese companies. China's African policy resembled that of European powers in the colonial and immediate post-colonial period. China was doing what France used to excel at.

In comparison, Europe's engagement in the politics of African oil looked increasingly low profile and even marginal. Countries such as the UK, France and the Netherlands focused heavily on a conflict-resolution agenda. Spain tripled aid to Africa, but in its diplomacy towards the continent was almost exclusively preoccupied with the issue of migration.[14] Reflecting the lack of overtly politicized, strategic engagement, the European focus was more on the developmental aspects of energy. A number of new initiatives were forthcoming and European diplomats recognized the need to correct the EU's weakened strategic position; but most new proposals retained a developmental feel rather than a directly political engagement on energy security. Indeed, EU policy-makers presented this as a strength of the evolving European approach towards Africa.

European diplomats concurred in stressing that, far more fundamentally than in other regions, energy partnership with Africa was to be understood through the lens of development policy and governance issues. Andris Piebalgs claimed that the EU's approach was distinctive in marrying European security of supply concerns with development policies, in particular through a focus on broadening access to energy within Africa itself.[15]

The EU Energy Initiative for Poverty Eradication and Sustainable Development was launched in 2002 at the World Summit for Sustainable Development in Johannesburg. It was significant that the EU's main energy initiative in Africa to date was about improving access to energy as part of poverty-reduction strategies. One instrument agreed under this Initiative was a 220 million euro Energy Facility, to support projects strengthening energy delivery to rural areas. This was coordinated from a Secretariat within the Commission's Development directorate. In a similar vein, the Dutch government developed an 'Energy for All' initiative to increase World Bank investment in improving energy access of the poorest communities in Africa.

The October 2005 EU Strategy for Africa attached priority to the funding of regional energy infrastructure, including links between Sub-Saharan and North Africa.[16] Energy was one of the 'fiches' of the statement on 'Policy Coherence for Development' (PCD) agreed in 2005, that committed the Commission and member states to tighten coherence between aid efforts and the range of other EU policy concerns in Africa. This statement insisted that, 'Non-development policies should respect development policy objectives and development cooperation should, where possible, also contribute to reaching the objectives of other EU policies.' The issue at stake was to look beyond 'the frontiers of development cooperation, and consider the challenge of how non-aid policies can assist developing countries in attaining the Millennium Development Goals'.[17] It also committed the EU to strengthen twinning programmes in the energy sphere, regulatory frameworks, regional cooperation and the integration of energy into poverty-reduction strategies. The underlying approach was said to be all about allowing developing states to make their own 'energy choices'.[18]

All this was interpreted as a pivotal commitment to 'integrating energy interventions into development cooperation'.[19] Energy was also a priority issue for discussions at the EU–Africa ministerial in Brazzaville in October

2006. Energy cooperation was for the first time identified explicitly as a priority focal area for the 23 billion euro EDF budget. This funding was to include a new Africa–Europe Partnership on Infrastructure, focusing in particular on energy projects.

A European Consensus on Development was agreed in 2006 as the first common set of guidelines for European-development policies. This reiterated a conviction in the two-way linkage between security and development: development was said to be necessary for security; security necessary for development. In line with the overarching PCD maxim, it was to be ensured that all security policies impacted positively on development policies and the attainment of the Millennium Development Goals. Crucially, development efforts were presented as the principal means to improve energy security.[20] At the December 2006 European Council, EU member states agreed to having their own national policies monitored with respect to this linkage between development, energy security and other policy aims.

Opening the Africa–Europe Energy Forum in March 2007, the Commission's director of development policy reiterated that the EU's focus was on 'access to energy' for poor communities.[21] An updated review of EU–Africa cooperation issued in April 2007 was nearly exclusively about infrastructure development; the extension of internal market principles to Africa; and means to ensure the use for development of oil and gas revenues. The proposed way forward was mainly for dialogue on these issues through an Africa–EU Energy Alliance.[22]

A ministerial meeting in May 2007 did appear to increase the level of political engagement and commitment. New high-level energy dialogue with African states would take shape as a special part of the EU's overall 2007–9 Energy Action Plan. The EU talked more explicitly about Africa being crucial to its own future security of supply, alongside the longer-standing language relating to security of local citizens' supply. At the same time, the EU would formalize an Energy Initiative for Sustainable Development and Poverty Eradication whose aim would be to push member states to increase the share of their aid cooperation allocated to energy issues. A new annual roundtable between European and African public and private bodes would review progress, especially on the 'development-oriented use of oil and gas revenues'. A particular effort would be made to use Economic Partnership Agreements (EPAs) to gain commitments to improve investment conditions in Africa's energy sector.[23]

These various initiatives and proposals were incorporated into a new Africa–EU Partnership on Energy that was formally signed at the EU–Africa summit held in December 2007. The document outlining this Partnership reiterated the familiar range of commitments relating to infrastructure links, supported through new African Energy Funds; cooperation on climate change; more senior-level political dialogue on energy; technology and know-how transfer, the latter through new 'twinning' programmes involving energy ministries; and the need for reform of national energy agencies in Africa. It also confirmed the aim of ensuring an 'increased development-oriented use of oil and gas'.[24] Just prior to the summit, development commissioner Louis Michel argued that all this represented a significantly upgraded strategic commitment, based on the fact that 'Africa is a safer producer than most other regions'.[25] Energy was identified as one of the priorities in a broad-ranging 'action plan' that would supposedly guide EU–Africa relations.

The issue of energy was overshadowed by other issues at the summit and did not receive the political 'push' some diplomats argued it required. The new energy-action plan agreed at the summit did not come with specifically allocated new money. Attention at the summit focused on two issues. First, Zimbabwe and the decision of UK Prime Minister Gordon Brown not to attend after Portugal, backed by other member states, insisted on waiving the EU's own visa ban to invite Robert Mugabe to the event. The UK lamented EU weakness on a key human rights question; other EU, and African, states complained that the UK was undermining the prospects of Europe regaining geo-strategic presence in Africa because of one specific post-colonial fixation. The second issue that dominated discussions was the rejection by approximately half of African states of the EPAs being offered – or, in African states' view, imposed – by the Commission. These required African economies gradually to open up their markets to European imports, after the WTO had ruled inadmissible the continuation of the EU's set of preferential trading provisions that had defined the post-colonial EU–ACP relationship. Whatever the merits of each side of the argument on these issues, the tensions that dominated the summit rendered questionable ministers' claims that the foundations of a new geo-strategic partnership had been laid. At the summit's close Senegalese President Abdulye Wade concluded, on behalf of African states: 'Europe has practically lost the battle against China in Africa.'[26]

The whole tone of official addresses was strikingly different from the equivalent statements related to Russia, the Caspian, Central Asia or the Middle East. Officials in the Commission's development directorate insisted that the new energy-action plan agreed at the December 2007 summit would not be dictated by the EU; rather, the latter would 'wait to see what ACP states want to do with it': language not likely to be heard in relation to policy on Russia or the Middle East. The question arose of how this poverty-reduction focus related to Europe's own energy security. The official European line was that the developmental approach was not only a coherent part of EU energy security strategy, but indeed the most sustainable means of pursuing Europe's own interests. The British prime minister listed as a new UK priority the provision of clean energy sources to Africa and linked this to broader UK energy interests. The primary effort to increase energy efficiency and productivity within ACP states would increase capacity and thus the amount available for export; the prospect of greater export to European markets would in turn drive improvements in capacity and efficiency, in a virtuous circle of better governance and resource allocation.

In practice tension was not entirely absent. The Council Secretariat's Africa unit lamented that in this region energy policy was jealously guarded and led by the Commission's Development directorate and consequently lacked 'political input'. Many energy policy-makers rejected the notion that African states' own development should be any part of their concern or remit.[27] Legal battles ensued between the Council and Commission over what type of projects could rightfully be funded out of the new Stability Instrument beyond traditional development sectors.[28] Tensions intensified as responsibility for many political issues were transferred from Relex to the Development directorate, making strategic direction more difficult.[29] EU diplomats revealed that during the German 2007 presidency African issues were led through a strongly development perspective, making coordination at the EU level harder in this period on the nominal linkage to security issues, including energy. Development experts bemoaned the increasing primacy, as they saw it, of security forums; security experts perceived an imbalanced primacy of development perspectives.

Most African producer states limited domestic supplies as rising international prices made it more attractive to increase exports. Several policy-makers pointed out that placing such an overwhelmingly priority focus on aid projects designed to boost local energy consumption risked reducing exports to the West. Diplomats attested to tension consequently increasing between DG TREN and DG Development. Like other producer states, African countries admonished the European governments' hypocrisy – as they saw it – in talking of new 'jointly owned' energy partnership while they poured new funds into their own efforts to develop alternatives to developing states' oil and gas. One influential report admonished the UK and other donors for, in practice, still devoting limited funds to improving access to energy in Africa or to helping African states develop alternative energy sources.[30] A key tension also arose over market liberalization: African governments accused the EU of pushing this as an instrumental fillip to their own supplies when combating local energy poverty was more a question of state intervention and redistribution. African governments often complained that what they wanted from Europe were long-term commitments to buy more significant amounts of oil and gas from Africa, not 'abstract partnerships'.

The role and effectiveness of EU conflict-resolution initiatives was also widely questioned. European documents routinely asserted that development and security concerns combined to require the EU to play a more active role in tempering African conflicts. Crucially, in Africa European policy-makers laid greater stress than in other regions on energy interests being linked to broader conflict-resolution efforts. As outlined in Chapter 2, European Security and Defence Policy (ESDP) instruments and capacities were gradually strengthened. A 250 million euro African Peace Facility was agreed for 2004–7, to coalesce conflict-related funding out of the EDF. Under the 10th EDF an increased 300 million euros was allocated to the Peace Facility for 2008–10. In May 2007 a commitment was made to speed progress in ongoing discussions on the 'EU concept for strengthening African capabilities for the prevention, management and resolution of conflicts', launched in June 2006.[31]

However, this wider European conflict-resolution engagement in practice remained relatively modest, with little obvious link to energy security strategy. There was no enhanced EU political will to undertake military interventions in conflict situations. The EU instead limited itself (with the exception of Chad, discussed below) to supporting 'multilateral subsidiarity', through support for the interventions of other organizations, particularly the African Union in the cases of Somalia and Sudan.[32] Experts pointed out that the new EU Battlegroups established in 2007 merely repackaged much existing military capacity.[33] According to one expert, ESDP settled itself into a comfortable niche of narrowly delineated military–civilian crisis management operations, divorced from broader security challenges, including that of energy.[34] Whatever the significance of this new conflict resolution strand of EU foreign policy, one energy official admitted that it had no link at all to deliberations or planning on energy policy. Reflecting the need for links to be strengthened between traditional development issues and security concerns, British development minister Douglas Alexander lamented that the Department for International Development (DfID) still needed to move from being 'an aid agency' to acting as 'a development ministry'.

Finally, the 'China factor' began to be reflected in European strategies. In 2007 new dialogue commenced in Brussels between the EU and China on Africa. While this was pushed hard by Louis Michel, the Chinese reaction was relatively cool and the initiative did not develop much systematic cooperation. Critics judged the new EPAs to be an ill-disguised geo-strategic counter to China, to the extent that they contained a clause requiring African states to grant the EU at least as generous commercial conditions as those offered to any other major trading partner.[35] Policy-makers suggested that one of the main challenges for the EU in Africa was to get China signed up to market rules, to bring down the energy prices Beijing was offering – which were squeezing medium-sized European companies out of the market. Pointing to events such as Angola's decision to break off negotiations with Sinopec over contractual differences, some European diplomats optimistically hoped that China's 'honeymoon period' in Africa was over. A range of views existed on this issue amongst member states and different departments of the Commission. At least for some diplomats the 'China threat' had been exaggerated: they highlighted the fact that much of the African oil extracted by Chinese companies found its way on to the open market and that the development packages that China offered to secure its deals helped share the aid burden with European donors.

Transparent governance and energy security

An associated strand of this same overarching philosophy appeared clear in Africa: helping development through more transparent governance structures was itself central to European energy interests. More stable, transparent and prosperous states would get more oil and gas out of the ground, manage it better and increase exports under more predicable conditions. But was this proclaimed linkage between energy interests and support for good governance really reflected in European policies? Did energy concerns indeed lead to or lie behind increased EU commitments to the promotion of more transparent governance structures? Or did more traditional realpolitik persist and prevail?

Of course, for long the standard line was that the search for energy supplies in Africa provided one of the clearest examples of nefarious Western influence in supporting 'friendly' dictators and trampling on local rights. As the energy potential of the Gulf of Guinea rose to international prominence one interpretation was that states in this region were far from being the 'failed states' they were normally classified as; rather, they were successful for energy interests precisely because their governance structures insulated international oil companies and provided them with benign operating conditions. European governments were said to be happy with this status quo, and indeed had continued actively to collude in hollowing out African states, as the latter focused all their competences on managing energy relationships with the outside world, through decisions taken by an ever-decreasing circle of political elites.[36]

As outlined in Chapter 3, the Extractive Industries Transparency Initiative (EITI) was widely seen as the key initiative in the linkage between energy and governance reform. But within the overall range of European policies this remained relatively limited in scope. By 2007 of 27 EU member states only the UK, France, Germany and the Netherlands had signed up to the EITI. A number of other member states such as Spain had resisted civil-society pressure to join, although four further states did commit in 2008 (Spain, Italy, Belgium, and Sweden). Key producer states such as Angola also rejected the EITI – indeed the latter appeared most needed precisely where governments were most flush with oil resources and thus assertive enough to rebuff the initiative. Moreover, the EITI only covered the transparency of payments into national budgets. A government might be able to account for all payments from MNCs and MNCs show that no bribes have been paid, but the underlying problem of patronage in the distribution of national budgets could proceed without censure. The EITI was widely lauded as a useful initiative, but it received no official EU-level backing; there was no combined European attempt to widen its scope; and most member states and the Commission (especially under development commissioner Louis Michel) rejected the notion that producer states should be pressured in any concrete fashion to join it. Revealingly, some diplomats saw it as a well-meaning development initiative but not of significant bearing to EU energy security. Indeed, at the December 2007 summit the EITI was transferred out of the EU–African energy plan and into the analogous governance action plan.

Beyond the EITI there was certainly a large number of European commitments and initiatives that focused on the issue of governance reform. The EU's principal conflict-prevention strategy stressed a priority focus on good governance, the rule of law and 'political inclusion'.[37] The 2005 Strategy for Africa included a Governance Initiative and an EU–Africa Forum on Human Rights.[38] And from the 10th EDF budget 2.7 billion euros (out of a total 22 billion for 2008–13) were set aside to be allocated as reward for those ACP states committed to cooperating with the EU on governance reforms. The Commission promised that absolute priority would be attached to 'good governance ... and democratization ... even in the most difficult country situations' in Africa.[39] Governance elements were increasingly incorporated into the EU's various conflict prevention/resolution initiatives, such as the Stability Instrument (that replaced the Rapid Reaction Mechanism in 2007), the EU Programme for the Prevention of Violent Conflicts and a Security Sector Reform initiative, which by 2007 was funding projects in 26 African countries.

France introduced a new Governance Strategy that included a commitment to devise a political reform strategy specifically for Africa's 'fragile states.'[40] This hinted at a broader rethinking in French African policy. France continued (haltingly) to move away from its traditional bilateral military agreements in the continent, in search of a new identity for its beleaguered post-Rwanda/ Zaire Africa policy. More of its aid went through the European Commission; more support was given for the Africanization of military peacekeeping; and more emphasis was placed on commercial links, especially with the big economies of Nigeria and South Africa, rather than solely on the cultural affinities of traditional Francophone *pré carré*. The 2007 presidential campaigns of both Nicolas Sarkozy and Segoléne Royal argued that France needed to design a more reform-oriented African policy.[41] In practice, a year into Sarkozy's presidency key French diplomats were still blocking any reduction in French military cooperation with African regimes, fiercely defending *la Francafrique*.[42]

As elsewhere, Europe's proclaimed support for democratic governance did not include any systematic use of punitive policies. No conditionality was linked to African governments' introducing more transparent management of energy revenues. Even if the EU's philosophy was that its own energy interests were directly tied to better governance structures in Africa, member states and the Commission resisted the suggestion made by some experts that aid and debt relief should be made conditional on concrete progress on these questions. One diplomat optimistically insisted that EU funding for access to energy would do more to assist democratization than any tough policy purposively labelled as democracy promotion.

The EU was sparing in its use of Article 96 of the Cotonou accord that provided formally for the suspension of aid and trade preferences. This was used to impose sanctions on only ten occasions between 2000 and 2007. The ten cases – Ivory Coast, Liberia, Zimbabwe, Central Africa Republic,

Guinea-Bissau, Togo, the Republic of Guinea and Mauritania, plus Haiti and Fiji of ACP partners outside Africa – did not include any of Africa's big energy producers. Sanctions were used in states that suffered widespread conflict and state breakdown, dramatic reversals in democratic rights, coups or interruptions to the constitutional process.

After much wrangling, the Cotonou accord included 'governance' as a 'fundamental' rather than 'essential' element – that is, not as grounds for triggering sanctions.[43] Contrary to EU promises, EDF money was not in practice shifted away from 'bad governance performers' to reformist governments.[44] In Cotonou's 2004 mid-term review, provisions were widened slightly for civil-society actors to receive funds directly, without government assent.[45] But, Cotonou was most notable in the political domain for introducing an additional layer of dialogue prior to any action being taken against democratic infringements – through a strengthened obligation to hold so-called 'Article 8' political dialogue before consideration was given to invoking Article 96 consultations – thus rendering sanctions more unlikely.[46]

In addition, the more 'positive' route to encouraging governance reform was pursued less than concertedly. Funds allocated to supporting democratic governance accounted for a modest proportion of overall official development assistance (ODA). Few European donors allocated more than 3 or 4 per cent of their development aid for political-governance projects. The Commission claimed that a massive 2 billion out of its total 10 billion euro aid budget was related to governance; this was certainly a hugely significant and strengthened commitment, but evaluations observed that this used a definition that included much funding that had little to do with making policy-making more accountable and transparent. Governance was understood still in a relatively apolitical sense, referring to the 'sound management of public affairs' not the far-reaching political reform of non- or semi-democratic regimes.[47] The Commission's own institution-building 'indicators of achievement' nearly all related to strengthening the capacity and procedural efficiency of the state, not to democratic plurality.[48] Analysts concluded that the EU still had some way to go to put in practice a concept of 'human security' that fully embraced human rights and individual participation in decision-making, as opposed to traditional state-oriented understandings of 'political stability'.[49]

Indeed, there were signs of official recognition that support for good governance had been limited and ineffectual. One of the central strands of DfID's 2007 Governance strategy was an acknowledgement that much technical governance support for state institutions had failed because it had neglected a more political understanding of democratic contestation. In the future DfID would, it was claimed, strike a better balance between state capacity-building and strengthening accountability, for example through citizen participation in public expenditure controls.[50] France's new Governance Strategy insisted that French governance programmes would also move away from a purely state-oriented approach.

However, by autumn 2008 there was limited evidence that such formal commitments were producing genuinely more assertive reform-oriented political aid in Africa's energy producing states. The overarching trend in EU development policy was towards more budgetary support provided directly to governments. Crucially, while governance reform was stated to be an integral part of the EU's approach to energy security in Africa, in practice there was little link made between policy-making in the two policy areas. The Governance unit in the European Commission had no meaningful input into energy-policy deliberations.

Energy and politics in Nigeria

More than anywhere else in Africa, Nigeria demonstrated the shortcomings of Europe's energy security policies and the fraught relationship between governance challenges and energy interests. The country's low-level conflict intensified in the wake of democratic elections held in 1999, one conflict deepening in the north between Christians and Muslims and another taking root between local communities, the government and oil companies in the Niger Delta.[51] Nigeria's importance was reflected in formal EU policy commitments. The country was identified as a priority target for democracy support; as warranting increased attention as a 'fragile state'; as a priority state in the battle against terrorism after 9/11; and, after the Delta conflict played such a palpable role in pushing up world oil prices, as a hitherto overlooked priority for energy security.[52]

In the 1990s, European relations with the dictatorship of General Abacha were limited, but not subject to comprehensive sanctions. The EU imposed a range of punitive measures against Nigeria in 1995 after the execution of a group of Ogoni campaigners, including writer Ken Saro Wiwa. Significantly, these sanctions did not include an oil embargo. In practice there was no significant injection of new European funding into Nigeria after the country's democratic transition in 1999. After the 1999 elections, the EU agreed a 100 million euro Quick Start Programme, which included 6.6 million euros of support to national and state assemblies and an additional 7 million euro democracy and human rights package. But the first projects under this programme began only at the end of 2001. Five million euros were allocated to support elections in 2003, along with 2.5 million euros from the EIDHR for 2002–4, while the aim of assisting democratic consolidation was enshrined in an EU–Nigeria Common Position.

Despite undergoing democratic transition and being of increasing importance for energy interests, the overall European involvement in the country remained relatively limited. Nigeria was Africa's most under-funded state in terms of its ODA/GNP ratio. The European Commission and the British government were the only two European donors of any meaningful size. In 2003 the UK allocated $43 million to Nigeria; a figure rising to $100 million by 2006. Commission aid for the period 2001–7 was just below 50 million euros a year.[53] No other European state donated more than $10 million a year. In 2004 a 'preventive strategy' was drawn up by the Council's Africa working group, but then not implemented due to the lack of engagement from member states.[54] Conversely, European arms sales increased, France extended its RECAMP military programme to Nigeria, and Germany stationed a team of officers for capacity-building.

By late 2006 the insurgency in the Delta region was worsening, with more frequent attacks on oil installations and kidnappings of Western oil workers (over 100 of which occurred in 2006–7). At points in 2006 and 2007 the conflict shut down 20 per cent of the country's oil production and seriously hampered the government's plans to double production. Huge amounts of oil were lost through siphoning or illegal 'bunkering', which helped fund militant groups. Attacks also increasingly targeted off-shore facilities, that international oil companies had assumed more secure. Militant groups, the most prominent of which was the Movement for the Emancipation of the Niger Delta (MEND), were driven by local communities' lack of control over and share in energy resources.

Unrest was fostered by government manipulation of local and national elections in 2003. The government of President Obasanjo introduced various schemes to increase investment in infrastructure in the Delta, but resources were siphoned off through corruption and most projects failed. After the breakthrough democratic transition of 1999, governance reform was halting. President Obasanjo launched an anti-corruption drive only after his re-election in 2003 and Nigeria was the first state to sign up to the EITI. In general, however, the country was awash with increased oil revenue that seemed simply to deepen corruption, as it increased the incentive for venal politicians to lay their hands on state revenues.

Rather than embedding the rule of law, the government sought to buy off militants in the Delta with oil contracts and government positions, providing incentive for a perpetuation of violence. Several companies linked to militant groups were granted security contracts. At the 2005 National Political Reform Conference groups from the Delta demanded that 25–50 per cent of oil revenues go direct to local communities in oil producing areas, and that this not be channelled through corrupt federal government bodies. This reform was also advocated by the Special Committee on Oil Producing Areas, which included representatives of the oil majors. The government offered only a 17 per cent transfer, further enraging local communities. Progress was made on the transparency of energy-related payments under the Nigerian EITI, but the latter became less effective as it was used as Obasanjo's personal political vehicle.[55] Observers noted the same kind of resource nationalism as in other producer states, as Obasanjo introduced new quotas on minimum Nigerian participation in oil licenses. Local administrations' spending on 'gifts' for oil executives increased.[56] In his final months in office in 2007 the president doled out licensing offers for 45 oil blocks to political cronies. Between 2003 and 2007 all major new oil contracts went to Asian companies who offered development packages in return. Chinese, Indian and other Asian firms were favoured expressly when their respective governments supported Obasanjo in his unconstitutional bid for a third term in office.[57]

As prices rose, oil companies channelled increased sums in bribes to local governors, which simply inflamed the population more as the distribution of such largesse was erratic and patronage-driven. Local governors may have stormed out of the 2005 national forum on political reform because the government refused sufficiently to increase the percentage of oil revenue to be retained in the Delta, but they themselves were responsible for siphoning off that share that did flow back into the Delta. As the 2007 elections approached, 33 of Nigeria's 36 state governors were under investigation.

Nigeria's 2007 elections confirmed the fragility of the country's democracy. The senate had to block Obasanjo's unconstitutional bid to stand for a third term, amid rumours of sizeable bribes changing hands. The president manoeuvred to exclude key opposition figure Atiku Abubakar from the election, clearing the way for his anointed PDP (ruling-party) successor. The electoral commission was denied autonomy. State elections on 14 April witnessed blatant manipulation in favour of the ruling party and presidential cronies. Despite the Supreme Court granting Abubakar last-minute permission to run, the PDP then swept back to power at the federal level with their presidential candidate Umaru Yar'Adua securing an improbable 70 per cent of the vote.

As Nigeria's internal strife worsened, the European funding that was forthcoming exhibited a strong security orientation. The Commission limited its assistance to working with Nigerian government programmes. Priority was placed on helping better equip Nigerian security forces both for internal security and for assuming leadership of African peacekeeping. Cooperation on or pressure for internal-security governance reform within Nigeria were negligible. The Commission acknowledged that it failed to put in place a broad ranging civil-society funding package. The UK DfID also admitted that its strategy was heavily government-focused and that little progress had been made on reducing the pervasive effects of patronage and corruption.[58] One British diplomat argued that the EU could not push for reform for fear that Nigeria would 'fracture ... and then we would lose *all* the oil'.

The UK Foreign and Commonwealth Office created the post of 'energy expert for West Africa' and indicated it would look favourably on requests from Nigeria for military training related to the protection of oil facilities.[59] British government representatives met several times with the US and Nigeria under the new Gulf of Guinea Energy Security Strategy (GGESS) body, to look at further enhancing security assistance;[60] it was significant that UK security cooperation in Nigeria took place to a far greater extent through the GGESS than with European partners. The UK trained Nigerian security units in techniques for preventing bunkering. In the summer of 2005, the UK pushed successfully for Nigeria to be offered the biggest ever debt relief package, just as President Obasanjo was mired in a series of domestic scandals and accused of unconstitutionally marginalizing political rivals. One of

Javier Solana's advisors admitted that the EU remained soft on governance issues because it did not want to 'rock the boat' for energy reasons. Most European diplomats insisted strongly that Nigeria was too powerful to be susceptible to European pressure exerted through threatened aid reductions. One observed that the EU had thrown away its moment of potential influence when offering the 2005 debt-relief package.

The overall level of European engagement did not increase significantly. Of member-state development agencies, only DfID had an office in Nigeria. The British government lamented that Nigeria was still conspicuously short of donor attention; one diplomat compared Nigeria to Pakistan where counter-terrorist concerns had engendered a significant influx of new EU funds and donors. While counting Nigeria as its second largest gas supplier, Spain was not a prominent or proactive player in EU policy towards Nigeria. The UK was looking to sign LNG deals but its energy dependence on Nigeria was actually low and its lead role here apparently explained more as either a development-led policy or a colonial hang-over. One European diplomat admitted that democratization had proved no magic solution for Nigeria but sanguinely opined that 'at least we can talk to them now' and that more critical engagement was not necessary. For one critic, EU detachment could be explained by the fact that the oil illegally bunkered in Nigeria increasingly found its way to Europe anyway.[61] It was US officials who mediated between Obasanjo and rebel leader Mujahid Dokubo Asari, and indeed pushed for the president effectively to buy-off Asari in return for a commitment to stop attacks on oil installations; European governments expressly stood back from such direct engagement.[62]

At the same time, European concerns grew over the impact of Nigeria's failure to consolidate its new democracy or to contain corruption. Obasanjo had looked highly beneficial for energy interests, rescinding contracts awar-ded to military cronies under the Abacha regime and clearing the field for international oil companies. But he gradually moved back to favouring his own cronies for contracts, most of whom had little expertise of the oil busi-ness. Shedding light on the oil–democracy relationship, Nigeria in this period provided a clear example of higher oil prices not having a quiescent effect, but in fact stoking more protest, anger and conflict – bloated revenues made it more unacceptable to citizens that governance reforms had not provided an open and fair way of distributing these additional resources.

Increasingly, European aid projects did take on more of a governance orientation. British development projects supported public scrutiny of federal budgets; NGOs in the Delta to track oil revenues; the Ministry of Finance to set up an Oil and Gas Accounting Unit; benchmark ranking between federal states on transparency; and the Economic and Financial Crimes Commis-sion.[63] The EU did strongly criticize the running of local elections in 2003 for failing to meet even minimal democratic standards. A Census Support project was the Commission's biggest initiative in Nigeria, providing over 100 million euros for a new and fairer census prior to the 2007 elections.

Both the UK and the Commission professed an intention to exert greater pressure for governance reform at the state level, including through shifting funds towards those states most committed to tackling corruption. DfID declined to offer new direct budgetary support, because of the likelihood of such funds being siphoned off to finance the nepotism that increasingly pervaded the Nigerian polity. DfID insisted that central to its new approach was a more systematic focus on the links between the development and security agendas, for example through increased efforts on transparency reforms in the Niger Delta. UK officials insisted that security cooperation also began to adopt a reform angle, with the aim to increase democratic control over the security forces and restrain the latter's tactics. European engagement was certainly not as securitized as that of the United States, as the latter provided new military hardware to the Nigerian government to patrol the Delta, and even began pushing NATO to get involved in the Gulf of Guinea.

The fears of violence and political manipulation surrounding Nigeria's April 2007 elections were responsible for driving international oil prices back up.[64] This conditioned European policy calculations. The EU criticized Obasanjo's grab for a third term. The UK and Commission worked with Canada and Japan on UN election preparation projects, in the face of government efforts to curtail external monitoring.[65] EU monitors were strongly critical after the poll, giving what they claimed was the EU's most damning election rebuke ever issued anywhere in the world.[66] However, there was universal agreement among EU policy-makers that punitive measures would not be desirable against Nigeria, with diplomats citing energy supply concerns as a primary reason for their reticence. The EU worked with the electoral commission trying to influence from 'inside', and a number of member states sought to water down the European electoral monitoring effort. And while some Nigerian protestors talked of emulating Ukraine's Orange revolution, they did not receive the kind of European backing that activists received in Kiev in 2004. Indeed European diplomats put the emphasis on cautioning the opposition to be 'responsible'.[67]

President Yar'Adua adopted a more conciliatory and consultative approach to the Delta conflict, offering militants an amnesty and dialogue. He did not, however, address the root grievances related to local control over oil and gas revenues.[68] Oil output in May 2007 was at its lowest level since 2003.[69] Militants briefly called a cease-fire after the elections, but from the autumn of 2007 attacks on oil installations and kidnappings actually increased in frequency. Yar'Adua promised to revisit some of the oil contracts doled out to Obasanjo cronies.[70] By late 2007, increasing popular anger was erupting at the details emerging of the corrupt management of the oil sector during the Obasanjo era; this prompted the new president to promise far-reaching governance reform of the oil industry.[71] Court rulings in late 2007 forced some senators and local officials elected in April to leave office. Further production increases in mid-2008 largely cancelled out the effect of Saudi supply increases within international markets.

Against this background the EP criticized EU governments for moving straight back to 'business as normal'. It also urged use of Article 96, but member states blocked this. The EU did not monitor local elections in late 2007, which were violent and unfree. UK diplomats were cool towards Yar'Adua and watched to see if he met EITI commitments to open up the Nigerian National Petroleum Corporation to publish transparent accounts. In this sense, reform dynamics suffered a major setback at the end of December 2007 when Yar'Adua removed the corruption-busting head of the Economic and Financial Crimes Commission.[72] In fact, the notable development was the president's call for a renegotiation of existing international contracts. With tensions growing, diplomats revealed that a new high-level EU–Nigeria political dialogue initiated in March 2008 – in large part due to energy security concerns – achieved few tangible advances.

Other country examples

The limits to European energy engagement and to the governance-orientation of EU policies could also be seen in other African states. It is beyond the scope of this chapter to examine every producer state in Africa, but it is illustrative to outline the challenges facing the EU in a select number of countries.

Angola provided one of the clearest cases of diminishing European influence. After UNITA rejected the results of the country's 1991 elections, European governments for the first time clearly switched allegiance to treat the MPLA as the only legitimate Angolan government. But MPLA hostility lingered on, given the West's support for UNITA during the Cold War. This enabled José Eduardo dos Santos to respond to every effort to nudge him into holding elections with cries of anti-imperial resistance. Angola's political development engendered serious challenges for Western states. Corruption intensified after the end of war: in 2006 the country was 151st out of 158 states on Transparency International's ranking. Elections were postponed, as dos Santos hung on to office, centralizing power, attacking opposition figures and with the argument that securing a few big oil deals first would secure him another term. Due to oil revenues, Angola was by 2005–6 the world's fastest growing economy: this growth massively increased wealth disparities and social tension. Sonangol functioned increasingly as the creature of a small cabal of the political elite. Revenues and deals were sewn up by the apocryphal '100 families'.

In early 2007 Angola joined OPEC which threatened to constrain the country's promised increase in production. Flush with funds it rejected an IMF liberalization package. Not only did the government reject the EITI but in fact tightened up laws prohibiting the release of energy-related information. A Global Witness campaigner was detained. Sixty per cent of Angola's oil production came from the Cabinda enclave, where (despite a peace deal in 2007) conflict deepened between separatists and government forces, revolving in large measure around differences over the sharing of oil revenue: here no local democracy was allowed, all officials appointed by central government. Angola provided one of the best examples of the tension between external and internal energy policy: as increasing quantities of oil and gas were shipped out of Angola, the majority of the country's population still lacked access to modern energy.

Donors did not rush into post-war Angola in the way they did in Afghanistan or the Balkans, despite the importance of its energy reserves. While the EU was Angola's biggest donor, this was a country where aid was negligible relative to other sources of funds and seemingly unable to wield influence. The 9th EDF budget allocated 146 million euros to Angola, up to 35 million of which was to be spent on democracy and good governance. OECD figures showed that overall European aid remained relatively low, as Angola reaped its oil wealth. In 2005 no donor gave Angola more than 30 million; France (23 million) and Portugal (21 million) were the two largest member-state donors – these modest amounts compared to the aid receipts of most African states. At governmental level, Angola cold-shouldered France after the Elf trials. When a key Total drilling licence came up for renewal it was transferred to a Chinese company. Indeed, Angola provided probably the most dramatic case of Sinopec, backed by Chinese state resources, bidding extremely high for exploration rights – over \$2 billion for three parcels in 2006 – driving out European firms.[73]

Gradually some signs emerged of greater effort on the part of some European governments, as the extent of Angola's energy reserves became more apparent. In 2006 Spain agreed new arms sales, a tied \$150 million credit line and doubled its annual aid to Angola – the oil-rich country becoming the second highest Sub-Saharan African recipient of Spanish aid and one of only five priority target states within Spain's new Plan Africa. Nicolas Sarkozy invested considerable effort to mend relations with dos Santos, in the hope of moving France's relations with Angola beyond the fall out from the Elf trials. As he did so Angola awarded Total with expanded operations in a key offshore block in January 2008.[74] It was argued that Paris's energy-driven rapprochement with dos Santos partly explained Sarkozy's desire to downplay *la francafrique* as the main basis for French relations with Africa.[75] In 2007 Germany offered Angola a new credit line that was second only to that awarded by China in 2004.[76] However, such efforts were still relatively modest. Even the US – once the fiercest of enemies of the Marxist MPLA – overtook the European presence, helped by Washington offering Angola new military cooperation.

European policy hardly seemed to react to the deepening malaise of bad governance and the connection between this and energy exploitation. As civil society and opposition parties were subject to increased repression in 2007, the EP criticized the EU for not contemplating firmer measures towards Angola. The European Commission insisted that it tried to use the Cotonou 'governance reward' to strengthen Angolan commitments to governance reform and increased the allocation for governance projects under the 10th

EDF. However, it admitted that it gained no real leverage. Senior EITI representatives admitted that one of their biggest disappointments, and the EITI's main Africa lacuna, was governments' failure to push hard enough to get Angola signed up to the initiative. Angola remained peripheral to the new energy cooperation initiatives and funds introduced by the European Union. One diplomat observed that Angola was one of the few Cotonou states with which political dialogue had not progressed and lamented that 'the EU is not focused on Angola'. In the summer of 2008 the EU sent a scoping mission to Angola ahead of elections scheduled for September 2008. These (largely democratic) elections served to consolidate the MPLA's hold on power.

In *Sudan* the combination of persistent conflict, human rights tensions and Chinese competition sufficed to undermine any European energy engagement. As far back as 1992 Chevron and a raft of Western independents had pulled out of Sudan and later the CNPC entered this market through taking 40 per cent of the Greater Nile Petroleum Operating Company. The EU's political engagement in Sudan's civil wars was sporadic and relatively limited, despite the country's energy potential. The EU imposed a limited range of sanctions from the early 1990s, but was not as punitive as the US and gave the impression of rather reluctantly following Washington's lead on those measures it did adopt. On the one hand, the EU did not make a concerted attempt to intervene robustly enough to temper Sudan's instability and provide the conditions for a productive energy partnership. On the other hand, it was not willing to support the kind of unconditional diplomatic engagement pursued by the Chinese. European policy was neither one thing nor the other, adopting neither strong critical pressure nor purely 'soft' engagement. All Sudan's big external contracts went to China; only a few small contracts stumbled on with European firms such as OMV and Nile White Water.

In the wake of the 2004 peace deal between North and South Sudan the EU agreed a 400 million euro aid package, ending 15 years of suspended European cooperation. However, there was little sustained focus on either energy cooperation or governance reform; nearly two-thirds of aid was allocated to basic food aid and humanitarian relief. Indeed, the peace deal shared out power but did not address underlying governance reform, and in fact was accompanied by additional restrictions on NGOs' ability to receive Western development funds.[77] The UK's Post Conflict Reconstruction Unit funded institution-strengthening projects in southern Sudan,[78] but few other donors did.

In short, the peace deal supported by Western governments legitimized an autocratic regime, freeing up the latter's military to move on Darfur. The regime awarded oil contracts mainly to its own supporters. North and south both engaged in patronage and favouritism to share out revenues, in the absence of a strong legal framework. Heavy government repression was used to protect southern oil fields from rebel activity. Under the peace deal oil revenues were supposed to be shared equally between north and south. In practice, the Khartoum government refused to devolve the full 50 per cent share to the south. In October 2007 the southern ruling party (SPLM) briefly left the national unity government over the south's loss of oil share. A lack of transparency in oil management was still seen as potential trigger for reigniting the north–south conflict.[79] The two sides did on this occasion pull back from the brink. The SPLM rejoined the government at the end of 2007 and the transfer of oil revenues improved. Despite the continuing problems with the energy aspects of the peace deal, EU aid flowed.

In relation to the crisis that then unfolded in Darfur, the EU declined directly to intervene and imposed only limited sanctions. Rather it provided financial support and training for the African Union. Little political pressure was exerted on the Sudanese government to rein in the Janjaweed militia; as much European criticism was aimed at the rebel factions that did not sign up to the 2004 Darfur peace agreement. By 2007, Tony Blair was well out front of – and some noted, out of step with – other European leaders in being more critical of the Sudanese government and advocating a no-fly zone. When the European Commission's ambassador to Sudan was thrown out of the country in late 2007 after calling for the release of a tribal leader, Louis Michel was effusive in apologizing to the Khartoum government.[80] Sudan only accepted a UN hybrid force because of China, who assured Khartoum that this would not be intrusive. In April 2007 China increased military aid to Sudan, just as the UK was pushing with the US to obtain a resolution in the UN critical of the Sudanese government on Darfur.

In all these policy deliberations, it was not clear that energy played a crucial role. Some critics argued that the West had 'imposed' the 2004 peace deal to increase the autonomy of the more pro-Western and Christian South as a means of gaining more secure access to oil contracts (this deal included the provision for a referendum in the south on independence in 2011). But others criticized the EU for being so 'soft' on the Bashir government because it hoped for oil contracts decided at Khartoum's behest. European governments did not impose the same range of commercial sanctions as the United States. The government of Southern Sudan struggled for autonomy to award its own oil contracts, and courted the Chinese in pursuit of this aim. In December 2006 Khartoum's industry minister won control over contracts in the south, leaving the SPLM without direct access to international deals: so, for European powers, good relations with Khartoum became more paramount.

However, as the north–south conflict threatened to re-ignite in late 2007, one respected organization expressed surprise at how 'dangerously disengaged' the international community remained on this oil-related challenge.[81] It was Washington's pressure that prompted the SPLM to return to government; the EU was conspicuously absent at the delicate juncture.[82] The UK's position 'softened' markedly after Gordon Brown succeeded Tony Blair. Even China appeared more aware of the energy implications of Sudan's governance pathologies, as it reportedly leaned on Khartoum to improve relations with the SPLM as a means of freeing up access to more southern reserves.[83] Total was caught in the cross-fire of simmering north–south tensions, as a deal it had negotiated in the south with the Khartoum government was rendered void by the SPLM; as of 2008 the French company was still biding its time waiting to be able to return to Sudan. Diplomats admitted that the EU's 'softness' on the Sudanese government reflected a desire to maintain counter-terrorist cooperation with a key information source on Al Qa'ida more than energy-related concerns. In 2008 the Sudanese government itself appealed to the EU to focus more on energy interests, Khartoum apparently keen to diversify away from increasingly toughly negotiated Chinese contracts.[84]

Equatorial Guinea was Africa's third largest producer, but by the mid-2000s was past its peak and set to be overtaken by Sudan and others. President Obiang's long and dictatorial rule over Equatorial Guinea did not work to the benefit of European governments. US firms succeeded in sewing up most of the significant deals in the country. ExxonMobil and a number of small US independent oil companies took the vast majority of Equatorial Guinea's production. The US had been critical of Obiang during the 1990s but reopened its embassy in 2006 and then invited Obiang to the White House to seal a revived energy partnership and offer new security cooperation. Obiang himself set up in business and went into commercial partnership with Mobil, the latter using the security agency run by Obiang's brother.

The Commission failed to establish a presence, as Obiang frustrated the dispersal of aid allocated under both the 9th and 10th EDF budgets; Equatorial Guinea was the only Cotonou partner not to sign the EDF action plan agreed at the December 2007 EU–Africa summit. The EU was still reluctant to engage on improving the transparency of energy governance in Equatorial Guinea – while Obiang was highly dictatorial, he increasingly found it difficult to get his orders obeyed and a crumbling institutional system meant effective implementation of presidential decisions had become impossible.[85] In May 2008, as the EU exerted strong pressure on Robert Mugabe in relation to the conduct of elections in Zimbabwe, a far more tightly manipulated election in Equatorial Guinea slipped by almost unnoticed in Europe.

Spain and France – the only EU member states fully engaged in debates on Equatorial Guinea – had an uneasy relationship with Obiang. Spanish companies were denied contracts in the early years of the oil boom. In 2004 Obaing accused Spain and the UK of supporting mercenary plots against him and planning to return the Madrid-based opposition to power. The Aznar government denied the charges, but during the botched mercenary coup attempt Spain moved warships close to Malabo. Accusations and rumours abounded of MI6 involvement; the UK government openly acknowledged that it did know of the plot but did not inform Obiang, not wanting to be seen to defend such a notorious human rights abuser.

After 2004 Spain in particular commenced a new drive to tighten energy partnership with Obiang. Spain's Socialist government ensured that there was little EU pressure on or criticism of Obiang – although in July 2008 prime minister José Luis Rodríguez Zapatero refused to meet Obiang in Madrid in protest at the conditions surrounding the elections of May 2008. A new 30 million euro Spanish aid package was offered in 2005. The opposition leader based in Madrid, Severo Moto, complained at increasingly hostile treatment from the Spanish government; Moto's political asylum was revoked by the PSOE government in 2005 (a move overturned by the Spanish supreme court in 2008) and he was eventually arrested in April 2008 on charges related to the possession of weapons. Obiang was received with full state honours in Madrid in 2006 and the Spanish government refused to restrict access to financial assets held by the president and his family in Spain. Oil exports from Equatorial Guinea to Spain increased by a third between 2005 and 2008.[86] Repsol made some in-roads with the regime – representatives of the company travelling to the country with Spanish ministers – and British Gas was awarded the first LNG contract with Equatorial Guinea in 2007.[87] Despite such developments, however, Europe's energy-related engagement with Equatorial Guinea remained limited and that which existed was antithetical to a focus on human rights.

In *Chad*, France suffered a period of tense relations with the government in early 2000s when Elf pulled out. Exxon ran the main oil exploration project, with Shell and Total as junior partners, winning World Bank backing on conditions of transparency in revenue management, including with civil-society oversight. In 1999 Shell and Total pulled out, apparently in response to increased social opposition to their presence. Chinese companies moved in. Oil bonuses then increasingly went to fund arms purchases. President Déby outfoxed the World Bank, who thought they had an agreement that revenues would be diverted to social expenditure. Déby clung to power unconstitutionally and in 2006 banned opposition parties. In 2006 the French government provided some military backing to ward off a coup attempt, to strengthen Déby's mandate and free up oil funding from growing instability.[88] A large 202 million euro allocation was made from the 9th EDF.

An ESDP mission to Chad was agreed in 2007 to help stem the spillover of Darfur's conflict. The mission was delayed for nearly six months, due both to a lack of helicopters and Germany (and some other member states) seeking a stronger UN mandate for the EU mission. It was reported that other member states were reluctant to commit troops because they perceived the EU mission to be a cover for French interests in propping up Déby and securing oil contracts.[89] Rebels attacked Déby in early 2008, in a putsch organized from Sudan; he put this down robustly and then tightened restrictions on political opposition and NGOs. France backed Déby, but more out of a concern with rebels moving out of Sudan and spreading that conflict and humanitarian disaster than a calculated play for oil contracts. As the ESDP mission began to function, only to a limited extent did this suggest a conjoining of conflict- and energy-related concerns. One official acknowledged that this mission had not been accompanied by any political strategy for Chad itself.

Conclusion

The European focus on energy security in Africa exhibited a tone distinctive in many respects from that which prevailed in other producer regions. The focus on energy grew out of development concerns and remained strongly oriented in philosophy towards issues of 'energy poverty'. Critics often charged the West with sucking out oil and gas from Africa's coastal regions and preventing the continent's energy wealth from ever making it into the African hinterland. All EU policy statements promised to avoid just this occurrence. This chapter demonstrates that it would be naïve to suggest that such harmful dynamics were completely absent from European policies, but also that the development strand of energy policy ran ahead of Europe's high-politics engagement. Some policy-makers interpreted this in positive light; others lamented that in Africa the EU still had a development policy but no energy security strategy relevant to its own supply needs.

The link made by the EU between energy and governance was apparently clearer in Africa than in other regions. Governance efforts in the Niger Delta provided perhaps the best example of this link being made in practice. However, elsewhere attempts at strong energy-related engagement approximated more to power-politics approaches. This was especially the case in Angola, Sudan and Chad. It was routinely argued that China was gaining influence by 'under-cutting' the West to the extent that it did not 'hector' African states on democracy and human rights. But in practice the EU's policies were themselves not strongly coercive and did not in overall terms impose conditionality related to political reform.

While the EU adopted the familiar rhetoric of integrating market and governance structures, in practice this dimension of policy was of lower profile than in other regions. In political terms, the EU still struggled to gain meaningful presence in Africa's main producer states. In Nigeria overall funding and diplomatic activity was limited. In Sudan the focus on Darfur diverted attention from the simmering tension between north and south that undermined any prospect of deeper energy cooperation. In Equatorial Guinea, the US gained the primary market share, encouraging Spain in particular to make new efforts to engage president Obiang. China's presence spurred greater EU interest after Europe had begun to neglect Africa from a security point of view. But the EU's incipient new political commitments in Africa required significant deepening before the EU could hope to regain some of its lost ground on the continent.

8   European energy companies

Oil companies' influence has always been pivotal to the politics of international energy. It is invariably, indeed, the target of the most trenchant criticisms of Western power. During World War II Shell actively pushed for the British Navy to be switched from coal to oil – a decision that was regularly cited by experts as that which fundamentally changed the geopolitics of energy and set the parameters for the modern era. International Oil Companies (IOCs) became routinely seen as the arbiters of Western foreign policies, and in particular the most pernicious aspects of those strategies. Yet while European governments struggled to meet the geopolitical challenges of energy security, European oil and gas companies faced their own fiercely competitive battles. National Oil Companies (NOCs) were in the ascendancy with respect to their western counterparts. Analysts mulled the emergence of a 'new seven sisters' – Saudi Aramco, Gazprom, the Chinese National Petroleum Corporation, the National Iranian Oil Company, Petróleos de Venezuela Sociedad Anónima, Petrobras and Petronas – and detected an 'existential crisis' amongst Western oil majors.[1] In November 2007 Petro China became the world's biggest company by market capitalization, overtaking Exxon-Mobil. By the end of 2007 only 7 per cent of reserves were in the hands of IOCs. The latter's comparative advantages had been reduced to two: first, the provision of advanced technology for the most difficult of drilling operations; second their development of integrated services, from extraction through to the market.[2]

This book's remit has been to outline and assess European governments' approaches to energy security; this chapter examines what role European energy companies sought to play in the definition of those policies. Cutting across the positions examined in this chapter is a concern with the nature of the relationship between energy companies and European governments and which way round the influence has run between these two actors. The chapter finds that, despite the new international challenges facing them, European oil and gas companies' engagement on the foreign policy dimensions of energy security was reactive and relatively limited during the early and mid-2000s. Multinationals' influence was felt on very specific policy issues, but suffered from companies' own uncertainties over the broader political dimensions of energy security. Companies differed on the role of markets, geo-politics and good governance standards. On some occasions on these issues companies sought to 'push' EU governments into adopting new positions; on other occasions they themselves were 'pulled' into policy outcomes by those governments; on still other occasions more of a partnership existed between the two sets of actors. By 2008 companies spoke of their intentions to engage more on the foreign policy dimensions of EU energy security, but it remained unclear how this would influence the overall nature of European policy.

Towards a foreign-policy dimension?

By common agreement, amongst company representatives themselves and diplomats, European multinationals were slow to engage with new debates over energy security. The main umbrella organizations – Business Europe, the Oil and Gas Producers (OGP), the European Petroleum Industry Asso-ciation (Europia) – acknowledged the reactive state of oil majors' input into foreign-policy debates. Companies' main focus from the mid-1990s had been on internal-market liberalization and environmental issues. The foreign-policy dimensions of energy security had not received systematic attention; the private sector recognized that it was in this sense reacting to rather than leading efforts to incorporate energy questions more fully into the Common Foreign and Security Policy (CFSP). The European business community tentatively started to focus on the external dimension of energy security only as energy prices began to hit record highs and after reflection was needed in reaction to the Commission's 2006 Green Paper. Prior to that, energy secur-ity concerns had been equated to internal market issues and specific trade-related instruments – the main focus of lobbying had been on the importance for European businesses of tackling the practice of dual pricing in producer states. If companies did engage on foreign-policy issues it was recognized as being in a very indirect, even circuitous fashion. For instance, concerns were expressed that the Kyoto Protocol would restrict any switch back to coal in Europe, placing an additional constraint not felt in the US, and thus increasing European vulnerabilities to external energy factors.

Formal forums incorporating the private sector into energy security delib-erations were relatively limited in nature. Arguably the most notable attempt was the US–UK Energy Dialogue created in 2002, aimed at 'bringing toge-ther the separate strands of international energy policy and foreign policy' and incorporating companies into this process of enhancing political stability for investment. This was notably not a 'Europeanized' initiative. European oil companies' inclusion in and influence over the design of European Union (EU) foreign policy was certainly weaker than that enjoyed by their US counterparts over United States strategic initiatives. Chevron Texaco, Exxon Mobil and Enron all had significant input into the Bush administration's new energy strategy.[3] The tightened relationship between the oil majors and the US government witnessed under the Bush administration embedded the notion of energy policy resting on a strategic partnership: in the Persian Gulf, the Caspian and West Africa US multinationals would back the government's geostrategic policies, while the administration would in return directly back the companies' interests – this linkage even being formally enshrined in the US's 2001 energy report.[4]

In Europe both government and company representatives characterized the relationship as more ad hoc and lamented the absence of formal mechanisms at the EU and nation-state level to facilitate formal dialogue between diplomats and IOC executives. The energy units in national foreign ministries revealed a dearth of contacts with oil companies on EU external policies. The same was true of geographical departments. Diplomats working on Iraq, for instance, revealed abiding uncertainty on both sides: companies remained unsure whether the EU was committed to increasing its role in Iraq, European governments claimed to have little idea of oil majors' intentions in the country. In relation to Africa, as new initiatives accumulated there was no forum gathering together oil majors and European diplomats. While multinational corporations' (MNCs') interest in the Gulf of Guinea deepened, one expert noted that governments and the oil majors had consulted little on the West's new strategic designs on this region.[5] Companies' were granted representation within the EU–Russia Energy Dialogue, but saw the utility of this as limited to essentially technical questions.

By 2006–7, a number of initiatives were forwarded aimed at rectifying this situation. Under the new EU–Africa action plan agreed in December 2007 the commitment was made to incorporate the private sector in discussions on Africa strategy, including on energy. The EU's new Strategy for Central Asia proposed a formal partnership between EU governments and multinationals to develop policy towards this area. UK officials insisted that BP and Shell were deeply involved in the elaboration of the 2007 UK White Paper. However, company representatives revealed that engagement mostly took place in relation to specific measures – the Commission's unbundling proposal, the 'reciprocity clause' – rather than on the EU's longer-term and overarching approach to energy security. Europia representatives highlighted that dialogue took place almost exclusively with officials in the Commission's energy and transport directorate (TREN), dealing with the more technical sides of energy, while the foreign policy nerve-centre of Relex remained a 'black hole' for companies. Much more engagement and coordination still occurred in relation to climate change and internal market reforms than on energy's external dimensions. Private-sector collective action could be observed in relation to climate change debates[6] in a way that was not evident on CFSP issues. For example, the business sector engaged in a systematic manner through formal dialogue mechanisms to express its concerns over the Commission's January 2008 '20/20/20 by 2020' proposals, gaining a presence in climate change debates that was not apparent in relation to foreign policy.

Some company statements – both public and private – suggested that the internally focused approach to energy security began to be questioned, at least rhetorically. One set of examples came from BP. One BP executive observed that, 'Energy security can be enhanced by actions taken within Europe but fundamentally European energy security is a matter of foreign policy'. Both the private sector and European governments needed to understand that the type of 'security' required for energy security, 'extends to the whole process of development and how it is advanced'.[7] Companies had been too heavily focused on the internal dimensions of energy policy, reflecting a worryingly defensive approach: energy concerns 'do not warrant a nervous retreat into self-sufficiency'. The same BP manager argued that the EU should focus most on pressing for 'a competition policy with a global dimension'.[8] The EU and its oil companies needed to become more outward-looking, one executive argued, and develop a much more sophisticated understanding of the factors that ensured stability and security.

In this sense, many private-sector representatives thought that the foreign-policy dimension of the EU Green Paper was the most important and the area where the most useful added-value could emerge. Deeper engagement was needed on the more political aspects of energy security in Russia, the Middle East, the Caspian and Africa. Crucially, this involvement needed to go well beyond the kind of technical dialogues that the EU had to date focused on initiating. Few in the private sector viewed the results of such dialogues as positive or particularly relevant. The EU–Russia Energy Dialogue in particular was seen as being of little worth: as one oil executive pointed out, Russia did not need dialogue, but rather a clearer roadmap from the EU of what it would get in return for strategic energy cooperation.

Only a more resolute foreign-policy dimension could, BP statements argued, knit together the diverse strands of energy security, providing an overarching framework for linking issues such as the physical security of infrastructure, the integrity of distribution systems, the use of strategic stockpiles and reserves, the need for new infrastructure to take advantage of Liquefied Natural Gas (LNG), the need for market openings and the incremental concentration of energy reserves in a more limited number of countries.[9] A Repsol executive outlined the evolution in thinking about energy security: first this was understood by oil companies simply as access to resources; then as diversification; then as being based around the role of the International Energy Agency and stock reserves; and now as requiring a truly global and political approach. Such an approach was not about unwarranted panic over oil supplies being cut off, but rather using and understanding the linkages between the EU's internal market and its foreign policy.[10] A common complaint was that there was inadequate 'strategic thinking' at the foreign-policy level on how to back up European private-sector interests. Business Europe and individual company representatives lamented what they perceived to be a lack of knowledge of energy issues in Brussels.

The OGP similarly suggested that its focus became more political and less 'technical', including through an engagement with European governments on more political issues. It criticized EU policy as ad hoc in approach and dependent on a proliferation of purely technocratic energy dialogues with different producers, subject to different rules and agreements, with little read over between them. The umbrella organization called for a more coherent and strategic EU approach to energy security. Europia representatives argued that the internal–external link was seen as crucial: while internal market regulations were ignored by many member states this created distortions that discouraged companies from supporting the notion of more common European foreign policies.

Indeed, in some cases companies were ahead of governments in pressing to diversify into new areas. By the early 2000s, Total was spending 30 per cent of its global exploration and production budget in Africa, and lamenting the lack of an EU geopolitical strategy in the continent. Central Asia provided a similar example, with several European companies that entered this high-risk frontier area in the 1990s complaining at how they had struggled to interest EU ministers and diplomats in the region until 2006–7.

The preceding chapters reveal how companies often sought bilateral deals with producer states that sat uneasily with the spirit, and sometimes even the letter, of common European rules and norms. In principle, the private sector expressed itself in favour of deeper European coordination. It was judged that individual European states could not now achieve much on their own; the current wave of high-energy prices must serve as a prompt to deeper European cooperation. At the same time, however, some company officials cautioned that EU policies should not constrain other forums of cooperation in the energy field; as one opined, the EU as such was unlikely to emerge as the most appropriate or prominent energy security actor; rather it would be more useful for smaller clusters of different states to take forward the energy dossier in the foreign-affairs domain. Generating something akin to a Prisoners' Dilemma, European energy companies appeared to desire a unified EU energy strategy but free manoeuvrability until that became an imminent prospect.

This related to what some spokesmen revealed was a certain 'schizophrenia' on the part of the private sector: firms wanted EU-level foreign-policy muscle to back them up much more than occurred at present, but at the same time complained strongly at specific issues where the national room for manoeuvre was constrained by European level policies. In particular, some European oil companies expressed serious concerns over the incipient Europeanization of energy policy leading to a regulation-heavy approach to energy issues. The main umbrella organizations representing the oil industry concurred that for many companies the desire was less for a stronger CFSP to back up energy investments and more for politicians to resist the temptation to 'interfere' in international energy matters. One business representative argued that national governments and companies felt forced to 'go their own way' because the Commission failed to give strong backing for the types of infrastructure projects the private sector saw as important – from a private-sector perspective, Nordstream was the result and not the cause of EU policy shortcomings.

Divisions between governments were often mirrored by similar differences between different states' private sector firms. Companies from a number of member states expressed particular anger at German business 'doing its own thing' and of Germany refusing to support the (Polish) proposal for a 'mutual support commitment'. Significantly, the traditionally more sceptical British private sector was seen as having shifted position notably, to become one of the firmest advocates of a common European energy policy, as a result of the UK moving towards being an energy importer. Smaller energy firms tended to be more strongly in favour of deeper European cooperation on energy. The vice president of Danish oil and gas company DONG lamented that member states' hindering of a common energy policy was adding to the uncertainty of his firm's international investment decisions.[11]

Companies also had different geographical priorities. Indeed, one high-profile group containing MNC representatives highlighted that for this reason there had been little united EU backing for European firms seeking to gain access to challenging markets and that there was little prospect of such unity in the future.[12] In overall terms, EU umbrella organizations acknowledged a certain over-concentration among the private sector on Russia. If companies had become more engaged on the political dimensions of energy security it was, spokesmen highlighted, because they had been jolted into reassessment as a result of Vladimir Putin's actions in Ukraine and Belarus and the growing competitive threat posed by Gazprom. In this sense, it was lamented that positions represented to some degree a knee-jerk response to worrying developments in one producer state and not a more careful and balanced look at political issues in general. Spanish and French firms sought to keep the focus on North Africa. And it was recognized that French companies were most influential and engaged over policies towards Iran, reflecting their erstwhile status as the principal source of investment in the Islamic republic.

Markets versus geopolitics

Generally, firms espoused a market-based approach. The smaller 'independent' energy firms tended to be most pro-market, in the hope of this tempering the dominant positions of the established oil giants. Most energy companies came out against the proposed 'reciprocity clause' on the grounds that this would provoke third countries into introducing retaliatory restrictions on access into their markets. Europia declared its main lobbying aim as increasing awareness amongst EU diplomats that Europe was not a 'self-contained energy island' and needed to think far more in terms of global competitiveness – this still seen by the private sector as a weakness of EU strategic planning.

One BP spokesman argued that EU policy-makers were in danger of confusing the need to manage price volatility with an assumption that drastic means were needed to defend against an imminent cut-off of supplies, which seemed mistakenly to be the subject of much policy deliberation.

European oil companies supported and took an active role in the Caspian Pipeline Consortium, on the grounds of 'market fundamentals', despite many diplomats complaining that this Russia-transversing pipeline undermined the viability of the various options backed by European governments for routes into the EU market that circumvented Russia.

But, while seeking a broader security focus to energy policy, the main practical desire was for the EU to focus on improving investment conditions. There was little evidence that the basic European approach of extending internal market rules and regulations was prioritized at the behest of oil companies. Indeed, one analyst argued that MNCs' espousal of free market solutions was often disingenuous: many in the private sector did not want extra competition, but rather to retain the high mark-ups they attained through their cosy, fixed contracts with national oil companies in producer states. One senior official noted that Shell and other oil giants sought long-term contracts as much as Gazprom did. After the Sakhalin experience, Shell chief executive Jeroen van der Veer questioned the appropriateness of market-extending approaches in Russia.[13] EU governments' aim to open markets was about making *both* European and producer state firms adhere to market rules and preventing them from sewing up the market in deals that – despite all the apparent tensions with producer state companies – both were reasonably content with.

Indeed, the head of the OGP stressed that the private sector strongly favoured government-backed long-term contracts. Given that these contracts were an invention of European MNCs, producer country diplomats argued that it was unfair of the EU to admonish the likes of Gazprom for offering them. Some oil company representatives highlighted that what they wanted most from an energy-sensitive EU foreign policy was for a clear signal to be given to individual producer states on future levels of demand, to make long-term relations more predictable rather than subject to market fluctuations. E.ON's chief executive thundered that the biggest threat to Europe's energy security came not from Russia but from the Commission's 'unbundling' proposals that would render geopolitical deal-making more difficult.[14] (Ironically, E.ON did 'unbundle' its own distribution networks in early 2008 in return for the Commission dropping anti-trust investigations against the company). Eni similarly opposed the 'unbundling' package of market liberalization on the grounds that it would weaken European companies' international leverage.[15] The European petrochemical lobby's demands for continued protection of home markets continued to be one of the main obstacles to the signing of an EU–GCC free trade area.

According to some critics, it was increasingly clear in this sense that the interests of European oil majors were diverging from those of overall EU energy security.[16] European companies certainly did not all appear to share a key tenet of the 'markets and institutions' storyline, namely that allowing national oil companies from producer states to buy up downstream assets was beneficial for energy security insofar as it increased producer countries' stakes in EU economic growth. Where such access was granted it was on the basis of government-negotiated bilateral deals, where downstream shares were bartered for long-term supply guarantees – and not as part of a de facto commitment to free market energy solutions. In this sense, and in particular as expressed through their bilateral deals with Gazprom, European energy majors in practice sought out cartel-like arrangements with producer country oil and gas companies, keeping prices high for consumers and accepting producer states' argument that investment in boosting productive capacity should be conditioned on long-term supply guarantees in European markets.

One significant example that touched directly on foreign policy was Repsol's opposition to Sonatrach being able to sell directly into Spain; here Repsol had a primary influence on Spanish policy, and in a way that appeared very different from the influence of UK MNCs over the British government, for example. In addition, in March 2008 Gas Natural took the Spanish government to court after the latter relaxed the conditions for Sonatrach to gain a greater participation in Medgaz. Nabucco chief executive Reinhard Mitschek opposed unbundling, appealing to European governments for preferential backing for the planned pipeline and measures to exempt the latter from rules relating to third party access rights.[17]

Following the oil and gas reserves

While advocating more strategic and politically-oriented approaches to energy security, oil companies continued to hunt down new investment opportunities where these became available in some of the world's most unstable, violent and politically repressive countries. In this sense, significant continuity was evident from some of the best known episodes in the controversial history of Western oil companies' strategic influence. The exploitation of oil in North Africa and the Middle East had long entailed collusion between Western governments, oil companies and Arab autocrats.[18] Standard Oil was found guilty of treason for dealing with the Nazis; Texaco supplied the Franco regime.[19] There was also a long history of 'big oil' propping up autocrats in Africa. This was demonstrated in particular by a spate of corruption cases in France during the 1990s. A huge scandal involving Elf, that uncovered a dense network of kickbacks and arms transfers across Africa, shook the French political elite and its whole edifice of *la francafrique*. As indicated in the previous chapter, in Angola and Congo Brazzaville Elf was found even to have been bank-rolling both sides of these countries' respective civil wars, while in Cameroon and Gabon direct payments had been made to governments in return for contracts being awarded to Elf rather than US or UK oil companies.[20]

Some of the fastest rising recipients of FDI during the late 1990s and into the new century included Algeria, Kazakhstan, Sudan and Angola.[21] Oil companies' own lists of what they saw as their most important new projects into the mid-2000s included sizeable new investments in countries that were neither democratic nor improving in terms of governance standards. In such markets many companies admitted to thinking little about structural governance issues and were rather concerned more narrowly with the ease of building-up relationships with individual pro-market officials. A common refrain from oil executives was still that of: 'We follow the oil, and stay out of politics.'

During the early- to mid-2000s Shell took 16 per cent of the Kashagan field consortium in Kazakhstan; invested in LNGs in Oman; signed an agreement with the Libyan National Oil Company with a view to partnership on gas and LNG development; and expanded offshore development in Nigeria. In early 2007 Shell finalized the biggest single investment ever made by a UK company, for LNG development in Qatar. It also won the contract to Gabon's largest oilfield, and listed other notable expansions of exploration in production in 2007 to include Algeria, Tunisia, Libya, Egypt, Oman, Saudi Arabia, Syria and the United Arab Emirates.[22]

Also in the mid-2000s BP launched four major projects in Azerbaijan, namely the Azeri–Chirag–Gunashli oil fields, the Shah Deniz gas field, and the BTC and South Caucasus pipelines; such was the scale of BP involvement in Azerbaijan in the wake of the 1994 'contract of the century' that opened up the country to foreign investors, that it was locally called 'the BP country'. The company won three blocks in Algeria's sixth international licensing round, consolidating BP's status as the largest investor in Algeria, this alongside its LNG collaboration with Sonatrach at UK terminals. BP increased its involvement in Egypt and embarked on a new offshore production facility in Angola. BP's sales pitch moved from 'beyond petroleum' to 'back to petroleum' as it tightened its focus on gaining access to remaining reserves of oil in challenging markets. In 2006–7 BP's production increased by a third in Algeria and by 50 per cent in Azerbaijan; new finds were made in Egypt; and new contracts signed in Libya and Oman.[23]

Total listed as its most significant initiatives a new oil discovery in Yemen and the launch of a Yemeni LNG project; a seventh oil discovery in Libya, accompanied by a new production sharing agreement with the Libyan National Oil Company in December 2005; a big increase in exploration investment in Africa, especially Nigeria and Angola; an 18.5 per cent stake in the Kashagan field; a reopened 30 per cent joint venture with Saudi Aramco for gas exploration; and a range of new projects in Iran, with high Total participation in many exploration consortia. While Total withdrew from its joint venture with Saudi Aramco in 2007 due to disappointing drilling results, in the same year the company significantly expanded exploration and production investment in Yemen, Qatar, Libya, Algeria, Venezuela, Nigeria and Angola (the latter attracting a near doubling of Total investment between 2005 and 2007).[24]

Repsol became the second largest energy operator in Libya, reaching a series of new deals in 2006.[25] Overall, however, 80 per cent of Repsol's reserves were still concentrated in Latin America. (The company declared an intention to move away from Latin America until, along with BP, it made a huge offshore oil field discovery in Brazil). Outside this region, Spain's leading company had, by the end of 2006, 16 blocks in each of Algeria and Libya; small investments in Angola, Saudi Arabia and Equatorial Guinea; and in 2006 reached new deals with Gazprom and in Kazakhstan.[26] In contrast to Repsol's disproportionate focus on Latin America, by the end of 2006 nearly half of Iberdrola's gas came from Nigeria.[27]

Agip was thrust into leading the Caspian Pipeline Consortium, developing the Kashagan field; US firms would not accept Total as leader of this consortium; Exxon Mobil was not chosen as it was hindered by US sanctions from cooperating with Iranian partners; and, so Agip was chosen to lead the project.[28] ENI teamed up with Gazprom further to consolidate its position as largest investor in Libya. After acquiring Yukos assets with ENI, ENEL became the first IOC to create a vertically integrated process covering the entire value chain in Russia. The company also signed a cooperation agreement with Saudi Arabia in 2007.[29] In June 2006 a 1 billion euro investment in Egypt was agreed for increasing gas liquification capacity, to be undertaken by BP, Unión Fenosa and ENI. In 2006–7 the BG Group became joint operator of Kazakhstan's giant Karachaganak gas field; signed a new LNG deal with Nigeria; and undertook new surveys in Libya and Algeria.[30]

MNCs in the oil sector were often seen as favoured with fast-track procedures outside domestic governance frameworks, especially in relation to judicial proceedings. Oil executives' list of states in which they judged the investment climate to have improved over the 2000s included countries with clear democratic limitations: Angola, Libya, Azerbaijan, Kazakhstan and Egypt. Azerbaijan was one of the most notable cases where the oil sector enjoyed special regulatory conditions with the authorities, even if the more general legal framework for investment was weak.

In the Middle East, many investors harboured negative concerns over possible political liberalization, expressing a mostly unfavourable view on the prospects of Islamists winning power.[31] Many thought reform would be particularly destabilizing in Saudi Arabia. The official EU line that Nabucco did not depend on Iranian supplies was countered by the chief executive of OMV, the Austrian company heading the Nabucco consortium, stating that, 'We are convinced that Iran would be a sustainable supplier for the future.'[32] Some insisted that hostile political conditions did not perturb oil companies, whatever their rhetoric to the contrary, as they simply increased margins and guarantees within their contracts to compensate for more politically difficult operating environments. Oil was still widely seen as the archetypal enclave; most companies reporting political concerns and changes in thinking were smaller firms and those more vulnerable to domestic conditions.

In Africa, many traditional practices persisted. BP committed itself to opening up information on its dealings in Angola as far back as 2001, but when threatened by the Angolan government withdrew its plan. BP signed a large new deep-water exploration deal with Angola in 2007. International oil companies were reported to see Angola – where the same government had been in place since independence – as providing some of the most stable political conditions of all producer states.[33] The Elf trials in France might have ended this strategic arm of the French state operating as 'one of Africa's great slush-funds',[34] but the investigations and subsequent change had been hindered by the French government and oil companies. The French magistrates' investigations had negative repercussions on French interests in both Angola and Gabon – the Angolan government ended a Total contract, Omar Bongo opened up to Anglo-Saxon oil companies – meaning that the new merged TotalFinaElf was never likely completely to forgo the benefits of France's networks of influence with autocratic regimes.[35] Both Shell Gabon and Total Gabon had the president's daughter on their boards.

Indeed, worldwide Total was especially exposed in 'challenging markets' – where its chief executive advocated increased presence despite, he claimed, the company having 'no love affair' with autocratic leaders – this making it the only oil major to register increased production in 2007.[36] Total's involvement in Myanmar clearly influenced French government policy towards the junta, Paris insisting on exempting oil and gas from EU sanctions in October 2004.

Other examples abounded. Amnesty International criticized the BP-led consortium that developed the Baku–Tblisi–Ceyhan pipeline. The agreement did include principles for the protection of human rights, which BP insisted were the most advanced of their kind. However, the oil companies had insisted on ring-fencing such protection from changes in the human rights provisions of the governments in question, leaving human rights protected only by a voluntary code of conduct overseen by the oil firms themselves. In addition the oil majors explicitly tasked the security forces of the governments in question with protecting the pipeline, these forces having notorious human rights records.[37]

If anything, the increasing tightness of international energy markets reinforced the search for and magnitude of 'first mover' advantages, the rents obtained by being first into politically risky markets. The margin for manoeuvre was also squeezed by competition from NOCs that in many places were now far better equipped to begin actually managing local resources: in this sense 'the political frontier niche [was] getting crowded', raising the prospect of IOCs having to move more towards becoming providers of technical and financial services to NOCs and having to hunt harder for profit margins.[38]

The rise of the Corporate Social Responsibility (CSR) agenda was commonly criticized as being about no more than improving companies' image and reducing their 'reputational costs'. An increasing number of multinationals agreed codes of conduct on a range of rights-based and environmental issues, while initiatives were enshrined officially at the level of the EU, UN and OECD. But all such commitments were subject to limitations. MNCs generally insisted on codes being no more than voluntary and relating only to their own internal operations and procedures. In this sense, some private-sector representatives admitted that CSR gave companies a 'good story' to tell on issues such as environmental and labour rights and thus actually deflected the problems of doing business with autocrats. One survey found that the range of initiatives addressing the problem of MNCs' support for armed groups had not forced companies into providing significantly more open information on their local security arrangements – this being true of the UN Global Compact, the OECD Guidelines for Multinationals and the Voluntary Principles on Security and Human Rights (the latter incorporating the UK, US, Norway and the Netherlands).[39]

Companies were keen to retain the narrow focus adopted by the Extractive Industries Transparency Initiative (EITI). Indeed, the latter had become relatively comfortable for MNCs, who were not obliged to disaggregate what they paid to governments or to publish any information on producer states not signed up to the EITI (non-signatories accounting for over four-fifths of world production). The influential campaigning group Global Witness highlighted that good progress was made under the EITI, but was critical of the fact that more focus had been placed on the corruption of developing countries than of European companies and governments.[40] Similarly, the 'Publish what you pay' campaign opined that the EITI had secured good progress in select countries such as Nigeria and Azerbaijan, but not on an overall, balanced basis across producer states.[41]

Only a narrow range of governance issues was of concern to many MNCs, in particular conditions governing the repatriation of profits and the sanctity of contracts; their only focus was on directly 'business enabling' governance issues, in the words of one executive.[42] For umbrella organizations such as Europia the 'rule of law' equated to little more than 'sanctity of contracts' and not the broader political conditions impacting on judicial process.

This could be seen in companies' own CSR programmes. Repsol provided one typical example. The company emphasized its participation in the EITI and the European CSR initiative from 2006, as well as its adoption of the UK–US Principles on Security and Human Rights. Its CSR statements and commitments were entirely free, however, of governance concerns within producer states' political systems.[43] ENI created a new Corporate Affairs and Governance Office; a new Corporate Governance Code; joined the EITI; and in 2006 spent 74 million euros on community development in host countries. But the company stated that it saw the main risk to its interests coming from 'changes to the political and economic frameworks in countries of activity', representing an apparently highly status quo oriented view on governance issues – even if a small number of its projects did touch indirectly on politics, for example funding and setting up village councils in Kazakhstan to deliberate on nearby oil projects.[44] Enel also introduced a new ethics code and an anti-corruption unit in 2006, but its CSR programme was similarly devoid of any reference to the impact on its interests of producer states' political structures.[45] The EU multi-stakeholder forum on CSR, created in 2002, to advance beyond the Global Compact, exhibited the same self-denying ordinance.

Probably the most high-profile case of a European energy company being seen as contributing to instability and bad governance was that of Shell's operations in Nigeria. After a long presence dating back to the 1930s, Shell was forced to leave Ogoniland in the Niger Delta in 1993 after pressure from the Movement for the Survival of the Ogoni People. The Shell Petroleum Development Company of Nigeria (SPDC) produced half the country's oil, and was made up of the Nigeria National Petroleum Corporation (NNPC) (55 per cent), Shell (30 per cent), Total (10 per cent) and Agip (5 per cent). The Delta accounted for 10 per cent of Shell's global production.[46] Formally, Shell said it had withdrawn because it could no longer operate in a way consistent with its business ethics. The company recognized it had lost its 'social license to operate', in the phrase adopted in subsequent statements and reports. But Shell was accused of being behind the sentencing and execution of Ogoni campaigners and of colluding with the then military regime in the provision of security measures. After the return of democratic government, Shell spent significant sums of its own money on building schools and offering scholarships in the Delta. But the company remained an overwhelmingly controversial spectre in the Delta, for example when it put limits on the amount of transparency it was willing to support under Nigeria's new corruption commission and the Nigerian Extractive Industries Transparency Initiative.

In sum, there remained examples of European companies being indifferent to political regime-types or actively preferring to deal with autocrats. The influence this had over EU energy policy varied. On some governance issues, governments sought a greater reformist commitment from their own multi-nationals. Policy-makers insisted that a distinctive part of the EU approach was the strong recommendations issued to IOCs about governance standards in the way they operated in non-democratic producer states. Ideas were floated in EU policy-making circles of CFSP offering firmer support to oil companies in return for a stronger commitment from the latter to CSR principles – but such proposals were not implemented. Energy industry employers' organizations agreed that companies invariably saw the lengthy horizons of oil and gas investments as making it necessary to build-up 'long-term relations' in preference to pushing for short-term market or governance reforms – and that they still felt that this point had not been adequately taken on board by diplomats. One EU advisor lamented that 'Brussels can preach about markets and governance' but it had little means of influencing the behaviour of companies, who remained completely 'disconnected' from EU security networks.

On other occasions, it was more a case of European governments and IOCs acting in partnership in a way that neglected any focus on good gov-ernance in producer states. In general, in southern member states stronger links existed between governments and oil companies than in northern member states. The close relationship in France between the political establishment and big multinationals was an integral part of the system of *pantouflage* (the interchange of personnel between the two worlds). Examples of two-way cooperation existed in northern member states as well, however. Shell used the Foreign and Commonwealth Office to move back into Libya: diplomats called this a 'model' operation, reflecting a 'symbiotic' public–private partnership, with the FCO opening way for IOCs, the latter's engagement itself oiling the wheels for European diplomacy. Moreover, EU governments backed their oil companies firmly over US extraterritorial sanctions in Iran and Libya. Tony Blair personally urged the Chinese government to buy its gas from BP – in battle against John Howard lobbying for the Australian Liquefied Natural Gas consortium – further diluting pressure on human rights issues in China.[47]

Good governance as self-interest?

Despite these trends, many oil and gas companies claimed that good governance was at the heart of their concerns and improvements in transparent, accountable and predictable decision-making crucial to their long-term interests. Oil executives commonly lamented that the 'resource nationalism' associated with non-democratic regimes was a major obstacle to the desired expansion of investment. It was pointed out in this sense that some of the countries with the largest remaining energy reserves were reluctant to open up to investors in part out of fear over the impact that a general process of liberalization would have on the control exerted by the incumbent regime. MNC representatives in Central Asia and the Caspian suggested that European companies' interest in the region had reached a plateau as more assertive regimes reopened contract conditions from the mid-1990s to insist on much lower premiums. It was noted dryly that European majors were questioning their commitment to this region just as European governments were discovering Central Asia, ten years too late for the private sector.

It was pointed out that in most producer states international oil companies were not given adequate incentives for secure, long-term investment. Countries such as Iran and Saudi Arabia were unable to attract bids from a large number of big players. Moreover, their capital needs were sacrificed to governments' budgetary needs. At the same time tensions grew between NOCs and their own governments, as the latter prioritized the quick development of fields to maximize short-term revenue.[48] The Saudi government's plan to open up gas contracts to international bidders was significantly diluted after disagreements with IOCs on the low rates of return being offered.[49]

Whatever its limitations, more companies than EU governments signed up to the EITI. Norwegian company Statoil insisted that transparency and financial disclosure were the linchpins for governance and better revenue management and committed itself to disclose its tax payments in all countries. BP introduced a formal ban on facilitation payments, within a new anti-corruption code of conduct: 478 employees were dismissed under this code in 2005.[50] BP funded a new centre to work on resource-management transparency and advocated better EU foreign policy rewards for those states making most progress within the EITI.

Some companies did refer to increasing concerns often related to lack of democratic quality. These included arbitrary decision-making; the nationalism at the root of autocrats' legitimacy; politically conditioned joint venture requirements; the narrowness of pro-market coalitions; and increasing security costs (which represented over 10 per cent of total operating costs in Algeria, for example). Measures of 'stability' in political risk assessments were recognized by MNCs to be not very helpful; most risk ratings focused on indicators such as the number of assassinations, not systemic level problems of conflict.[51] The head of the OGP admitted that 'we are bad at assessing political risks'; the private sector tended to look at the solidity of fiscal regimes, but this was recognized as being woefully inadequate as a measure of longer-term stability.

Total insisted that there had been a genuine and big improvement in the dismantling of the 'Elf system' across Africa, one of the most incestuous of all relationships between big oil and government until the end of the 1990s. Total's chief executive insisted that as IOCs had been squeezed by the rise of NOCs they had been forced to revise their short-term and paternalistic attitudes. International oil companies, he argued, needed to consider their own challenge of remaining competitive as integrally linked to producer states' broader process of economic and political development.[52]

Some insisted that semi-authoritarianism and low-intensity democracy in fact gave the worst of both worlds. The high-profile disputes that occurred in Russia have already been mentioned in Chapter 4. Shell was forced to surrender overall control of Sakhalin II to Gazprom, and saw its share reduced to 25 per cent of the project. BP then suffered the same fate at the Kovykta gas field in the spring of 2007. In March 2007, BP failed in its bid for a major stake in Rosneft, in an auction set to favour state-controlled energy champions.[53] The chief executive of BP complained that Russia was an increasingly 'dark and hostile place' to many oil investors; indeed, BP itself tried to initiate a regular dialogue with Russian authorities to express concerns.[54] In July 2007 Total was granted a licence for the Shtokman field, accepting a similarly reduced participation to Shell and BP in their deals: no ownership rights over the resources, rather simply technological help to Gazprom, which the latter realized it could not do without. IOCs had also experienced problems in Russia in the 1990s, during the Yeltsin era[55] and despite the high-profile 'problematic' cases a plethora of bilateral deals accumulated between European companies and Gazprom – those signed by ENI and E.ON being of particularly notable reach. But companies recognized that these were deals requiring hefty quid pro quos, in the shape of downstream access in European national markets, in lieu of an open and objective rule of law prevailing in Russia. In September 2007, for example, Shell felt obliged to relinquish its stake in Germany's largest oil-industry complex to Rosneft in order to be allowed to participate in new field development in Siberia.[56] BP and its Russian subsidiary, BP–TNK suffered further harassment from various state ministries in the summer of 2008.

While in Nigeria much was written on the harm done by Shell and other companies to local communities, the country's post-1999 'low intensity' democracy itself served to dissuade more significant rises in European investment. Multinationals complained at being squeezed by two interrelated factors in Nigeria. First, the ever-rising tax take from the federal government – Shell frequently claimed that with the rise in oil prices the Nigerian government was by the mid-2000s collecting 95 per cent of its profits, the highest take in the whole of Africa and a direct reflection of governmental graft and institutional weakness. Second, IOCs were disadvantaged by the de facto need to compensate for the lack of effective law and order provision by paying for local security services, which often amounted to little more than old-fashioned protection money.[57] In 2004 Shell's own consultants argued that if the next presidential elections were not more democratic and again fostered conflict the company would have to abandon on-shore production.[58] Companies and local communities increasingly dealt directly with each other – reaching informal memorandums of understanding – as the Nigerian state was so venal and corrupt. However, trying to placate opposition through development projects also failed to assuage, but rather simply dragged Shell and other companies into acrimonious conflicts between different regions and villages and ethnic groups over who should receive such funds.[59] Shell dropped plans to resume operations in the western Niger Delta after the elections in 2007 and in June 2008 closed an off-shore oil production vessel after it was attacked by rebels; the company also employed a high-level advisor to devise a comprehensive peace initiative for the Delta.[60] Oil majors expressed increasing concern over president Yar'Adua's plans to renegotiate existing contracts and a Nigerian government report in April 2008 admitted that oil production was likely to fall because of declining interest from IOCs.[61]

Turkmenistan remained virtually impenetrable, except for small exploratory investments by independents such as Burren Energy. Total made strenuous efforts to sign a deal after president Niyazov's death, but to little avail by 2008. In Kazakhstan Repsol complained that arbitrary rule-making delayed its entry into the country, which was only secured at the end of 2006 after many years of negotiation and political procrastination.[62] In early 2008 IOCs had to reduce their stakes in the Kashagan field to allow the Kazakh state monopoly to assume an equal share; as the international members of the consortium intimated at further delays to starting production the Kazakh government declared an intention to take over control of the project.[63]

In 2006 the highly confident Angolan government launched a new licensing round with exorbitant signing bonuses for the dos Santos government. In

Africa, Shell had significant upstream presence only in Gabon, Cameroon and Nigeria. While Total had its rights to an exploration permit in southern Sudan upheld in 2007, the company could not move to begin operations in the country.[64] In general, in Africa it was the smaller European energy independents, such as Tullow Oil, that had pushed hardest and taken the greatest risks for new finds.[65] While Venezuela was not a significant supplier to the EU market, several European oil companies saw their interests seriously affected by the resource nationalism that helped sustain Hugo Chávez's Bolivarian revolution. After one round of confiscations, Chávez hoisted the Venezuelan flag over fields until then operated by ENI and Total.[66]

In Iraq a split emerged between small independents and the majors. By 2008 it was only the smaller independents that had risked involvement in Iraq, certainly in any direct contact with the Kurdish regional government. The small UK independent Gulfsands teamed up with a Syrian firm to develop energy projects in Iraq. By spring 2008 the bigger European companies had begun to engage with the Iraqi government and in September 2008 Shell became the first western firm to commit to a project in Iraq. But their presence remained a cautious one. In contrast, Russia used diplomatic offers, including a $10 billion debt-relief package, to reawaken Lukoil's Saddam-era deal and less risk-averse Chinese companies began to make more significant in-roads. By summer 2008, of 35 applicants short-listed for licences by the Iraqi government only seven were from the European Union.[67]

As explained in Chapter 3, IOCs were discouraged from engagement in Iran by the uncertainties of the international diplomacy related to the nuclear programme. EU diplomats revealed that this was one case where they had been subject to strong lobbying from European energy companies, against tighter sanctions being imposed on Iran that might interfere with longer-term energy cooperation. Total, Shell, Statoil, Repsol, Eni, E.ON and Centrica had by 2007 all signed initial exploratory memorandums with Iran, but desisted from signing definitive contracts while the prospect of US – and potentially broader international – sanctions remained. However, while in some sense this implied that European companies were straining at the leash to 'get into' Iran, firms also cited governance problems as increasingly acute. The biggest problem, according to one Total executive, was not the nuclear impasse but the contractual terms imposed by Iran.[68] One observer concurred that the biggest impingement on multinationals was the limited 'buy back' contracts on offer from the Iranian regime.[69] In early 2008 Eni moved to sign a firm contract, but other European companies remained uncertain as Iran established its June 2008 deadline for IOCs to sign contracts.

How far all these governance concerns impacted on policy was not clear. Significant variation existed between different companies, even within the same producer state. On CSR issues experts placed Statoil at one extreme, the Italian energy giants at the other end of the spectrum. Variation and uncertainty existed on the part of MNCs over how their interests related to local political conditions; views often depended simply on whether the company in question had good personal links with the regime or not. Little unity existed, for example, in the Gulf of Guinea, where established players used patronage links to keep 'new arrivals' at bay, producing a variety of private-sector views on governance questions.[70] Despite their growing concerns over the collapse of the rule of law in Russia, multinationals' lobbying efforts focused on gaining firmer rules on supply guarantees (to prevent Russia from reducing supplies to European customers where it had overestimated reserves) not on reform issues.

Nevertheless, on at least some occasions some MNCs argued that they were more interested in the governance dimension than their own governments. One French official admitted that 'EU governments have not listened enough' to private-sector concerns over simplifying frameworks for investment in producer states. A UK official revealed that governments had been increasingly lobbied by oil companies to push for governance reforms in banking and for regulations to render commercial operations more secure in places such as Nigeria and Angola. The reopening of Kashagan contracts by the Nazarbayev government provoked strong complaints from the European Business Association, urging stronger European governmental involvement and successfully pushing Javier Solana to visit Kazakhstan in autumn 2007.[71] The aspect of governance where European MNCs did lobby actively in EU institutions and began to gel together something of a network structure with officials was on regulatory structures. MNCs pushed to make sure that it was EU regulatory structures adopted in developing markets, especially in the Neighbourhood and Cotonou partners, rather than US standards, so as to make investment and trade easier; MNCs acknowledged this very strategic perspective on the way that a focus on governance structures was incorporated into EU foreign policy.[72]

Conclusion

European oil and gas companies engaged in a reactive and ad hoc fashion with EU efforts to strengthen the external dimension of energy security policy during the early and mid-2000s. It cannot be concluded that the plethora of new EU commitments on external energy security were agreed at the behest of oil giants. The course of energy-related EU foreign policy was not the 'creature' of oil and gas multinationals. The latter did engage more assertively on very specific policy issues, such as the 'unbundling' debate or the 'third country reciprocity clause'. Yet even here, their views often did not prevail, trumped by the differing positions of many European governments. At the more general conceptual level, companies' input was even more circumscribed in relation to the broad philosophy of energy security to be pursued by the Union.

A number of EU policy initiatives did increasingly seek to build in more structured engagement with and participation from oil and gas companies. In their discourse many energy companies recognized the need for an enhanced strategic, foreign-policy dimension to energy security. But many company representatives still expressed a pervasive scepticism over the actual and potential role of CFSP in international energy matters. Reflecting such variation between – and indeed within – companies a strikingly schizophrenic attitude could be said to exist amongst energy multinationals. On the one hand, these commonly lamented the divisions that existed between member states and the failure of the EU 'to speak with one voice' on energy. On the other hand, when incipient EU unity could be detected many company executives perceived this more as unwelcome interference than useful political backing. Even as they called for greater EU foreign-policy unity, European companies often battled to out-compete each other in forming alliances with third-country energy giants – the priority goal in practice being to gain an advantage over their EU rivals.

In principle, oil and gas firms most commonly espoused a 'markets and institutions' approach to energy security. The EU internal market was perceived to be the platform for European companies' own international extension and presence. Supporting the spread of EU regulations and standards to third-country markets would facilitate European investment and operations in those countries. However, at the same time, many company actions and pronouncements questioned and sought to impede the free-market orientation of energy policy. European energy multinationals were the architects of many cartel-like alliances and cooperative arrangements with third-country suppliers. At times the division was increasingly clear between 'European energy security interests' and 'European energy companies' interests'.

Significantly, despite the paucity of formal dialogue mechanisms between governments and the private sector over energy-related foreign policy, companies' respective positioning on the 'markets versus geopolitics' spectrum most often approximated to that of their own national governments: UK companies were more market oriented in their advocacy, French and German firms more geopolitical. Some companies, in some markets, were dismissive of issues of human rights and good governance; in such cases EU governments sometimes pushed against European multinationals on human rights issues, but on other occasions formed more of a partnership with them in seeking deeper engagement with highly autocratic regimes. In other markets there were more signs of IOCs pushing for transparent governance standards out of self-interest and complaining that EU governments were actually failing to press hard enough for such improvements. In short on issues relating to markets, geopolitics and democracy a range of different relationships existed between governments and European energy companies – this recalling on-going debates over the general relationship (and especially, degree of autonomy) between the state and business in Western economies.

9   Conclusions

The European Union's (EU) commitment systematically to incorporate energy security into its foreign-policy cooperation has raised a number of policy challenges in recent years. This book set out to address six main questions related to the external dimensions of EU energy security. First, the extent to which energy security has influenced changes in EU foreign policies. Second, whether energy security challenges have strengthened or weakened internal European unity. Third, what kind of approach the EU has adopted to energy security. Fourth, whether the EU has succeeded in gaining any notable influence over international energy questions relative to the role played by other actors. Fifth, the relationship between energy imperatives and EU positions on governance and human rights reforms in producer states. Sixth, the role played by European energy companies in the evolution of EU energy security strategy. With the book having explored the evolution of European policies in detail across the principal producer states and regions, a summary overview can be attempted of the light shed on each of these six questions.

The impact of energy security on EU foreign policy

Chapter 2 outlined the way in which many experts have urged energy security to be understood as one element integrally embedded within the broader set of security challenges facing Europe. A step change was indeed witnessed in EU policy from the mid-2000s. Prior to this energy security was strikingly absent from Common Foreign and Security Policy (CFSP) deliberations and from the standard menu of issues addressed as security challenges. Energy security assumed a priority place within external relations dialogues, while high-level political impulse was injected through a series of new policy papers and strategic reviews produced by the European Commission and national governments.

To some degree the new focus on energy security represented a panicky reaction to Russia's assertiveness, especially in the dispute with Ukraine in January 2006. This led to much of the new 'security' focus centring on the question of potential supply shut-offs. This was despite the EU's rhetorical insistence on the greater importance of basing strategy on longer-term planning. Gradually, from this moment of perceived crisis many actors in the EU did seek to construct a longer-term philosophy of energy security. However, many of the most notable concrete initiatives – such as the creation of the network of energy correspondents and the new 'solidarity' clause in the Lisbon Treaty – still betrayed more of a 'crisis management' mode of thinking.

The declared aim was to move beyond an erstwhile technocratic approach to external energy policy. This was achieved only to a partial degree, in select instances. Energy security established its place as another item on the CFSP agenda, but was not fully 'nested' within foreign policies aimed at other aims, such as conflict resolution or programmes of regional cooperation. If anything the trend was in the reverse direction, with energy being separated out and pursued through stand-alone memorandums of understanding, agreements and initiatives.

While several new initiatives and policy instruments were introduced, other proposals were blocked – including those for a 'Mr EU Energy Security' post and for an essential elements 'energy clause' to be included in all third-country agreements. The external dimensions of energy security were still subject primarily to consensus policy-making, despite the attempts of a small number of member states to bring qualified majority voting to this sphere – to instil the more dynamic decision-making witnessed in policies related to climate change.

Indeed, the foreign-policy dimensions of energy security remained – policy-makers concurred – of a decidedly secondary order compared with the EU's more prominent and 'vanguard' role in relation to climate-change policies. In 2008 the linkage between climate-change policies and CFSP geo-strategy began to be explored for the first time. At the time of writing this had produced few concrete policy changes – save some commitments to finance renewables development within third-country partners – but the relationship between these two strands of energy policy looked set to attract increasing attention in future deliberations. However, tension persisted between these two agendas, one dominated by a concern for greater energy *in*dependence, the other focused on the better management of *inter*dependence. The balance between these two dynamics was fiercely debated in the allocation of finite EU resources.

Concerns over the external dimensions of energy policy had the most notable impact on policy towards Russia. They had least effect on policy in Africa; here a number of new EU energy initiatives were introduced from 2005 but the EU's policy response was still slower and more limited than that of China, the United States and other countries. Central Asia undoubtedly attracted more attention, albeit from a small number of member states. In this region, new funds were provided for energy infrastructure links and diplomatic engagement, although other security issues – and especially counter-terrorism – tended to cut across the focus on energy.

EU efforts in the Middle East exhibited much variation. New partnerships, funds and dialogues were offered to North African producers. Conversely, EU strategy in the Gulf failed to register significant advances. In this region, still the most crucial for international energy supplies, trade problems and counter-terrorism impeded greater progress on energy cooperation. Even in North Africa, southern EU member states complained that the EU remained insufficiently engaged due to its fixation with Russia, while these states themselves saw migration as by far the most pressing security priority. In Iran, priority was attached to containing the Islamic Republic's nuclear activities – although there was some evidence to suggest that the EU softened its punitive measures with energy considerations in mind. The beginnings of an energy cooperation programme were seen in Iraq in 2007–8, albeit still overshadowed by the broader geopolitical and security factors militating against deeper engagement in this country.

Increasing or decreasing unity?

Chapter 2 outlined some of the general factors alleged by analysts to be pushing in the direction of deeper EU unity: the on-going processes of 'socialization' within CFSP; the emergence of a 'network' of common security perspectives within Europe; the influence of convergent 'transborder' linkages between functionaries, including in the energy sphere. This book's study of the external dimensions of energy security suggests that such dynamics of convergence were weaker in this sphere than analysts have detected in other areas of the CFSP agenda. Common European approaches were adumbrated and certainly created the frameworks for potential socialization. But, in practice governments' pursuit of energy security told a more varied story.

It was commonly claimed that the gradual deepening of the internal market would drive convergence in the external dimensions of energy security policy. The evidence presented in this book suggests that this occurred only to a limited extent. Some member states resisted even the most basic principles of transparency and information sharing with their EU partners. Such divergence existed at the political level but also amongst diplomats and technical experts – if a transborder epistemic community existed in the energy sphere it was no more than incipient and still often diluted by the disparate winds of fierce national competition.

France's external energy dependency was relatively low, undercutting its commitment to foreign-policy unity. Germany was even more the 'spoiler' through its Russia policy and increasingly its bilateral efforts in Central Asia. Italy gave increasingly explicit political backing to national, bilateral energy deals. Conversely, the traditionally sceptical UK became more supportive of EU cooperation, as its own energy dependency was set to increase fast. The Netherlands – the EU's remaining significant gas producer – advocated a balance between unity and retaining scope for bilateral policies.

Russia provided the most conspicuous examples of disunity. Member-state governments backed their respective national energy champions in signing long-term bilateral contracts with Gazprom – and were indeed minded to argue that such deals represented a success for energy security. Even in the case of Russia, however, the pull of EU cooperation was not entirely absent, and unity did tighten to some degree as Russia adopted increasingly heavy-handed tactics in the wielding of its new energy-based international power. Differences over Russia additionally engendered contrasting views among member states on how assertive the EU should be in prioritizing Central Asia within its energy security strategy. This was witnessed at a very general level – in differences over how far the EU should challenge Russian primacy in Central Asia – and in relation to more specific policy decisions – such as whether to offer Kazakhstan a place in the European Neighbourhood Policy (ENP) or whether sanctions should be lifted against Uzbekistan. At the other end of the spectrum to Russia, energy strategy in Sub-Saharan Africa was least subject to high political tensions between member states, as the EU sought to take the first steps towards regaining its lost influence on the continent.

Policy in the Middle East and North Africa did benefit from more institutionalized long-term partnerships that the EU sought to use as a base from which to deepen energy cooperation. While this undoubtedly rendered common EU-level initiatives of great significance, even under the rubric of the Euro-Mediterranean Partnership (EMP) – the most strongly institutionalized EU framework embracing oil and gas producer states – competitive dynamics were at least as evident as collusion. As the chapter on the Middle East demonstrates, member states increasingly undercut each other in an effort to gain access to Algerian energy supplies, this compounded by the latter's rejection of the ENP action plan offered to it. Spain and Italy in particular justified such bilateralism by expressing frustration at the lack of north European backing for deeper EU-level engagement in North Africa. Outside the scope of the EMP, Libya attracted even more of an open rivalry between member states keen to gain early preference with the internationally rehabilitated Colonel Gaddafi – even as they talked of enticing Libya into the EMP and/ or Neighbourhood Policy.

In the Gulf, the weight of national diplomacy was even more pronounced in relation to the impact of common EU forums and initiatives. This was due to a combination of factors: the determination of the larger member states to safeguard their national deals and channels of access; the relative disinterest in the region of most other member states; the tendency of Gulf Cooperation Council states themselves still to prioritize their links with national capitals rather than conceive the EU as primary interlocutor; and the limited purchase in the area of traditional EU economic, developmental and regulatory policy instruments. EU unity was notable in relation to Iran's nuclear programme, but differences predominated over the prospect of energy cooperation with the Islamic Republic. Here Italy was increasingly the most forward-leaning state in seeking to deepen energy ties on a bilateral basis with Tehran. A limited degree of 'Europeanization' took shape in policy towards Iraq but – even aside from the original differences over the 2003 invasion – the nature of this country's security situation and political challenges continued to engender contrasting views among member states. These militated against the possibility of establishing the foundations for a common energy strategy towards Baghdad.

Markets versus geopolitics

Chapter 2 examined one of the most central on-going debates between energy experts. For one school of thought the traditional geopolitics of energy have been surpassed; market dynamics have deepened and extended from the oil to the gas sector; and security is now about governing international markets to ensure that they can work with sufficient efficacy to correct shocks and demand-supply imbalances. In contrast, another school of thought has argued that it is geopolitics that is increasingly in the ascendancy, with the primacy attached to bilateral deals, the use of hard power to protect supplies and the rise of new consumers such as China not adhering to market governance principles. Debates over the nature of EU foreign policy reveal an apparently close approximation between the 'markets and institutions' school of thought and the way that most analysts see the EU as drawn to the reproduction of certain constituent norms and values.

The evidence presented in this book suggests that, as it developed its new external energy strategies, in practice the EU hovered uncertainly between a 'market-governance' and 'geopolitical' philosophy. The rules and regulations of the internal market were certainly presented as the key foundation to the EU's international projection in energy matters. The Energy Charter Treaty was supported as embodiment of rules-based multilateralism. New EU energy partnerships offered cooperatively to draw producer states into a European market-governance area rather than – officials insisted – playing geopolitics *against* them. The internal market was to serve as the model for regulatory rules and standards to be extended to producer states; the means of breaking up powerful third-country actors within Europe itself; an incentive for producer states to sign up to the principle of energy interdependence; and, in this sense, the EU's best negotiating tool to win concessions from producers. That is, strongly rationalist calculations (as opposed to a purely identity-driven logic) lay behind EU efforts to export energy-sector norms to producer states.

However, member state governments sought to have the best of both worlds, seeking the benefits of the influence flowing from European-wide market rules while simultaneously pursuing short-term gain from highly geopolitical behaviour. When governments backed their respective national champions in signing bilateral contracts, EU competition law was rarely invoked against such deals. Observers doubted that the internal market was integrated enough – even at the level of basic infrastructural links within Europe itself – either to serve as a common regulatory-governance magnet for producer states or to absorb external shocks. While market principles were espoused, most member states' governments and the Commission attached at least equal importance to the aims of carefully negotiating market access in reciprocal fashion and to a politically inspired diversification of supplies (the latter anathema to those insisting that for fungible energy supplies markets would clear and self-correct at any given price). The increasing salience of gas supplies – shaped by political deals over fixed supply routes rather than, as in the case of oil, supplies onto an open international market – helped further tip the scales towards geopolitical dynamics. It must be suspected that the market norm-based approach was emphasized in EU-level discourse in part to mask the extent of member states' geopolitical actions.

European diplomats asserted that one clear difference between EU and US strategies was the former's eschewal of any hard power, military component. While this certainly represented a key aspect of EU self-identity, the distinction was not quite as clear cut as many suggested. Many officials admitted that internal EU deliberations revealed a logic of coat-tailing on US military protection of energy supply routes in several regions; that the 'soft power' approach had emerged as much by accident as by carefully rationalized strategic design; and that some member states did begin to push for the European Security and Defence Policy (ESDP) to develop a more assertive deployment of European power capable of backing up energy security imperatives. Moreover, some member states' new military deployments and agreements did seem related to energy concerns, even though governments insisted this was not the case.

In North Africa the EU offered increasing amounts of technical cooperation to boost energy links, while also pressing for regulatory harmonization in the energy sector, based on the existing acquis of the EMP. However, North African producers were resistant to many aspects of the market-governance model. Elements of European cooperation with Algeria clearly cut across market principles. The reach of EU internal market norms was even more limited in the Gulf; here member-state governments rather sought energy cooperation on the back of traditional geopolitical forms of engagement, such as security cooperation and arms sales. The same situation pertained in Central Asia, where the EU's vague offer of inclusion in a system of market norms was no match for Russian influence. In the Caspian Basin the one partial exception was Azerbaijan, whose inclusion in the ENP did help at least to some degree bring the country into a more European rules-based sphere of influence.

Russia resisted market norms and complained at the EU's double standards over such principles. Energy dialogue with Russia from 2000 aimed to extend market rules, deepen regulatory convergence and improve the governance of foreign investment, but it proved difficult to insulate such low-politics cooperation from the high-politics tensions with President Putin. Russia was the case where member states argued most openly that a 'geopolitical dimension' was required. They differed on what that dimension should consist of: confrontation or uncritical engagement. As Russian heavy-handedness intensified the EU's focus was increasingly on the need to 'take a stand' geopolitically as the key to better energy security. The EU's offer to incorporate Ukraine into the EU internal energy market was certainly a Russia-related, geopolitical use of market principles. A curious situation pertained: there were instances of

EU 'weakness' or 'appeasement' towards Russia, but because the approach was more political than in other areas in some ways Putin was demonized more than autocrats in other producer states.

In Sub-Saharan Africa too the EU's stated aim was to extend market principles, but here energy policy was in practice approached far more through the lens of development cooperation. The EU's development policy-making community took greater charge of energy cooperation in Africa than did either the 'energy technocrats' or CFSP diplomats. In Africa, the EU to some degree resisted an instrumental focus on its own energy security in favour of incorporating a concern with local communities' access to energy into its range of development aid funding. This represented a notable contrast to the way that US efforts were led by the Pentagon in the Gulf of Guinea. Indeed, most in the EU resisted cooperation with the US in Africa as the means of confronting China's rising influence. EU officials insisted that the focus on 'energy poverty' within Africa was consistent with its own energy security concerns, but this link remained doubtful and was not articulated in any concrete fashion. Certainly the development focus did not sit entirely easily with the declared aim of market liberalization, in the eyes of many African interlocutors. In some cases, more of a political angle did emerge: in Angola the focus was more on strengthening diplomatic engagement; but in Sudan the EU's conflict resolution concerns cut across the prospects for enhanced energy cooperation.

European influence

A common theme to emerge from the book's chapters is that of the EU's increasing difficulties in asserting influence over international energy issues relative to other powers. This was most clearly the case away from the EU's immediate periphery. Africa provided the starkest example of Europe's declining influence. Competition and active investment campaigns not only from China by also increasingly from India, Malaysia, Brazil and other states diminished European market shares and diplomatic clout. Collaboration with the US was spurned more than cultivated. Reacting belatedly, the EU introduced a raft of new Africa initiatives, but these struggled to regain the ground lost. Chapter 7 shows how Nigeria provided a particularly notable example of limited European engagement in a persistent low-level conflict that had major implications for international energy security. By 2008 there were faint signs that the geopolitical pendulum was perhaps just beginning to swing back: several African states that had for a decade been courting China as a counter-weight to traditional European influence started to encourage more EU involvement in order to off-set China's newly powerful position.

In Central Asia, the EU was a markedly secondary player, unwilling and/or unable to challenge either Russian primacy or US geo-strategy (for example, on the question of pipelines taking Central Asian supplies across Iran). Many European diplomats indeed opined that 'challenging' Russia in this region was neither necessary nor desirable, and that 'security' was compatible with

Russia holding a monopoly over supply routes from Central Asia. By 2008, a great deal of new activity was afoot relating to the development of additional pipeline capacity from Central Asia into Europe, but European governments' preferences remained balanced overall between support for routes involving Russia and those designed to exclude Russia. China's influence in Central Asia was not as marked as in Africa, but also began to appear as an additional challenge to EU aims. The region presented the question of how far the EU was willing to extend its most advanced policy instruments: the decision not to offer Kazakhstan the prospect of participating in the European Neighbourhood Policy was – however valid the EU's reasons – a dint to influence over this most important of energy players in Central Asia. At most, here the EU gained influence in a relatively vague sense as a counter-weight to Moscow and Beijing, offering a model of cooperation based on democratic and market norms.

In relation to Russia itself, much has been written on the EU's divisions and ineffectiveness in confronting the more assertive foreign policies that took shape under Vladimir Putin. Nevertheless – and perhaps paradoxically – compared with the EU's secondary status in other producer regions, it was still the case that for Russia Europe was the key market and the most important international actor effecting Russian interests. The depth of transatlantic cooperation in policy towards Russia was again limited; indeed, several member states even advocated partnership with Russia to enhance EU security and preferential treatment vis-à-vis the United States.

It was also the case that for North African producers, the EU remained the most influential international actor. Even here, however, there were signs that the EU failed to maximize its influence. Algeria rejected the notion of a neighbourhood action plan that enshrined a commitment to energy cooperation based on market and governance norms. Instead it chose a new strategic alliance with Gazprom – this representing one of the clearest instances indicating that Russia presented a challenge not only in relation to its own supplies but also by virtue of its wider international actions. In both the Arabian Peninsula and Iran the different 'blockages' to EU policy enabled China to begin making in-roads and win new energy contracts at Europe's expense. In both North Africa and the Gulf the EU eschewed energy partnership with the US, as the latter remained the key reference point for 'hard security' challenges. Chapter 2 outlined the debate between those who saw the EU's security identity as increasingly 'leash-slipping' away from the US and those who characterized it as 'slip-streaming' US hard power. The evidence presented in this book suggests that, in an effort to gain energy-related influence vis-à-vis the United States, European policies exhibited an uneasy mix of both these dynamics. It was not clear that this produced any notable success.

Energy security and governance

Chapter 2 sketched debates over the relationship between energy security and issues relating to the support of democratic norms and human rights. Received wisdom suggests that heightened concern over energy dependence leads to a diminished focus on democracy in producer states. In contrast to this, some analysts have stressed more the way in which better governance is essential for long-term stability in producer states, arguing that support for political reform should be part of European energy policies, not a trade-off against them. Still other analysts insist that the nature of political systems in producer countries makes little difference one way or the other, and has little link to external energy interests.

Chapter 3 found that EU policy statements and commitments placed significant stress on the EU's 'added-value' being that of a 'rules-based governance' approach to energy security. As energy security rose up the foreign-policy agenda, the EU continued to introduce new democracy and human rights initiatives and in most places increased the amount of funding it devoted to such governance concerns. Deliberations in many states indeed focused on the way in which poor governance standards undermined the security of supplies to European markets. However, in general there was little systematic linkage made between energy policy and democracy support in any concrete sense. Most European diplomats rejected the kind of instrumental link advocated *inter alia* by US neo-conservatives, who saw support for democratic change in producer states as desirable precisely for reasons of energy security. Europeans still tended to pose the question in reverse: not 'how important is democratic governance for energy security?', but rather 'how much scope is left for human rights policy given the concern with energy security?' One feeling was that financial transfers to producer states had increased so much since 2002 that European strictures on human rights and governance would count for little. This left a striking disconnect and apolitical bent at the heart of EU foreign policy, as seen, for example, in the relatively weak overall European commitment to the Extractive Industries Transparency Initiative (EITI).

The internal politics of North Africa and the Middle East continued to be seen as largely unproblematic for European energy interests. Incipient pressure for change within the region, while still far from producing clear democratic breakthroughs, suggested underlying political conditions were rather less stable than European policy-makers judged to be the case. Heightened concerns over energy security did not completely override support for political liberalization in this region, but neither did it in practice produce a step-change increase in support consistent with the supposedly governance-oriented approach to energy security. Iran was the exception, where European governments did increasingly see a link between this country's deteriorating human rights situation and the desirable conditions for EU energy engagement. However, in this case, little reform-oriented effort was made because of the priority attached to containing Iran's nuclear activities.

Several European governments self-evidently raced to strengthen energy alliances with an increasingly autocratic Russian regime. However, at the same time, there was actually more of a critical focus on Putin's autocratic misdemeanours than on those of the non-democratic regimes of other producer states. Curiously, those states with the highest energy dependence on Russia adopted the toughest line on Russia's abuse of democratic rights. Despite a continuing strand of uncritical engagement within member states' bilateral policies, Putin's fusing of economic and political power was increasingly recognized as problematic for longer-term EU energy interests. Again, notwithstanding the much-commented and undoubted 'softness' of many European policies towards Russia, this was a link not made in many other equally autocratic producer states.

In Central Asia, the EU aspired at most to press regimes to manage energy resources in a slightly more transparent fashion, without risking the potential instability of broader political change. Azerbaijan and Kazakhstan in this sense implemented some reforms under the rubric of the EITI; at the same time they were offered energy partnerships with the EU that by-passed democracy and human rights strictures. President Nazarbayev was given strong and largely uncritical support, as a supposedly enlightened 'soft authoritarian' who had personally used his control of Kazakhstan's state machinery to facilitate European investments. As of 2008, such support appeared to be backfiring against European interests, as the president aimed to renegotiate contracts in order to wrest control of the Kashagan field from foreign operators. The EU did sacrifice engagement with Uzbekistan after the 2005 Andijan massacre, although here Germany and several other states sought to dilute such measures and open the way for energy cooperation with the brutal Karimov regime. The race to engage with Turkmenistan after the death of president Niyazov was presented as a step towards encouraging more open governance in this most closed of post-Soviet states; in practice the immediate EU focus was on securing energy contracts and a commitment that Turkmen gas would flow into European markets.

In Sub-Saharan Africa the development focus led to an apparently tighter link between energy and governance, insofar as the latter had already been incorporated into much new thinking on development cooperation. But here too, the EU in practice pursued a cautious approach to democratic reform; did not as a united bloc support the EITI; and failed to design policy-making processes that actually ensured coordination between energy and governance specialists. In cases such as Angola, the concern was increasingly with diplomatic engagement without any attempt to influence political reform. In the Niger Delta, the Commission and the UK Department for International Development did implement new initiatives that centred on improving the governance of energy resources. However, in this case other donors declined to engage in significant measure and the overarching EU diplomatic position was highly supportive of president Obasanjo, despite his being the source of many of Nigeria's governance-related problems.

Chapter 2 suggested that in terms of broader international relations debates it remained unclear how different positions on the energy–governance relationship would be explained by traditional theories. Realism might predict *either* Western 'counterbalancing' of autocratic producer states *or* 'bandwagoning' with those countries. Liberalism might predict *either* a Western focus on economic interdependence only *or* on pressure for convergent ('liberal') international governance norms. This book demonstrates that the EU espoused an approach to energy security based on liberal interdependence, constructed around democratic governance norms; it equally shows how in its implementation such policy exhibited a muddied mixture of counterbalancing and bandwagoning.

The role of European energy companies

European energy companies found themselves under increasingly intense competition from producer states' national oil companies as well as from Chinese, Indian and other investors. Yet Chapter 8 demonstrates that EU firms were less than fully convinced that a Europeanized energy security strategy was the best means of dealing with this challenge. Even if their rhetoric often suggested that they did support deeper EU cooperation, their actions belied a narrower outlook. European oil and gas companies mostly retained a distance from EU governments' efforts to strengthen the external dimension of energy security policy. This contrasted with the active involvement of multinationals in the design of the strategic elements of the Bush administration's energy security policy. European energy companies engaged more systematically on specific and especially more technocratic issues, this reinforcing the technocratic flavour of EU external energy initiatives. They also attached greater priority to influencing debates over climate-change measures than EU security policies. Where energy concerns were affected by other security concerns – counter-terrorism, conflict resolution – companies were reluctant to engage in these related areas of EU foreign policy.

Oil and gas companies routinely complained of EU governments' lack of strategic leadership on energy security; these governments in turn lamented multinationals' limited engagement on the broader political dimensions of security. Companies commonly criticized governments and the European Commission for being insufficiently pro-market and for increasingly intervening in political fashion; but their own behaviour in practice prioritized alliance-building and the protection of existing dominant market positions. Beyond the general features of companies' actions, much variation existed between smaller and larger firms. The former tended to offer more genuine support for European coordination and market liberalization, as a means of enhancing their own position in relation to the bigger energy players.

Notwithstanding such variation, overall it cannot be concluded that multinationals determined a market-based approach to EU energy security – this finding sitting uneasily with some of the recent work on international political economy outlined in Chapter 2. Indeed, where companies' did exert influence was in gaining backing from their respective national governments to secure long-term preferential deals with individual third-country producers on a bilateral basis. On the broader geopolitical aspects of energy security national champions commonly followed, more than they influenced the positions of their respective governments.

Energy companies mostly 'followed the oil' and were keen to keep out of the political challenges that beset producer states. Corporate Social Responsibility commitments did not have great impact on oil and gas companies' investment patterns. At the same time, a growing concern with 'resource nationalism' could be detected and companies' saw this phenomenon as linked in most cases to autocratic governance. Company representatives insisted that they now understood the 'stability' that was key to investors as being tied into long-term political and economic reform in producer states. This did at the margins encourage EU policy-makers to focus on rule of law issues in some countries: the 'export' of governance and regulatory rules directly pertinent to the energy sector was seen by companies as an important means of enhancing their own prospects in third-country markets. Companies did not though strongly relate their own interests to the question of whether EU foreign policies were supportive of or inimical to democratic reform in producer states. The democracy agenda was neither pursued at the behest of European energy companies, nor were the latter responsible for the *limits* to its implementation. Chapter 2 outlined the argument that multinationals have been primary players in the spread of 'low intensity' democracy; this book has not found significant evidence that EU energy security policies in the 2000s accorded to such an analytical framework.

The writing of this book closes as the Commission prepares a further strategic energy review, with the stated aim of finding ways of making EU energy security policies more effective. It does this against the background of growing concerns over energy security within member states' domestic political debates. The six elements of EU energy security outlined above demonstrate that some relatively fundamental aspects of energy strategy are still under design; that policies are being driven by internal and external dynamics that do not always push in the same direction; that in energy matters the EU remains unsure of its most effective source of international power; and that it remains unclear which actors should really be running the foreign-policy dimensions of energy security. Some actors express doubts even over whether the EU is an appropriate level at which to coordinate energy policies; in energy matters some implicitly pose the question of whether the EU is too large-scale for immediate national aims and too small-scale to contribute to broader multilateral coordination. The EU struggles to strike the correct balance between over- and under-reacting to the 'new energy paradigm'. European commissioners and ministers might claim that energy has returned to the 'heart of European cooperation', but firmly united, coherent and sustainable policy outputs remain elusive.

Notes

1 Introduction

1 H. Franssen, 'Oil Supply Security through 2010', in L. Bloomfield Jr. (ed.) *Global Market and National Interests: The New Geopolitics of Energy, Capital, and Information,* Washington, DC: Centre for Strategic and International Studies, 2002, p. 59.
2 CIEP, *Study on Energy Supply Security and Geopolitics,* The Hague: Clingendael International Energy Programme, January 2004, p. 45.
3 Financial Times, *Special Report: Energy,* 9 November 2007, p. 2. ONLINE. Available HTTP: http://www.ft.com/reports/energynov2007
4 N. Butler, 'European Energy Security', presentation at the International Institute for Strategic Studies, Geneva, 17 September 2005. ONLINE. Available HTTP: http://www.bp.com/genericarticle.do?categoyId = 98&contentId = 7010497
5 P. Isbell, 'La Dependencia Enerética y los Intereses de España', *Análisis del Real Instituto,* Madrid: Real Instituto Elcano, 3 March 2006, p. 5.
6 Commission of the European Communities, *European Energy and Transport Trends to 2030 – Update 2007,* Brussels: European Commission, 2007, p. 16.
7 K. Al-Rodhan and A. Cordesman, 'The Geopolitics of Energy: Geostrategic Risks and Economic Uncertainties', Washington, DC: Centre for Strategic and International Studies, 20 March 2006, p. 18.
8 Commission of the European Communities, *Green Paper: A European Strategy for Sustainable, Competitive and Secure Energy,* COM(2006) 105, Brussels: European Commission, 8 March 2006, Annex, pp. 19 and 24.
9 GMF, *Transatlantic Trends 2007,* Washington, DC: The German Marshall Fund of the United States, 2007.
10 Commission of the European Communities, *An Energy Policy for Europe,* COM (2007) 1, Brussels: European Commission, 10 January 2007.
11 Commission of the European Communities, *Green Paper: A European Strategy for Sustainable, Competitive and Secure Energy,* p. 3; and Commission of the European Communities, *An External Policy to Serve Europe's Energy Interests,* paper from the Commission/SG/HR for the European Council, Brussels: European Commission, 2006.
12 A. Missiroli, 'Disasters Past and Present: New Challenges for the EU', *Journal of European Integration* 28/5, 2006, 423–36.
13 One exception being J. Gault, 'EU Energy Security and the Periphery', in R. Dannreuther (ed.) *European Union Foreign and Security Policy: Towards a Neighbourhood Strategy,* London: Routledge, 2004, p. 172.

2 Concepts of energy security and EU foreign policy

1 CIEP, *Study on Energy Supply Security and Geopolitics,* The Hague: Clingendael International Energy Programme, January 2004.

2 P. Fusaro, 'The Future Importance of Oil: Geopolitical Lynchpin or Common Commodity', in L. Bloomfield Jr. (ed.) *Global Market and National Interests: The New Geopolitics of Energy, Capital, and Information,* Washington, DC: Centre for Strategic and International Studies, 2002.

3 J. Mitchell, K. Morita, N. Selley and J. Stern, *The New Economy of Oil: Impacts on Business, Geopolitics and Society,* London: Royal Institute for International Affairs, 2001, pp. 176, 179, 181 and 207.

4 J. Mitchell, 'A New Era for Oil Prices', *Chatham Rouse Report,* London: Royal Institute of International Affairs, August 2006, pp. 4–7.

5 D. Clarke, *The Battle for Barrels: Peak Oil Myths and World Oil Futures,* London: Profile Books, 2007.

6 James A. Baker III Institute for Public Policy, 'The Geopolitics of Natural Gas', *Baker Institute Study* 29, Houston: James A. Baker III Institute for Public Policy, Rice University, March 2005, p. 2.

7 P. Noël, 'Time to Challenge the Myths of Energy Security', *Financial Times,* 11 January 2008.

8 J. Mitchell, 'Energy Supply Security: Changes in Concepts', speech to the French Ministry of Economy, Finance and Industry, Paris, November 2000.

9 J. Nye, 'The Wrong Way of Thinking about Oil', *The Korea Herald,* 27 February 2006.

10 D. Yergin, 'Energy Security and Markets', in D. Goldwyn and J. Kalicki (eds) *Energy and Security: Toward a New Foreign Policy Strategy,* Washington, DC: Woodrow Wilson Center, 2005, p. 56.

11 J. Mitchell, 'Renewing Energy Security', *RIIA Working Paper,* London: Royal Institute of International Affairs, July 2002, pp. 4–5 and 23.

12 Ibid., p. 5.

13 CIEP, *Study on Energy Supply Security and Geopolitics,* pp. 24, 26 and 91.

14 A. Jaffe, 'The Outlook for Future Oil Supply from the Middle East and Price Implications', speech, Tokyo, 20 July 2005, available from the James Baker III Institute for Public Policy, Rice University, p. 9.

15 B. Mommer, *The Governance of International Oil: The Changing Rules of the Game,* Oxford: Oxford Institute for Energy Studies, WPM 26, 2000, p. ii.

16 P. Roberts, *The End of Oil: The Decline of the Petroleum Economy and the Rise of a New Energy Order,* London: Bloomsbury, 2005, p. 94.

17 C. Van der Linde, 'Energy in a Changing World', inaugural lecture as Professor of Geopolitics and Energy Management at the University of Groningen, *Clingendael Energy Papers* 11, The Hague: Clingendael Institute for International Relations, December 2005, pp. 6 and 13–14.

18 R. Armitage, L. Bloomfield Jr. and J. Kelly, 'Preserving US and Allied Interests in a New Era', in Bloomfield Jr. (ed.) *Global Market and National Interests,* p. 211.

19 D. Yergin, 'Ensuring Energy Security', *Foreign Affairs* 85/2, 2006, 69–82.

20 M. Leonard, *Divided World: The Struggle for Power in 2020,* London: Centre for European Reform, 2006.

21 P. Isbell, 'Revisiting Energy Security', *Análisis del Real Instituto,* Madrid: Real Instituto Elcano, 23 November 2007, p. 2.

22 CFR–James A. Baker III Institute for Public Policy, 'Strategic Energy Policy Challenges for the 21st Century', report of an Independent Task Force, Houston: James A. Baker III Institute for Public Policy, Rice University, and the Council on Foreign Relations, 2001, p. 29.

23 Yergin, 'Ensuring Energy Security', pp. 69–70.

24 J. Gault, 'EU Energy Security and the Periphery', in R. Dannreuther (ed.) *European Union Foreign and Security Policy: Towards a Neighbourhood Strategy,* London: Routledge, 2004, p. 170.

25 M. Humphreys, J. Sachs and J. Stiglitz, 'Introduction: What is the Problem with Natural Resource Wealth?' in M. Humphreys, J. Sachs and J. Stiglitz (eds) *Escaping the Resource Curse*, New York: Columbia University Press, 2007, pp. 11–13.
26 M. Ross, 'Does Oil Hinder Democracy?' *World Politics* 53/3, 2001, 325–61.
27 T. Friedman, 'The First Law of Petropolitics', *Foreign Policy*, May–June 2006.
28 W. Engdahl, *A Century of War: Anglo-American Oil Politics and the New World Order*, London: Pluto, 2004.
29 Jaffe, 'The Outlook for Future Oil Supply from the Middle East and Price Implications', p. 4.
30 CFR–James A. Baker III Institute for Public Policy, 'Strategic Energy Policy Challenges for the 21st Century', p. 30.
31 A. Hurrell, *On Global Order: Power, Values and the Constitution of International Society*, Oxford: Oxford University Press, 2007.
32 J. Gray, *Black Mass: Apocalyptic Religion and the Death of Utopia*, London: Penguin, 2008, pp. 4, 43 and 235.
33 CIEP, *Study on Energy Supply Security and Geopolitics*.
34 Gault, 'EU Energy Security and the Periphery', p. 170.
35 N. Elhefnawy, 'The Impending Oil Shock', *Survival* 50/2, 2008, 43.
36 Jaffe, 'The Outlook for Future Oil Supply from the Middle East and Price Implications', p. 12.
37 M. Kaldor, T. Karl and Y. Said, 'Introduction', in M. Kaldor, T. Karl and Y. Said (eds) *Oil Wars*, London: Pluto Press, 2007.
38 M. Ross, 'Blood Barrels: Why Oil Wealth Fuels Conflict', *Foreign Affairs* (87/3), 2008, 2–8.
39 J. Deutch, 'Security and Energy: Short-term Implications of a Long-term View', in B. Mossavar-Rahmani (ed.) *Thinking the Unthinkable*, proceedings of XIII Repsol YPF–Harvard Seminar on Energy Policy, 9–10 May 2003, p. 24.
40 For an overview of this lack of linkage, see R. Youngs, *International Democracy and the West: The Role of Governments, Civil Society and Multinationals*, Oxford: Oxford University Press, 2004, Ch. 2. Also, A. Walter, 'Do They Really Rule the World?', *New Political Economy* 3/2, 1998, 289.
41 Jaffe, 'The Outlook for Future Oil Supply from the Middle East and Price Implications', p. 6.
42 CFR–James A. Baker III Institute for Public Policy, 'Strategic Energy Policy Challenges for the 21st Century', p. 7.
43 W. Robinson, *Promoting Polyarchy*, Cambridge: Cambridge University Press, 1996; N. Chomsky, *Deterring Democracy*, London: Vintage, 1992; B. Gills, J. Rocamora and R. Wilson, 'Low Intensity Democracy', in B. Gills, J. Rocamora and R. Wilson (eds) *Low Intensity Democracy: Political Power in the New World Order*, London: Pluto Press, 1993; N. Chomsky, *World Orders, Old and New*, London: Pluto Press, 1997; and R. Cox, 'Global Restructuring: Making Sense of the Changing International Political Economy', in R. Stubbs and G. Underhill (eds) *Political Economy and the Changing Global Order*, Basingstoke: Palgrave Macmillan, 1994.
44 R. Blanton and S. Blanton, 'Human Rights and Foreign Direct Investment: A Two-Stage Analysis', *Business and Society* 45/4, 2006, 464–85.
45 Youngs, *International Democracy and the West*, Chaps 1 and 3.
46 P. Cerny, 'Political Agency in a Globalizing World: Toward a Structurational Approach', *European Journal of International Relations* 6/4, 2000, 435–63; C. Hay and B. Rosamond, 'Globalization, European Integration and the Discursive Construction of Economic Imperatives', *Journal of European Public Policy* 9/2, 2002, 147–67; and B. Rosamond, 'Babylon and On? Globalization and International Political Economy', *Review of International Political Economy* 10/4, 2003, 661–71.

47 M. Gritsch, 'The Nation-state and Economic Globalization: Soft Geo-politics and Increased State Autonomy?', *Review of International Political Economy* 12/1, 2005, 1–25.

48 A. Slaughter, *A New World Order*, Princeton: Princeton University Press, 2004, Chaps 1 and 2.

49 A. Stern, *Who Won the Oil Wars? Why Government Wage War for Oil Rights*, London: Collins and Brown, 2005, p. 20.

50 CIEP, *Study on Energy Supply Security and Geopolitics*, p. 89.

51 Van der Linde, 'Energy in a Changing World', pp. 15–16.

52 A. Young and J. Peterson, 'The EU and the New Trade Politics', *Journal of European Public Policy* 13/6, 2006, 795–814.

53 F. Schimmelfennig and U. Sedelmeier, 'Governance by Conditionality: EU Rule Transfer to the Candidate Countries of Central and Eastern Europe', *Journal of European Public Policy* 11/4, 2004, 661–79.

54 S. Lavenex, 'EU external governance in "wider Europe"', *Journal of European Public Policy* 11/4, 2004, 693

55 J. McCormick, *The European Superpower*, Basingstoke: Palgrave Macmillan, 2007, pp. 12, 32 and 174.

56 J. Neyer, 'The Deliberative Turn in Integration Theory', *Journal of European Public Policy* 13/5, 2006, 779–91.

57 A. Linklater, 'A European Civilising Process', in C. Hill and M. Smith, *International Relations and the European Union*, Oxford: Oxford University Press, 2005.

58 C. Hill and M. Smith, 'International Relations and the European Union: Themes and Issues', in Hill and Smith, *International Relations and the European Union*, p. 12.

59 Selected examples of this strand of thinking included T. Christiansen and B. Tonra, 'The Study of European Union Foreign' in T. Christiansen and B. Tonra (eds) *Rethinking European Union Foreign Policy,* Manchester: Manchester University Press, 2004; M. Smith, 'Toward a Theory of EU Foreign Policy Making: Multi-level Governance, Domestic Politics, and National Adaptation to Europe's Common Foreign and Security Policy', *Journal of European Public Policy*, 11, August, 2004, 740–58; J. Checkel, 'Why Comply? Social Learning and European Identity Change', *International Organization* 55/3, Summer 2001, 553–88; R. Ginsberg, *The European Union in International Politics: Baptism by Fire*, Lanham, MD: Rowman and Littlefield, 2001; and B. Rosamond, 'Conceptualizing the EU Model of Governance in World Politics', *European Foreign Affairs Review* 10/4, 2005, 463–78.

60 M. Smith, 'Institutionalization, Policy Adaptation and European Foreign Policy Cooperation', *European Journal of International Relations* 10/1, 2004, 95–136.

61 B. White, *Understanding European Foreign Policy*, Basingstoke: Palgrave Macmillan, 2001.

62 B. Kohler-Koch and B. Rittberger, 'The "Governance Turn" in EU Studies', *Journal of Common Market Studies* 44, Annual Review, 2006, 27–49.

63 S. Croft, J. Howarth, E. Krahmann, T. Terriff and M. Webber, 'The Governance of European Security', *Review of International Studies* 30, 2004, 3–26.

64 E. Kirchner, 'The Challenge of European Union Security Governance', *Journal of Common Market Studies* 44/5, 2006, 947–68.

65 M. Koenig-Archibugi, 'International Governance as New *Raison d'État*? The Case of the EU Common Foreign and Security Policy', *European Journal of International Relations* 10/2, 2004, 147–88.

66 S. Collard-Wexler, 'Integration under Anarchy: Neorealism and the European Union', *European Journal of International Relations* 1273, 2006, 397–432.

67 Council of the European Union, *A Secure Europe in a Better World: European Security Strategy*, Brussels: European Council, 12 December 2003, p. 12.

68 I. Manners, 'Normative Power Europe Reconsidered: Beyond the Crossroads', *Journal of European Public Policy* 13/2, 2006, 182–99.

69 A. Hyde-Price, '"Normative" Power Europe: A Realist Critique', *Journal of European Public Policy* 13/2, 2006, 217–34. Kupchan backs up this view, in C. Kupchan, 'The Rise of Europe, America's Changing Internationalism, and the End of U.S. Primacy', *Political Science Quarterly* 118/2, Summer, 2003.

70 European Parliament, 'The Future of the European Security Strategy: Towards a White Book for Defence?', paper at the workshop organised by the EP Sub-Committee on Security and Defence, Brussels, 6 March 2008.

71 R. Cooper, *The Breaking of Nations*, Boston: Atlantic Monthly Press, 2003, pp. 62, 78 and 160.

72 B. Hettne and F. Söderbaum, 'Civilian Power or Soft Imperialism? The EU as a Global Actor and the Role of Interregionalism', *European Foreign Affairs Review* 10/4, 2005, 535–52; and M. Farrell, 'A Triumph of Realism over Idealism? Cooperation between the European Union and Africa', *Journal of European Integration* 27/3, 2005.

73 J. Zielonka, *Europe as Empire: The Nature of the Enlarged European Union*, Oxford: Oxford University Press, 2006, pp. 148 and 160.

74 From the 17 January 2005 edition, quoted in J. Zielonka, 'Europe as a Global Actor: Empire by Example?', *International Affairs* 84/3, 2008, 471–84.

75 A. Hyde-Price, 'A "Tragic Actor?" A Realist Perspective on "Ethical Power Europe"', *International Affairs* 84/1, 2008, 39–44.

76 A. Magen, 'Transformative Engagement through Law: The Acquis Communitaire as an Instrument of EU External Influence', *European Journal of Law Reform* 9/3, 2007, 361–92.

77 E. Barbé et al., 'Exporting Rules to the Neighbourhood? A Framework for the Analysis of Emerging Patterns of Europeanisation, Internationalisation and Coordination between the EU and its Neighbours', paper presented at the EUPROX seminar 'Interlocking Dimensions of European Security Neighbourhood: Energy, Borders and Conflict Management', Barcelona, 9 October 2007, p. 5.

78 V. Dimier, 'Constructing Conditionality: The Bureaucratization of EC Development Aid', *European Foreign Affairs Review* 11/2, 2006, 263–80.

79 Van der Linde, 'Energy in a Changing World', pp. 15–16.

80 C. Layne, 'The Unipolar Illusion Revisited: The Coming of the United States' Unipolar Moment', *International Security* 31/2, 2006, 7–41.

81 A. Mañé-Estrada, 'European Energy Security: Towards the Creation of the Geo-energy Space', *Energy Policy* 34/18, 3773–86.

82 D. Stokes, 'Blood for Oil? Global Capital, Counter-insurgency and the Dual Logic of American Energy Security', *Review of International Studies* 33/2, 2007, 245–64.

83 Including one notable 'constructivist' interpretation of the European Security and Defence Policy: C. Meyer, 'Convergence Towards a European Strategic Culture? A Constructivist Framework for Explaining Changing Norms', *European Journal of International Relations* 11/4, 2005, 523–49.

84 S. Duke and H. Ojanen, 'Bridging Internal and External Security: Lessons from the European Security and Defence Policy', *Journal of European Integration* 28/5, 477–94.

85 One example being J. Howarth, *Security and Defence Policy in Europe*, Basingstoke: Palgrave Macmillan, p. 248.

86 R. Whitman, 'Road Map for a Route march? (De-)civilianizing through the EU's Security Strategy', *European Foreign Affairs Review* 11/1, 2006, 1–15.

87 Smith, in conclusions in M. Smith, 'Toward a Theory of EU Foreign Policy Making: Multi-level Governance, Domestic Politics, and National Adaptation to Europe's Common Foreign and Security Policy', *Journal of European Public Policy* 11, August, 2004, and outlined in the new book O. Elgström and M. Smith (eds) *The European Union's Roles in International Politics. Concepts and Analysis*, London: Routledge, 2006.

88 CIEP, *Study on Energy Supply Security and Geopolitics*, p. 15.
89 L. Dobson, 'Normative Theory and Europe', *International Affairs* 82/3, 2006, 511–23.
90 T. Garton Ash, *Free World: Why a Crisis of the West Reveals the Opportunity of Our Time*, London: Penguin Books, 2005, pp. 135 and 151.

3 The policy response

1 Council of the European Union, *A Secure Europe in a Better World: European Security Strategy*, Brussels: European Council, 12 December 2003.
2 C. Grant, *Europe's Blurred Boundaries: Rethinking Enlargement and Neighbourhood Policy*, London: Centre for European Reform, 2006, p. 65.
3 Commission of the European Communities, *Green Paper: A European Strategy for Sustainable, Competitive and Secure Energy*, COM(2006) 105, 8 March 2006, p. 4.
4 Ibid., pp. 15–20.
5 Council of the European Union, *Presidency Conclusions 23–24 March 2006* (7775/1/06 REV 1), Brussels: European Council, 18 May 2006, p. 16, para. 49.
6 Commission of the European Communities, *An External Policy to Serve Europe's Energy Interests,* paper from the Commission/SG/HR for the European Council, Brussels: European Commission, 2006.
7 Benelux Position Paper, *External Energy Policy for Europe*, February 2007, mimeo.
8 B. Ferrero-Waldner, 'The European Neighbourhood Policy: The EU's Newest Foreign Policy Instrument', *European Foreign Affairs Review* 11/2, 2006, 139–42.
9 R. Dannreuther, 'Developing the Alternative to Enlargement: The European Neighbourhood Policy', *European Foreign Affairs Review* 11/2, 2006, 183–201.
10 See B. Ferrero-Waldner, opening speech, European Neighbourhood Policy Conference, Brussels, 3 September 2007. ONLINE. Available HTTP: http://europa.eu/rapid/pressReleasesAction.do?reference = SPEECH/07/500
11 European Commission Eurobarometer Unit, *Eurobarometer Survey*, Brussels: European Commission, March 2007.
12 J. M. Barroso, opening speech at the External Energy Policy Conference, Brussels, 20 November 2006.
13 F. Barabaso, cited in *Platts EU Energy*, 23 March 2007.
14 *Platts EU Energy*, 20 October 2006.
15 Commission of the European Communities, *An Energy Policy for Europe*, COM (2007) 1, Brussels: European Commission, 10 January 2007, pp. 18–19.
16 Council of the European Union, *Presidency Conclusions, March 8/9 2007, European Council Action Plan (2007–2009): Energy Policy for Europe*, Brussels: European Council, 2 May 2007.
17 The Dutch Energy Council, *Energised Foreign Policy: Security of Energy Supply as a Key Objective*, The Hague: The Dutch Energy Council, December 2005, p. 39.
18 FCO, *UK International Priorities. A Strategy for the FCO*, Foreign Policy White Paper presented to Parliament by the Secretary of State for Foreign and Commonwealth Affairs by Command of Her Majesty, London: Foreign and Commonwealth Office, December 2003.
19 DTI, *Our Energy Future: Creating a Low Carbon Economy. Energy White Paper,* London: Department for Business, Enterprise and Regulatory Reform, 25 February 2003, p. 79.
20 FCO–DTI–DEFRA–SEPN, *UK International Priorities: The Energy Strategy*, London: Foreign and Commonwealth Office, Department for Business, Enterprise and Regulatory Reform, Department for Environment, Food and Rural Affairs and Sustainable Energy Policy Network, 2004, p. 5 and p. 28.
21 DTI, *Meeting the Energy Challenge: A White Paper on Energy*, London: Department for Business, Enterprise and Regulatory Reform, May 2007.

22 European Parliament, *Draft Report on Towards a Common European Foreign Policy on Energy*, Brussels: European Parliament, 22 May 2007.
23 W. Patterson, 'Loft Insulation as Foreign Policy', *The World Today* 63/7, July 2007, 7–18.
24 J. Gault, 'European Energy Security: Balancing Priorities', *FRIDE Comment*, Madrid: Fundación para las Relaciones Internacionales y el Diálogo Exterior, May 2007. ONLINE. Available HTTP: www.fride.org
25 D. Miliband, 'New Diplomacy: Challenges for Foreign Policy', speech at the Royal Institute for International Affairs, London, 9 July 2007.
26 J. Henningsen, 'Rising to the Energy Challenge: Key Elements for an Effective EU Strategy', *Issue paper* 51, Brussels: European Policy Centre, December 2006, p. 11.
27 *Platts EU Energy*, 25 January 2008, p. 4.
28 *The Economist*, 19 January 2008, p. 30.
29 M. Renner, 'The New Geopolitics of Oil', *Development* 49/3, 2006, 56–63.
30 Keynote address to Chatham House, London, 8 February 2008. ONLINE. Available HTTP: http://www.cfr.org/publication/15701/keynote_address_to_chatham_house _by_he_abdalla_salem_elbari.html
31 C. Egenhofer, 'Integrating Security of Supply, Market Liberalisation and Climate Change', in M. Emerson (ed.) *Readings in European Security* 4, Brussels: Centre for European Policy Studies, 2007, p. 93.
32 C. Pascual, 'The Geopolitics of Energy: From Security to Survival', Washington, DC: Brookings Institute, January 2008.
33 D. Keohane, 'The Absent Friend: EU Foreign Policy and Counter-terrorism', *Journal of Common Market Studies* 46/1, 2008, 125–46.
34 Council of the European Union, *Climate Change and International Security 7249/ 08,* paper from the High Representative and the European Commission to the European Council, Brussels: European Council, 3 March 2008.
35 Commission of the European Communities, *Green Paper: A European Strategy for Sustainable, Competitive and Secure Energy*, COM(2006) 105, Brussels: European Commission, 8 March 2006, pp. 15–20.
36 Commission of the European Communities, *An External Policy to Serve Europe's Energy Interests*, paper from the Commission/SG/HR for the European Council, Brussels: European Commission, 2006.
37 Henningson, 'Rising to the Energy Challenge: Key Elements for an Effective EU Strategy', p. 12.
38 CEPS, 'G8 Chair's Summary', G8 Summit Saint Petersburg, 17 July 2006 in *CEPS European Neighbourhood Watch* 18, Brussels: Centre for European Policy Studies, July 2006, p. 10.
39 A. Konoplyanik, 'Energy Charter: The Key to International Energy Security', *Petroleum Economist*, February 2006, pp. 19–20.
40 Barroso, opening speech at the External Energy Policy Conference.
41 J. Gault, 'EU Energy Security and the Periphery', in R. Dannreuther (ed.) *European Union Foreign and Security Policy: Towards a Neighbourhood Strategy*, London: Routledge, 2004, p. 177.
42 J. Lamy, 'Que Signifie Relancer la Politique Énergétique Européenne?', *Revue du marché común et de l'Union européenne* 506, March 2007, 141–45.
43 DTI, 25 February 2003, *Meeting the Energy Challenge: A White Paper on Energy*, p. 77.
44 Czech Ministry of Industry and Trade, *State Energy Policy of the Czech Republic 2004*, approved by Government Decision no. 211 of 10 March 2004, Prague: Czech Ministry of Industry and Trade, 2004.
45 Polish Ministry of Economy, *Guidelines for Energy Policy of Poland until 2020*, document approved by the Council of Ministers on 22 February 2000, Warsaw: Polish Ministry of Economy, 2000.

46 Baltic Council of Ministers' Energy Committee, *Baltic Energy Strategy 1999*, Vilnius, Riga, Tallinn: Baltic Council of Ministers' Energy Committee, 1999.
47 S. Vos, 'Europe's Infant Energy Strategy Looks Muddled and Unclear', *Europe's World* 4, Autumn 2006, 133–37.
48 French Ministry of the Economy, Industry and Employment, 'Commentaires de la France sur les propositions du Livre vert', Paris: French Ministry of the Economy, Industry and Employment, March 2006. ONLINE. Available HTTP: www.industrie.gouv.fr/energie
49 Quoted in *Financial Times*, 4 September 2007.
50 Dutch Ministry of Foreign Affairs and Economy Ministry, *Security of Energy Supply and Foreign Policy*, The Hague: Dutch Ministry of Foreign Affairs and Economy Ministry, 19 May 2006.
51 *BBC Panorama*, 5 November 2006.
52 *EU Observer*, 24 August 2007.
53 Ibid., 3 December 2007.
54 French Ministry of the Economy, Industry and Employment, *French Memorandum for Revitalising European Energy Policy with a view to Sustainable Development*, Paris: French Ministry of the Economy, Industry and Employment, 17 January 2006, reproduced on Euractiv.com
55 French Ministry of the Economy, Industry and Employment, 'Commentaires de la France sur les propositions du Livre vert', p. 1.
56 *Financial Times*, 12 February 2007.
57 *Eurasia Daily Monitor*, 14 May 2007.
58 B. Bot, 'Realistic Multilateralism in the 21st Century: The Netherlands and the EU between International Law, Politics and Power', speech at Roosevelt Academy, Middelburg, 29 January 2007.
59 Conservative Party, 'An Unquiet World', submission to the Shadow Cabinet, London: Conservative Party, July 2007, p. 165.
60 'The EU: Ending Doubts on Energy and Climate Change', speech at the Energy Security, Environment and Development: Three Issues for the G8 Conference, Institut Français des Relations Internationales (IFRI), Brussels, 24 May 2007, (emphasis added).
61 K. Barysch, 'Reciprocity will not Secure Europe's Energy', *CER Bulletin* 55, London: Centre for European Reform, August–September 2007.
62 *Platts EU Energy*, 7 March 2008, p. 3.
63 J. Solana, address to the EU External Energy Policy Conference, Brussels, 20 November 2006.
64 J. Stern, 'Security of European Natural Gas Supplies: The Impact of Import Dependence and Liberalization', *RIIA Working Paper*, London: Royal Institute of International Affairs, July 2002, p. 4.
65 G. Austin and D. Bochkarev, 'Energy Sovereignty and Security: Restoring Confidence in a Cooperation International System', in G. Austin and M. Schellekens-Gaiffe (eds) *Energy and Conflict Prevention*, Brussels: Madariaga European Foundation, 2007, p. 36.
66 M. Klare, *Blood and Oil*, London: Penguin, 2004, p. 7.
67 Ibid., pp. 71 and 174.
68 S. Kern, 'How the Demand for Oil Drives American Foreign Policy', *Análisis del Real Instituto*, Madrid: Real Instituto Elcano, 23 June 2006.
69 L. Kleveman, *The New Great Game: Blood and Oil in Central Asia*, London: Atlantic Books, 2004, pp. xix and 263.
70 W. Engdahl, *A Century of War: Anglo-American Oil Politics and the New World Order*, London: Pluto, 2004, p. 248.
71 D. Goldwyn and J. Kalicki, 'Introduction: The Need to Integrate Energy and Foreign Policy', in D. Goldwyn and J. Kalicki, *Energy and Security: Toward a*

New Foreign Policy Strategy, Washington, DC: Woodrow Wilson Center, 2005, p. 14.

72 S. Biscop, 'The ABC of European Union Security Strategy: Ambition, Benchmark, Culture', *Egmont Paper* 16, Brussels: Egmont Institute, October 2007.

73 J. Howarth, *Security and Defence Policy in the European Union*, Basingstoke: Palgrave Macmillan, 2007, p. 107.

74 A. Bailes, 'The EU and a "Better World": What Role for the European Security and Defence Policy?', *International Affairs* 84/1, 2008, 115–30.

75 L. Fox, 'Energy Security and Military Structures', speech at Chatham House, London, 22 May 2006.

76 Dutch Ministry of Foreign Affairs and Economy Ministry, *Security of Energy Supply and Foreign Policy*, p. 18.

77 A. Monaghan, 'Energy Security: NATO's Limited, Complementary Role', *Research Paper* 36, Rome: NATO Defence College, May 2008, p. 9.

78 B. Ferrero-Waldner, opening address at the External Energy Policy Conference, Brussels, 20 November 2006.

79 B. Ferrero-Waldner, 'The European Neighbourhood Policy: The EU's Newest Foreign Policy Instrument', *European Foreign Affairs Review* 11/2, 2006, 139–42.

80 E. Landaburu, European Parliament hearing on 'Towards a Common European Foreign Policy on Energy', Brussels, 28 February 2007.

81 FCO, *Good Governance in the Energy Sector,* London: Foreign and Common Wealth Office. ONLINE. Available HTTP: http://www.fco.gov.uk/servlet/Front?pagename = OpenMarket/Xcelerate/ShowPage&c

82 DTI, 'Joint Energy Security of Supply Working Group (JESS)', Sixth Report, London: Department for Business, Enterprise and Regulatory Reform, April 2006, p. 12.

83 FCO–DTI–DEFRA–SEPN, *UK International Priorities: The Energy Strategy*, p. 14.

84 Benelux Position Paper, *External Energy Policy for Europe.*

85 F. Steinmeier, 'Interaction and Integration', *Internationale Politik* 8/1, Spring 2007.

86 Solana, address to the EU External Energy Policy Conference.

87 See, for example, S. Wood, 'Energy and Democracy: The European Union's Challenge', *Current History* 107/707, 133–38.

88 I. Kolstrad and A. Wiig, 'Transparency in Oil Rich Economies', *U4* 2, Bergen: Chr. Michelsen Institute, 2007, p. 19.

89 DTI, *Energy Act 2004, Second Annual Report to Parliament on the Security of Gas and Electricity Supply in Great Britain by the Secretary of State for Trade and Industry*, London: Department for Business, Enterprise and Regulatory Reform, 11 July 2006, p. 18.

4 The Middle East

1 BP, *Statistical Review of World Energy 2007*, London: British Petroleum, 2007, p. 7.

2 Ibid., p. 30.

3 EIA, *US National Oil and Gas Imports by Country*, Washington, DC: Energy Information Administration, 2007. ONLINE. Available www.eia.doe.gov

4 Commission of the European Communities, *European Energy and Transport Trends to 2030 – Update 2007,* Brussels: European Commission, 2007, p. 27.

5 *Financial Times*, 19 April 2007.

6 *Financial Times*, 16 May 2007.

7 P. Roberts, *The End of Oil: The Decline of the Petroleum Economy and the Rise of a New Energy Order*, London: Bloomsbury, 2005, p. 257.

8 G. Nonneman, 'EU–GCC Relations: Dynamics, Patterns and Perspectives', *GRC Working Paper*, Dubai: Gulf Research Centre, June 2006, p. 37.

9 F. Halliday, *100 Myths about the Middle East*, London: Saqi, 2005, p. 124.

10 J. Barnes and A. Jaffe, 'The Persian Gulf and the Geopolitics of Oil', *Survival* 48/1, 2006, 143–62.

11 J. West, 'Saudi Arabia, Iraq, and the Gulf', in D. Goldwyn and J. Kalicki (eds) *Energy and Security: Toward a New Foreign Policy Strategy*, Washington, DC: Woodrow Wilson Center, 2005.

12 All this in G. Nonneman, 'Political Reform in the Gulf Monarchies: From Liberalisation to Democratisation? A Comparative Perspective', *Durham Middle East Papers*, Sir William Luce Fellowship Paper 6, Durham: Institute for Middle Eastern and Islamic Studies, August 2006.

13 A. Ehteshami and S. Wright, 'Political Change in the Arab Oil Monarchies: From Liberalisation to Enfranchisement', *International Affairs* 83/5, 2007, p. 916.

14 M. Al-Rasheed, 'Circles of Power: Royals and Society in Saudi Arabia', in P. Aarts and G. Nonneman (eds) *Saudi Arabia in the Balance: Political Economy, Society, Foreign Affairs*, London: Hurst and Company, 2005, pp. 201 and 208; I. Glosemeyer, 'Checks, Balances and Transformation in the Saudi Political System', in ibid., p. 231.

15 A. Hamzawy, 'The Saudi Labyrinth: Evaluating the Current Political Opening', *Carnegie Working Paper* 68, Washington, DC: Carnegie Endowment for International Peace, April 2006, p. 6.

16 I. Glosemeyer, 'Checks, Balances and Transformation in the Saudi Political System', in Aarts and Nonneman, *Saudi Arabia in the Balance: Political Economy, Society, Foreign Affairs*, p. 224.

17 A. Sager, 'Political Opposition in Saudi Arabia', in Aarts and Nonneman, *Saudi Arabia in the Balance: Political Economy, Society, Foreign Affairs*, p. 239.

18 I. Rutledge, *Addicted to Oil: America's Relentless Drive for Energy Security*, London: I.B. Tauris, 2006, p. 190.

19 T. Niblock, *Saudi Arabia: Power, Legitimacy and Survival*, London: Routledge, 2006, p. 5.

20 Glosemeyer, 'Checks, Balances and Transformation in the Saudi Political System', p. 233.

21 G. Luciani, 'Arab States: Oil Resources and Transparency', *Arab Reform Bulletin* 6/2, Washington, DC: Carnegie Endowment for International Peace, March 2008, p. 7.

22 A. Mañé Estrada, 'Argelia: ¿Retorno al Nacionalismo Energético?' *Aálisis del Real Instituto*, Madrid: Real Instituto Elcano, September 2006, p. 5.

23 Commission of the European Communities, *Commission Staff Working Document – Annex to the Green Paper, A European Strategy for Sustainable, Competitive and secure Energy*, SEC(2006), 317/2, Brussels: European Commission, 8 March 2006, p. 43.

24 Council of the European Union, *8th Euro-Mediterranean Conference of Ministers of Foreign Affairs, Tampere, 27–28 November 2006 – 'Tampere Conclusions'*, Brussels: European Council, 30 November 2006.

25 ENPI, *Regional Strategy Paper (2007–2103) and Regional Indicative Programme (2007–2010) for the Euro-Mediterranean Partnership*, Brussels: European Neighbourhood and Partnership Instrument, pp. 31–32.

26 *Platts EU Energy*, 30 November 2007, p. 13.

27 *Platts EU Energy*, 11 January 2008, p. 3.

28 Commission of the European Communities, *A Strong European Neighbourhood Policy*, COM(2007) 774, Brussels: European Commission, 5 December 2007.

29 ENPI, *Regional Strategy Paper (2007–2103) and Regional Indicative Programme (2007–2010) for the Euro-Mediterranean Partnership*, p. 55.

30 OECD Statistics, DAC Database, www.oecd.org/statsitics

31 AECI, *La Agencia Española de Cooperación Internacional en Cifras*, Madrid: Agencia Española de Cooperación Internacional, 2007, pp. 5 and 11.

32 *El País*, 5 February 2008.
33 Z. Baran, 'PESC y Seguridad de los Suministros Energéticos', *Política Exterior* 177, May–June 2007, p. 150.
34 'Press Conference at the European Council Summit in Brussels, 13 March 2008', in *CEPS Neighbourhood Watch* 36, Brussels: Centre for European Policy Studies, March 2008, p. 2.
35 G. Joffé, 'The European Union, Democracy and Counter-Terrorism in the Maghreb', *Journal of Common Market Studies* 46/1, 2008, 147–71.
36 C. Browning and P. Joenniemi, 'Geostrategies of the European Neighbourhood Policy', *DIIS Working Paper* 2007/9, Copenhagen: Danish Institute for International Studies, 2007.
37 *El País*, 30 July 2007.
38 *Global Insight Daily Analysis*, 21 September 2007.
39 *Platts EU Energy*, 8 February 2008, p. 18.
40 J. Farés and F. Pérez, 'España en la Génesis de una Nueva Política Europea de Energía', *Working Paper*, Barcelona: Observatorio de Política Exterior Europea, Universidad Autónoma de Barcelona, March 2008, p. 4.
41 *El País*, 18 December 2007.
42 L. Martinez, 'European Union's Exportation of Democratic Norms: The Case of North Africa', in Z. Laïdi (ed.) *European Union Foreign Policy in a Globalized World: Normative Power and Social Preferences*, London: Routledge, 2008, p. 131.
43 A. Baabood and G. Edwards, 'Reinforcing Ambivalence: The Interaction of Gulf States and the European Union', *European Foreign Affairs Review* 12/3, 2007, 537–54.
44 C. Ungar, *House of Bush, House of Saud*, London: Gibson Square, 2007, 4th edition, p. 261.
45 R. Bronsen, *Thicker than Oil: America's Uneasy Partnership with Saudi Arabia*, Oxford: Oxford University Press, 2006, p. 251.
46 Nonneman, 'Political Reform in the Gulf Monarchies: From Liberalisation to Democratisation? A Comparative Perspective', June 2006, p. 14. See also his article of same title in the *International Spectator* 3, 2006, 1–16.
47 A. Echagüe, 'The European Union and the Gulf Cooperation Council', *FRIDE Working Paper* 39, Madrid: Fundación para las Relaciones Internacionales y el Diálogo Exterior, May 2007.
48 G. Luciani, 'The Economics and Politics of the "Dire Straits"', *GRC Security and Terrorism Research Bulletin 6*, Dubai: Gulf Research Centre, August 2007, p. 15.
49 Echagüe, 'The European Union and the Gulf Cooperation Council'.
50 C. Koch, 'GCC–EU Relations: The News Again is "No News"', *GCC–EU Research Bulletin 5*, Dubai: Gulf Research Centre, July 2006, p. 3.
51 *Gulf Times*, 17 April 2008.
52 Nonneman, 'Political Reform in the Gulf Monarchies: From Liberalisation to Democratisation? A Comparative Perspective', p. 20.
53 J. Heliot, 'France and the Arabian Gulf', *GCC–EU Research Bulletin 5*, Dubai: Gulf Research Centre, July 2006, p. 12.
54 Baabood and Edwards, 'Reinforcing Ambivalence: The Interaction of Gulf States and the European Union', p. 549.
55 R. Aliboni, 'Europe's Role in the Gulf: A Transatlantic Perspective', *GRC Gulf Paper*, Dubai: Gulf Research Centre, August 2006, p. 8.
56 GRC, *The GCC Yearbook 2006*, Dubai: Gulf Research Centre, 2006.
57 *Financial Times*, 28–29 October 2006, p. 9.
58 For more on EU–Iran relations in the late 1990s see R. Youngs, *Europe and the Middle East: In the Shadow of September 11*, Boulder: Lynne Reinner, 2006, Ch. 3.

59 A. Gheissari and V. Nasr, *Democracy in Iran: History and the Quest for Liberty*, Oxford: Oxford University Press, 2006, p. 136.
60 *Financial Times*, 20 December 2006.
61 *Financial Times*, 6 March 2007.
62 Italian Ministry of Foreign Affairs, *Energy*. ONLINE. Available HTTP: http://www.esteri.it/MAE/EN/Politica_Estera/Temi_Globali/Energia/
63 *EU Energy*, 4 May 2007.
64 *Financial Times*, 14 February 2007.
65 *Energy Economist*, 1 April 2007.
66 Gheissari and Nasr, *Democracy in Iran: History and the Quest for Liberty*, pp. 142–44.
67 *EU Energy*, 6 April 2007.
68 *The Economist, Special Report on Iran*, London: *The Economist*, 21 July 2007, p. 6.
69 *New Europe*, 7 April 2008.
70 *EU Observer*, 17 September 2007.
71 *Platts EU Energy*, 16 May 2008, p.28
72 *New Europe*, 4 January 2008.
73 *The Economist*, 2 February 2008, p. 30.
74 *The Economist,* 22 March 2008, p. 47.
75 Rutledge, *Addicted to Oil: America's Relentless Drive for Energy Security*, p. 177.
76 L. Kleveman, *The New Great Game: Blood and Oil in Central Asia*, London: Atlantic Books, 2004, p. 262.
77 V. Marcel, 'Total in Iraq', *Policy brief*, Washington, DC: Brookings Institution, August 2003.
78 For one UK account revealing these points, see H. Synott, *Bad Days in Baghdad: My Turbulent Time as Britain's Man in Southern Iraq*, London: I.B. Tauris, 2008, pp. 46, 148 and 162.
79 N. Brown, A. Hamzawy, M. Ottaway, K. Sadjadpour and P. Salem, *The New Middle East,* Washington, DC: Carnegie Endowment for International Peace, 2008, p. 5.
80 *The Economist*, 19 January 2008, p. 36.
81 *Platts EU Energy*, 8 February 2008, p. 32.
82 Y. Said, 'Political Dynamics in Iraq within the Context of the Surge', submission to the US Senate's Foreign Relations Committee, 2 April 2008, p. 29.

5 Russia

1 A. Andrés, *Russia and Europe: Mutual Dependence in the Energy Sector, Working Paper* 2007/9, Madrid: Real Instituto Elcano, 2007, p.16; and EU–Russia Centre, *The Bilateral Relations of Member States with Russia*, Brussels: EU–Russia Centre, January 2008.
2 EIA, *US Oil Imports by Country,* Washington, DC: Energy Information Administration, 2007. ONLINE. Available HTTP: www.eia.doe.gov
3 EU–Russia Energy Dialogue, *Fifth Progress Report*, presented by Russian Minister of Industry Victor Khristenko and European Commission Director-General François Lamoureux, Moscow/Brussels, November 2004, p. 2.
4 D. Johnson, 'EU–Russia Energy Links', in D. Johnson and P. Robinson (eds) *Perspectives on EU–Russia Relations*, London: Routledge, 2005, pp. 189–90.
5 EU–Russia Energy Dialogue, *Sixth Progress Report*, presented by Russian Minister of Industry Victor Khristenko and European Commission Director-General François Lamoureux, Moscow/Brussels, October 2005, p. 2.
6 M. Emerson, 'From an Awkward Partnership to a Greater Europe? A European Perspective', in M. Emerson, I. Kobrinskaya and E. Rumer, 'Russia and the West', *Working Paper* 16, Brussels: Centre for European Policy Studies, September 2004, p. 2.

7 CEPS, 'European Commission Approves Terms for Negotiating New EU–Russia Agreement', press release, 3 July 2006, in *CEPS European Neighbourhood Watch* 18, Brussels: Centre for European Policy Studies, July 2006, p. 8.

8 From M. Emerson et al., 'A New Agreement between the EU and Russia: Why, What and When?', *CEPS Policy Brief* 103, Brussels: Centre for European Policy Studies, May 2006.

9 *El País*, 10 November 2006.

10 *New Europe*, 24 March 2008.

11 *WPS Russia Media Monitoring Agency*, 29 November 2006.

12 EU–Russia Energy Dialogue, *Seventh Progress Report*, presented by Russian Minister of Industry Victor Khristenko and European Commissioner for Energy Andris Piebalgs, Moscow/Brussels, November 2006.

13 M. Vahl, 'A Privileged Partnership? EU–Russian Relations in a Comparative Perspective', *Working Paper* 2006/3, Copenhagen: Danish Institute for International Studies, 2006, pp. 9, 13 and. 25.

14 Ibid., p. 17.

15 Interview in *Die Welt*, 25 January 2007, reproduced in *CEPS European Neighbourhood Watch* 23, Brussels: Centre for European Policy Studies, January 2007, pp. 4–6.

16 *Eurasia Daily Monitor*, 16 March 2007.

17 *The Economist*, 14 April 2007, p. 29.

18 *New Europe*, 12 January 2008.

19 Andrés, *Russia and Europe*, p. 18.

20 *Agence France Presse*, 5 December 2006.

21 *EUObserver*, 26 February 2007.

22 *Agence Europe*, 21 September 2007.

23 *Dow Jones International News*, 24 May 2007.

24 On these points, see transcript of the press conference following the Samara summit, reprinted in *CEPS Neighbourhood Watch* 27, Brussels: Centre for European Policy Studies, May 2007.

25 Quoted in *The Economist*, 1 September 2007, p. 23.

26 *El País*, 4 October 2007.

27 M. Leonard and N.Popescu, *A Power Audit of EU–Russia Relations*, London: European Council on Foreign Relations, 2007 p. 20.

28 Ibid., p. 16.

29 EIU, *Country Monitor*, London: The Economist Intelligence Unit, 24 September 2007.

30 For summit statement and leaders' press conference, see *CEPS European Neighbourhood Watch* 31, Brussels: Centre for European Policy Studies, October 2007, pp. 4–7.

31 S. Hanke and J. De Jong, *Energy as a Bond: Relations with Russia in the European and Dutch Context*, The Hague: Clingendael Institute for International Relations, 2007, p. 62.

32 *Financial Times*, 7 November 2007.

33 M. Emerson, 'Time to Think of a Strategic Bargain with Russia', *Policy Brief* 160, Brussels: Centre for European Policy Studies, May 2008, p. 4.

34 J. Sherr, 'Energy Security: At Last, A Response from the EU', *UK Defence Academy* 07/10, March 2007, p. 4.

35 *New Europe*, 11 February 2008.

36 *New Europe*, 5 February 2008.

37 *European Voice*, 27 March–2 April 2008, p. 9.

38 V. Milov, 'The Use of Energy as a Political Tool', *The EU–Russia Review* 1, Brussels: EU–Russia Centre, May 2006, p. 20.

39 Quoted in ibid., p. 18

40 EU–Russia Energy Dialogue, 'The Energy Dialogue EU–Russia', presentation of Christian Cleutinx, Director, European Commission Coordinator of the EU–Russia Energy Dialogue, Luxembourg, October 2005.
41 C. Maynes, 'A Soft Power Tool-kit for Dealing with Russia', *Europe's World* 3, Summer 2006, p. 22.
42 D. Johnson, 'EU–Russia Energy Links', in Johnson and Robinson, *Perspectives on EU–Russia Relations*, p. 183.
43 A. Monaghan and L. Montanaro-Jankovski, 'EU–Russia Energy Relations: The Need for Active Engagement', *EPC Issue Paper* 45, Brussels: European Policy Centre, p. 21.
44 *The Economist*, 25 August 2007, p. 27.
45 K. Kausch, 'Europe and Russia, beyond Energy', *FRIDE Working Paper* 33, Madrid: Fundación para las Relaciones Internacionales y el Diálogo Exterior, March 2007, p. 5.
46 *The Economist*, 1 March 2008, p. 26.
47 *The Economist*, 15 July 2006, p. 23.
48 *Eurasia Daily Monitor*, 30 June 2008, p.2
49 R. Lyne, 'Russia at the Crossroads: Again?', *The EU–Russia Review*, Brussels: EU–Russia Centre, May 2006, p. 9.
50 FCO–DTI–DEFRA–SEPN, *UK International Priorities: The Energy Strategy*, London: Foreign and Commonwealth Office, Department for Business, Enterprise and Regulatory Reform, Department for Environment, Food and Rural Affairs and Sustainable Energy Policy Network, 2004, p. 15.
51 A. Monaghan, 'EU–Russia Energy Co-operation', *EU–Russia Review* 2, Brussels: EU–Russia Centre, November 2006, p. 31.
52 S. Fischer, 'The EU and Russia: Conflicts and Potential of a Difficult Partnership', *SWP Research Paper*, Berlin: Stiftung Wissenschaft und Politik, January 2007, p. 17.
53 *Eurasia Daily Monitor*, 2 May 2006.
54 At press conference following the 17th EU–Russia Summit, Sochi, 25 May 2006, reported in *CEPS Neighbourhood Watch* 16, Brussels: Centre for European Policy Studies, May 2006, p. 5.
55 *El País*, 24 November 2006.
56 *EU Observer*, 23 November 2006.
57 Leonard and Popescu, *A Power Audit of EU–Russia Relations*, p. 42.
58 Monaghan, 'EU–Russia Energy Co-operation', p. 27.
59 *EUObserver*, 14 March 2007.
60 The Parliament Magazine, 'EU says Russian Oil and Gas Decision "Highly Problematic"', *The Parliament Magazine*, 19 September 2006. ONLINE. Available HTTP: http://www.theparliament.com/latestnews/news-article/newsarticle/eu-says-russiannbspoil-and-gasnbspdecision-highly-problematic/
61 CEPS, *CEPS Neighbourhood Watch* 20, Brussels, Centre for European Policy Studies, October 2006.
62 *EUObserver*, 12 February 2007.
63 *Financial Times*, 21 May 2007.
64 Quoted in *Democracy Digest*, Washington, DC: National Endowment for Democracy, May 2007, p. 6.
65 K. Barysch, 'The EU and Russia: From Principle to Pragmatism?' *Policy Brief*, London: Centre for European Reform, November 2006.
66 *The Economist*, 26 January 2008, p. 36.
67 *The Economist*, 16 February 2008, p. 62.
68 C. Grant and T. Valasek, *Preparing for the Multipolar World: European Foreign and Security Policy in 2020*, London: Centre for European Reform, 2007, p. 20.
69 Monaghan and Montanaro-Jankovski, 'EU–Russia Energy Relations: The Need for Active Engagement, pp. 10 and 24.

6 The Caucasus and Central Asia

1 Commission of the European Communities, *Energy Statistics Pocketbook 2007*, Brussels: European Commission, p. 14.

2 Turkmenistan Project, *Turkmenistan News Brief* 12, New York: Open Society Institute, 16–22 March 2007.

3 I. Rutledge, *Addicted to Oil: America's Relentless Drive for Energy Security*, London: I.B. Tauris, 2006, p. 119.

4 ICG, 'Central Asia's Energy Risks', *Asia Report* 133, Brussels: International Crisis Group, 24 May 2007.

5 For background on Central Asia energy issues, see S. Hansen, *Pipeline Politics: The Struggle for Control of the Eurasian Energy Resources*, The Hague: Clingendael Institute for International Relations, 2003.

6 Commission of the European Communities, *Strategy Paper 2002–2006 and Indicative Programme 2002–2004 for Central Asia*, Brussels: European Commission, 30 October 2002, p. 129.

7 S. Cornell, 'Europe's Energy Security: The Role of the Black Sea Region', in G. Austin and M. Schellekens-Gaiffe (eds) *Energy and Conflict Prevention*, Brussels: Madariaga European Foundation, 2007, p. 129.

8 A. Warkotsch, 'The European Union and Democracy Promotion in Bad Neighbourhoods: The Case of Central Asia', *European Foreign Affairs Review* 11/3, 2006, 509–24.

9 S. MacFarlane, 'The Caucasus and Central Asia: Towards a Non-strategy', in R. Dannreuther (ed.) *European Union Foreign and Security Policy: Towards a Neighbourhood Strategy*, London: Routledge, 2004, pp. 127–28 and 130.

10 L. Jonavicius, 'The Democracy Promotion Policies of Central and Eastern European States', *FRIDE Working Paper* 55, Madrid: Fundación para las Relaciones Internacionales y el Diálogo Exterior, March 2008.

11 B. Ferrero-Waldner, 'Azerbaijan', speech to the European Parliament, Strasbourg, 26 October 2005.

12 G. Bahgat, 'Europe's Energy Security: Challenges and Opportunities', *International Affairs* 82/5, 2006, 961–75.

13 Commission of the European Communities, *Strategy Paper 2002–2006 and Indicative Programme 2002–2004 for Central Asia*, pp. 15–16 and p. 22.

14 B. Ferrero-Waldner, opening address, External Energy Policy Conference, Brussels, 20 November 2006.

15 *BBC Monitoring Central Asia*, 30 November 2006.

16 Commission of the European Communities, *Strategy Paper 2002–2006 and Indicative Programme 2002–2004 for Central Asia*.

17 MacFarlane, 'The Caucasus and Central Asia: Towards a Non-strategy', pp. 130–32.

18 ICG, 'Central Asia: What Role for the European Union?', *Asia Report* 113, Brussels: International Crisis Group, April 2006, p. 15.

19 R. Aliboni, 'Globalization and the Wider Black Sea Area: Interaction with the European Union, Eastern Mediterranean and the Middle East', *Southeast European and Black Sea Studies* 6/2, 2006, 157–68.

20 ICG, April 2006, op. cit., p. 17.

21 *Eurasian Daily Monitor,* 24 January 2006 and 8 May 2006.

22 *Eurasia Daily Monitor,* 3 March 2006.

23 ICG, April 2006, 'Central Asia: What Role for the European Union?', p. 35.

24 Quoted in *EUObserver.com*, 2 June 2007.

25 E. Nuriyev, *The South Caucasus at the Crossroads: Conflicts, Caspian Oil and Great Power Politics*, 2007, Berlin: Lit Vertag, p. 267.

26 *Eurasia Daily Monitor,* 14 May 2007.

27 *Econews*, 18 September 2007.

28 *Eurasia Daily Monitor,* 10 June 2008, p.2
29 *Eurasia Daily Monitor,* 17 March 2008, p. 1.
30 *Platts EU Energy,* 8 February 2008, p. 29.
31 *Eurasia Daily Monitor,* 8 February 2008.
32 B. Ferrero-Waldner, 'The European Approach to Democracy Promotion in Post-communist Countries', speech to the Institute for Human Sciences, Vienna, 19 January 2007.
33 N. Kassenova, 'The New EU Strategy towards Central Asia: A View from the Region', *CEPS Policy Brief* 148, Brussels: Centre for European Policy Studies, January 2008, p. 5.
34 Warkotsch, 'The European Union and Democracy Promotion in Bad Neighbourhoods: The Case of Central Asia'.
35 A. Matveeva, 'EU Stakes in Central Asia', *Chaillot Paper* 91, Paris: EU Institute for Security Studies, July 2006, p. 61.
36 ICG, April 2006, 'Central Asia: What Role for the European Union?', p. 19.
37 H. Wegener, 'Central Asia: At Last Europe may be Getting its Act Together', *Europe's World* 5, Spring 2007, p. 16.
38 Nuriyev, *The South Caucasus at the Crossroads,* p. 249.
39 For figures, see Commission of the European Communities, *The EU's Relations with Azerbaijan.* ONLINE. Available HTTP: http://ec.europa.eu/comm/external_relations/azerbaijan/intro/index.htm (accessed 28 August 2006).
40 ENPI, *Azerbaijan Country Strategy Paper 2007–2013,* Brussels: European Neighbourhood and Partnership Instrument.
41 *EUObserver,* 7 November 2006.
42 Commission of the European Communities, *Memorandum of Understanding on a Strategic Partnership between the European Union and the Republic of Azerbaijan in the Field of Energy,* Brussels: European Commission, 2006.
43 B. Ferrero-Waldner, 26 October 2005, 'The European Approach to Democracy Promotion in Post-communist Countries'.
44 Cornell, 'Europe's Energy Security: The Role of the Black Sea Region', p. 124.
45 ENPI, *Azerbaijan Country Strategy Paper 2007–2013,* p. 38. The six donors listed being Germany, Italy, Sweden, France, Denmark, the UK and Greece.
46 J. Boonstra, 'Is the EU Serious about Promoting Democracy and Human Rights? The Case of Azerbaijan', *FRIDE–ECFR Working Paper,* Madrid: Fundación para las Relaciones Internacionales y el Diálogo Exterior and European Council on Foreign Relations, May 2008.
47 L. Alieva, 'EU and the South Caucasus', *C.A.P Discussion Paper,* Munich: Centre for Applied Policy Research, December 2006.
48 Commission of the European Communities, *Implementation of the European Neighbourhood Policy in 2007: Progress Report on Azerbaijan,* COM(2008) 164, Brussels: European Commission, 3 April 2008, pp. 2 and 6–7.
49 *Platts EU Energy,* 4 April 2008, p. 22.
50 *Eurasia Daily Monitor,* 1 May 2006.
51 Commission of the European Communities, *Memorandum of Understanding on Cooperation in the Field of Energy between the European Union and the Republic of Kazakhstan,* Brussels: European Commission, 2006.
52 Commission of the European Communities, *The EU's Relations with Kazakhstan.* ONLINE. Available HTTP: http://ec.europa.eu/comm/external_relations/kazakhstan/intro/index.htm (accessed 28 August 2006).
53 For summaries of national policies, see ICG, April 2006, 'Central Asia: What Role for the European Union?', p. 23.
54 Commission of the European Communities, *The EU's Relations with Kazakhstan,* p. 4.
55 Ibid., p. 6.

56 Rutledge, *Addicted to Oil: America's Relentless Drive for Energy Security*, p. 62.
57 T. Carothers, *US Democracy Promotion during and after Bush*, Washington, DC: Carnegie Endowment for International Peace, 2007, p. 9.
58 P. Baker, 'As Democracy Falters, Bush Feels Like a "Dissident"', *Washington Post*, 20 August 2007.
59 B. Dave, 'The EU and Kazakhstan: Balancing Economic Cooperation and Aiding Democratic Reforms in the central Asian Region', *CEPS Policy Brief* 127, Brussels: Centre for European Policy Studies, May 2007, p. 3.
60 N. Melvin, 'Building Stronger Ties, Meeting New Challenges: The European Union's Strategic Role in Central Asia', *CEPS Policy Brief* 128, Brussels: European Centre for Policy Studies, March 2007, p. 3.
61 *EUObserver.com*, 5 December 2006.
62 *Eurasia Daily Monitor*, 28 November 2005.
63 L. Kleveman, *The New Great Game: Blood and Oil in Central Asia*, London: Atlantic Books, 2004, pp. 81–82.
64 Ibid., p. 85.
65 Rutledge, *Addicted to Oil: America's Relentless Drive for Energy Security*, p. 111.
66 Kleveman, *The New Great Game: Blood and Oil in Central Asia*, p. 115.
67 Matveeva, 'EU Stakes in Central Asia', p. 63.
68 *Dow Jones International News*, 8 December 2008.
69 *The Economist*, 19 January 2008, p. 29; D. Bochkarev, 'El Acceso a los Recursos Energéticos de Asia Central en el Nuevo Contexto Energético Global: Retos y Oportunidades para la Unión Europea', in A. González and C. Claudín (eds) *Asia Central y La Seguridad Energética Global*, Barcelona: CIDOB, 2008, p. 141.
70 M. Von Gumppenberg, 'Kazakhstan: Challenges to the Booming Petro-Economy', *Working Paper* 2, Bern: Swiss Peace Foundation, 2007, p. 37.
71 *The Times of Central Asia*, 25 September 2007.
72 Commission of the European Communities, *The EU's Relations with Uzbekistan*. ONLINE. Available HTTP: http://ec.europa.eu/comm/external_relations/uzbekist an/intro/index.htm (accessed 28 August 2006).
73 C. Murray, *Murder in Samarkand: A British Ambassador's Controversial Defiance of Tyranny in the War on Terror*, Edinburgh: Mainstream, 2007, p. 53.
74 Ibid., pp. 133 and 344.
75 *EUObserver*, 10 November 2006.
76 ICG, 'Uzbekistan: Europe's Sanctions Matter', *Asia Briefing* 54, Brussels: International Crisis Group, November 2006, p. 3.
77 *Eurasia Daily Monitor*, 10 April 2006.
78 Commission of the European Communities, 30 October 2002, *The EU's Relations with* Uzbekistan, p. 41.
79 Commission of the European Communities, *The EU's Relations with Turkmenistan*. ONLINE. Available HTTP: http://ec.europa.eu/comm/external_relations/ turkmenistan/intro/index.htm (accessed 28 August 2006).
80 M. Denison, 'Turkmenistan in Transition: A Window for EU Engagement?', *CEPS Policy Brief* 129, Brussels: Centre for European Policy Studies, April 2007.
81 *Lithuanian News Agency*, 26 September 2007.
82 ICG, 'Turkmenistan after Niyazov', *Asia Briefing* 60, Brussels: International Crisis Group, February 2007, pp. 14–15.
83 *Eurasia Daily Monitor*, 14 December 2007, pp. 4–5.

7 Sub-Saharan Africa

1 *Agence Europe*, 9 October 2007.
2 Commission of the European Communities, *European Energy and Transport Trends to 2030 – Update 2007,* Brussels: European Commission, 2007, p. 27.

3 See N. Shaxson, *Poisoned Wells: The Dirty Politics of African Oil*, Basingstoke: Palgrave Macmillan, 2007.

4 Commission of the European Communities, *Energy Statistics Pocketbook 2007*, Brussels: European Commission, 2007, p. 14.

5 *El País*, 7 January 2008.

6 J. Marriott, A. Rowell and L. Stockman, *The Next Gulf: London, Washington and Oil Conflict in Nigeria*, London: Constable, 2005, p. 29.

7 EIA, *US National Oil and Gas Imports by Country*, Washington, DC: Energy Information Administration, 2007. ONLINE. Available HTTP: www.eia.doe.gov

8 M. Burrows and G. Treverton, 'A Strategic View of Energy Futures', *Survival*, 49/3, 2007, 79–90.

9 J. Solana, 'Energy in the Common Foreign and Security Policy', in G. Austin and M. Schellekens-Gaiffe (eds) *Energy and Conflict Prevention*, Brussels: Madariaga European Foundation, 2007, p. 14.

10 J. Frynas and M. Paulo, 'A New Scramble for African Oil? Historical, Political, and Business Perspectives', *African Affairs* 106/243, 229–51.

11 J. Ghazvinian, *Untapped: The Scramble for Africa's Oil*, Orlando: Harcourt, 2007, p. 237.

12 A. Vines, 'How Heavy are the Anchors?', *The World Today* 64/2, February 2008, 15–18.

13 The Stanley Foundation, 'Africa at Risk or Rising? The Role of Europe, North America and China on the Continent', *Policy Dialogue Brief*, Muscatine: The Stanley Foundation, May 2007, pp. 4–5 and 8.

14 F. Guerrero, 'Las Relaciones España-África Subsahariana: ¿A Remolque o en la Vanguardia de la UE', *Working Paper*, Barcelona: Observatorio de Política Exterior Europea, Universidad Autónoma de Barcelona, March 2008.

15 A. Piebalgs, 'Energy and Development', speech to the External Energy Policy Conference, Brussels, 21 November 2006.

16 Commission of the European Communities, *EU Strategy for Africa: Towards a Euro-African Pact to Accelerate Africa's Development*, COM(2005) 489, Brussels: European Commission, 12 October 2005, pp. 5 and 37.

17 Commission of the European Communities, *Communication from the Commission to the Council, the European Parliament and the European Economic and Social Committee, Policy Coherence for Development*, COM(2005) 134, Brussels: European Commission, 12 April 2005, pp. 3, 4 and 10.

18 Ibid., p. 18.

19 L. Van Schaik, 'Policy Coherence for Development in the EU Council: Strategies for the Way Forward', *Fiche on EU Energy Policy*, Brussels: Centre for European Policy Studies, June 2006, p. 118.

20 European Parliament–Council–Commission, *The European Consensus on Development*, 2006/C 46/01, Brussels: European Parliament–Council–Commission, 24 February 2006, pp. 4, 7, 13 and 14.

21 A. Theodorakis, keynote speech at the Africa–Europe Energy Forum, Berlin, 6–7 March 2007.

22 Council of the European Union, *Presidency-Commission Joint Background Paper on Energy Cooperation between Africa and Europe*, 8376/07, Brussels, European Council, 17 April 2007.

23 *Conclusions of the Council and the Representatives of the Governments of the Member States Meeting Within the Council on Energy Cooperation between Africa and Europe*, 9562/07, Brussels: European Council, 15 May 2007.

24 EU–Africa Summit, *The Africa–EU Strategic Partnership*, adopted by the Lisbon Summit, 9 December 2007, pp. 56–58.

25 Speech at the European Policy Centre, Brussels, 5 December 2007.

26 *Financial Times*, 9 December 2007.

27 Van Schaik, 'Policy Coherence for Development in the EU Council: Strategies for the Way Forward', p. 121.
28 C. Gourlay, 'Community Instruments for Civilian Crisis Management', in A. Nowak (ed.) 'Civilian Crisis Management: The EU Way', *Chaillot Paper* 90, Paris: EU Institute for Security Studies, June 2006, p. 59.
29 J. Kotsopoulous, 'The EU and Africa: Coming Together at Last?', *EPC Policy Brief*, European Policy Centre, July 2007, p. 3.
30 High-Level Task Force on UK Energy Security, Climate Change and Development Assistance, *Energy, Politics and Poverty*, Oxford: Oxford University Press, June 2007.
31 Council of the European Union, *8th EU–Africa Ministerial Troika Meeting, Final Communiqué*, 9678/07, Brussels: European Council, 15 May 2007, p. 4.
32 M. Gibert, 'Monitoring a Region in Crisis: The European Union in West Africa', *Chaillot Paper* 98, Paris: European Union Institute for Security Studies, January 2007, p. 30.
33 C. Mölling, 'EU Battle Groups 2007: Where Next?', *European Security Review* 31, December 2006, p. 7.
34 J. Howarth, *Security and Defence Policy in Europe*, London: Palgrave Macmillan, 2007.
35 B. Stocking, 'Seismic Rupture', *The World Today* 64/1, January 2008, 21–22.
36 R. Soares de Oliveira, *Oil and Politics in the Gulf of Guinea*, London: Hurst, 2007, pp. 120 and 128.
37 Commission of the European Communities, *Communication from the Commission on Conflict Prevention,* COM(2001) 211, Brussels: European Commission, 11 April 2001.
38 Commission of the European Communities, 12 October 2005, *EU Strategy for Africa: Towards a Euro-African Pact to Accelerate Africa's Development,* p. 25.
39 Commission of the European Communities, *Communication from the Commission to the Council and European Parliament, Proposal for a Joint Declaration by the Council, the European Parliament and the Commission on the European Development Policy,* COM(2005) 311, Brussels: European Commission, July 2005.
40 DGCID–MAE, *Governance Strategy for French Development Assistance*, Paris: Direction Générale de la Coopération Internationale et Development, Ministère des Affaires Étrangères, 5 December 2006.
41 T. Chafer, 'From Confidence to Confusion: Franco-African Relations in the Era of Globalisation', in M. Maclean, and J. Szarka. (eds) *France in the World*, Basingstoke: Palgrave Macmillan, 2008.
42 *Africa Confidential* 49/7, 28 March 2008, p. 7.
43 ECDPM, *Cotonou Infokit: Essential and Fundamental Elements (20)*, Maastricht: European Centre for Development Policy Management, 2001.
44 ECDPM, *InBrief* 5, Maastricht: European Centre for Development Policy Management, October 2003.
45 Commission of the European Communities, *Information Note on the Revision of the Cotonou Agreement,* Brussels: European Commission, 2004.
46 ECDPM, *InfoCotonou 7: The Review of the Cotonou Partnership Agreement: What's at Stake?*, Maastricht: European Centre for Development Policy Management, 2004.
47 Commission of the European Communities, *Communication from the Commission, Governance in the European Consensus on Development: Towards a Harmonised Approach in the EU*, COM(2006) 421, Brussels: European Commission, 30 August 2006.
48 ECDPM, *Governance Impact Assessment*, SEC(2006) 1021, Maastricht: European Centre for Development Policy Management, March 2006.
49 M. Kaldor, M. Martin and S. Selchow, 'Human Security: A New Strategic Narrative for Europe', *International Affairs* 83/2, 2007, p. 280.
50 DfID, *Governance, Development and Democratic Politics*, London: UK Department for International Development, 2007, p. 48.

51 International Alert, *Strategising for Peace and Social Justice in West Africa,* London: International Alert, 2004, p. 13.
52 *Africa Confidential* 45/20, 8 October 2004.
53 Nigeria–European Community, *Country Support Strategy and Indicative Programme for the Period 2001–2007,* Brussels: European Commission, 2001.
54 Saferworld–International Alert, *Developing an EU Strategy to Address Fragile States: Priorities for the UK Presidency of the EU in 2005,* London: Saferworld–International Alert, 2005, p. 10.
55 For a comprehensive account of the dynamics of conflict in the Delta, see ICG, 'Fuelling the Niger Delta Crisis', *Africa Report* 118, Brussels: International Crisis Group, 28 September 2006.
56 *The Economist,* 21 October 2006, pp. 71–72.
57 *Africa–Asia Confidential* 1/1, 2 November 2007, p. 3.
58 DfID, *Nigeria, Draft Country Assistance Plan 2004,* London: UK Department for International Development, 2007, pp. 3–18.
59 Marriott, Rowell and Stockman, *The Next Gulf: London, Washington and Oil Conflict in Nigeria,* p. 205.
60 ICG, 'Fuelling the Niger Delta Crisis', p. 25.
61 Shaxson, *Poisoned Wells: The Dirty Politics of African Oil,* p. 202.
62 Ghazvinian, *Untapped: The Scramble for Africa's Oil,* p. 56.
63 DfID, 2007, *Nigeria, Draft Country Assistance Plan 2004,* pp. 17–18.
64 A. Perry, 'Africa's Oil dreams', *Newsweek,* 11 June 2007, p. 24.
65 J. Ibrahim, 'Nigeria's 2007 Elections: The Fitful Path to Democratic Citizenship', *Special Report* 182, Washington, DC: United States Institute for Peace, January 2007, p. 8.
66 *The Economist,* 28 April 2007, p. 45.
67 *Africa Confidential* 48/9, 27 April 2007.
68 ICG, 'Nigeria: Ending Unrest in the Niger Delta', *Africa Report* 135, Brussels: International Crisis Group, December 2007, p. 1.
69 Ibid., p. 9.
70 *Africa Confidential* 48/12, 8 June 2007.
71 *Africa Confidential* 48/23, 16 November 2007, p. 6.
72 R. Joseph, 'Challenges of a "Frontier" Region', *Journal of Democracy,* 19/2, 2008, p. 103.
73 *The Economist,* 15 March 2008, p. 12.
74 *New Europe,* 4 January 2008.
75 *Africa Confidential* 49/7, 28 March 2008, p. 6.
76 *Africa Confidential* 48/18, 7 September 2007, p. 12.
77 *Africa Confidential* 48/3, 2 February 2007; and *Africa Confidential* 46/19, 23 September 2005.
78 DfID, *Nigeria, Draft Country Assistance Plan 2004,* 2007.
79 *Africa Confidential* , 20 July 2007, p. 4; ICG, 'Sudan's Comprehensive Peace Agreement: Beyond the Crisis', *Africa Briefing* 50, Brussels: International Crisis Group, March 2008, p. 1.
80 *Africa Confidential* 48/18, 7 September 2007, p. 9.
81 ICG, 'Sudan's Comprehensive Peace Agreement: Beyond the Crisis', p. 1.
82 Ibid., p. 9.
83 *Africa Confidential* 49/5, 24 February 2008.
84 *Africa Confidential* 49/7, 28 March 2008, p. 12.
85 Shaxson, *Poisoned Wells: The Dirty Politics of African Oil,* pp. 36, 143 and 125.
86 E. Burke, 'Spain and Equatorial Guinea – Different Views, Same Interest', *FRIDE Comment,* Madrid: Fundación para las Relaciones Internacionales y el Diálogo Exterior, June 2008.
87 *Global Insight Daily Analysis,* 10 October 2007.

88 *Africa Confidential* 47/9, 28 April 2006.
89 *The Economist*, 9 February 2008, p. 34.

8 European energy companies

1 *Financial Times*, 11 March 2007.
2 *Financial Times, Special Report: Energy*, 9 November 2007. ONLINE. Available HTTP: http://www.ft.com/reports/energynov2007
3 M. Klare, *Blood and Oil*, London: Penguin, 2004, p. 35.
4 I. Rutledge, *Addicted to Oil: America's Relentless Drive for Energy Security*, London: I.B. Tauris, 2006, p. 66.
5 R. Soares de Oliveira, *Oil and Politics in the Gulf of Guinea*, London: Hurst, 2007, p. 210.
6 A. Kolk and J. Pinkse, 'Multinationals' Political Activities on Climate Change', *Business and Society* 46/2, 2007, 201–28.
7 N. Butler, 'European Energy Security', presentation at the International Institute for Strategic Studies, Geneva, 17 September 2005. ONLINE. Available HTTP: http://www.bp.com/genericarticle.do?categoyId = 98&contentId = 7010497
8 N. Butler, 'Energy Security: A New Agenda for Europe', *CER Bulletin* 38, October–November 2004.
9 BP Global Press, 'European Energy Security', speech by Nick Butler at the International Institute for Strategic Studies, Geneva, 17 September 2005. ONLINE. Available HTTP: http://www.bp.com/genericarticle.do?categoryId = 98&contentId = 7010497
10 A. Cortina, 'Welcome and Introduction', in B. Mossavar-Rahmani (ed.) *Thinking the Unthinkable*, proceedings of XIII Repsol YPF–Harvard Seminar on Energy Policy, Salamanca, 9–10 May 2003, pp. 18–20.
11 Reported in *Platts EU Energy*, 4 April 2008, p. 10.
12 CEPS Task Force Report, 'Energy Policy for Europe: Identifying the European Added-Value', Brussels: Centre for European Policy Studies, March 2008, p. 25.
13 *Platts EU Energy*, 7 March 2008, p. 20.
14 *Platts EU Energy*, 16 November 2007.
15 *Reuters News*, 20 September 2007.
16 F. Müller, 'Energy Security: Demands Imposed on German and European Foreign Policy by a Changed Configuration in the World Energy Market', *SWP Research Paper*, Berlin: Stiftung Wissenschaft und Politik, January 2007, p. 18.
17 *Platts EU Energy*, April 2008, p. 3.
18 O. Noreng, *Oil and Islam: Social and Economic Issues,* Chichester: John Wiley, 1997.
19 A. Stern, *Who Won the Oil Wars? Why Government Wage War for Oil Rights*, London: Collins and Brown, 2005, pp. 76–77.
20 Ibid.
21 R. Youngs, *International Democracy and the West*, Oxford, Oxford University Press, 2004, p.188
22 Royal Dutch Shell, *Delivery and Growth: Annual Review and Summary of Financial Statements 2007*, The Hague: Royal Dutch Shell plc, 2007; and Royal Dutch Shell, *2004 Royal Dutch/Shell Group of Companies Annual Report*, The Hague: Royal Dutch Shell plc, 2004, pp. 17–23.
23 BP, *Annual Accounts and Reports 2007,* London: British Petroleum, 2007, pp. 23–24; and BP, *Making Energy More. Annual Review 2005,* London: British Petroleum, 2005, pp. 12–13.
24 Total, *Registration Document 2007,* Courbevoie: Total, 2007, p. 9; and Total, *Global Report 2005*, Courbevoie: Total, 2005, pp. 25–38.
25 Repsol-YPF, *Annual Report 2006,* Madrid: Repsol-YPF, 2006; and A. Estrada and A. Lorca, 'África del Norte: Su Importancia Geopolítica en el Ámbito

Eneroético', *Working Paper* 11/2007, Madrid: Real Instituto Elcano, April 2007.

26 Repsol-YPF, *Áreas de Negocio 2006*, Madrid: Repsol-YPF, 2006.

27 Iberdrola, *Presencia del Grupo Iberdrola en el Mundo*, Madrid: Iberdrola, 2006, p. 78.

28 L. Kleveman, *The New Great Game: Blood and Oil in Central Asia*, London: Atlantic Books, 2004, p. 76.

29 ENEL, *Annual Report 2007*, Rome: ENEL, 2007, pp. 11 and 24.

30 BG Group, *Annual Report and Accounts 2007*, Reading: BG Group, 2007, pp. 5 and 20.

31 R. Youngs, *International Democracy and the West*, p. 90

32 *Platts EU Energy*, 22 February 2008.

33 P. Le Billon, 'Drilling in Deep Water: Oil, Business and War in Angola', in M. Kaldor, T. Lynn Karl and Y. Said (eds), *Oil Wars*, London: Pluto Press, 2007, pp. 120–21.

34 *Africa Confidential* 48/5, 2 March 2007.

35 N. Shaxson, *Poisoned Wells: The Dirty Politics of African Oil*, Basingstoke: Palgrave Macmillan, 2007, pp. 93 and 181.

36 *The Economist* 12 January 2008, p. 57.

37 Amnesty International, *Human Rights on the Line: The Baku–Tblisi–Ceyhan Pipeline Project*, London: Amnesty International, 2003.

38 V. Marcel, 'Investment in Middle East Oil: Who Needs Whom?', *Chatham House Report*, London: Royal Institute of International Affairs, February 2006, p. 6.

39 Global Witness, *Oil and Mining in Violent Places: Why Voluntary Codes for Companies Don't Guarantee Human Rights*, London: Global Witness, October 2007.

40 Global Witness, 'EITI on the Right Track: Let's Go Further and Master', press statement, London: Global Witness, March 2005.

41 TI Norge, 'Publish What You Pay, New Report Finds Action Needed to Manage Natural Resource Revenues', press release, Oslo: Transparency International Norge, 11 October 2006.

42 R. Youngs, *International Democracy and the West*, p. 89

43 Repsol-YPF, *Informe de Responsabilidad Corporativa 2006*, Madrid: Repsol-YPF, 2006.

44 ENI, *Sustainability Report 2006*, Milan: ENI, 2006, p. 17.

45 ENEL, *Code of Ethics*, Rome: ENEL, 2006.

46 A. Rowell, J. Marriott and L. Stockman, *The Next Gulf: London, Washington and Oil Conflict in Nigeria*, London: Constable, 2005, p. 97.

47 P. Roberts, *The End of Oil: The Decline of the Petroleum Economy and the Rise of a New Energy Order*, London: Bloomsbury, 2005, p. 186.

48 Marcel, 'Investment in Middle East Oil: Who Needs Whom?' p. 4.

49 K. Stephens, 'Oil Companies and the International Oil Market', in A. Schiffrin and S. Tesalik (eds) *Covering Oil*, New York: Revenue Watch, 2005, p. 52.

50 BP, 2005, 'European Energy Security', p. 18.

51 R. Youngs, *International Democracy and the West*, p. 106

52 *Financial Times*, 4 May 2006.

53 *Financial Times*, 27 March 2007.

54 J. Browne, 'Energy Security: A European Perspective', speech at the European Policy Centre, Brussels, in *EPC Policy Briefing*, Brussels: European Policy Centre, 17 February 2005.

55 D. Johnson, 'EU–Russia Energy Links', in D. Johnson and P. Robinson (eds) *Perspectives on EU–Russia Relations*, London: Routledge, 2005, p. 183.

56 *Eurasia Daily Brief* 4/172, 18 September 2007.

57 ICG, 'Fuelling the Niger Delta Crisis', *Africa Report* 118, Brussels: International Crisis Group, 28 September 2006, p. 10.

58 *African Confidential* 46/23, 18 November 2005.
59 J. Ghazvinian, *Untapped: The Scramble for Africa's Oil*, Orlando: Harcourt, 2007, p. 46.
60 ICG, 'Nigeria: Ending Unrest in the Niger Delta', *Africa Report* 135, Brussels: International Crisis Group, December 2007, p. 9.
61 *Financial Times*, 31 January 2008 and 17 April 2008.
62 *El Pais Negocios*, 29 April 2007, p.16.
63 *New Europe*, 19 May 2008
64 Total, *Registration Document 2007*, p. 18.
65 *The Africa Report*, number 11, June/July 2008, p. 85
66 *Financial Times*, 4 May 2006.
67 *Platts EU Energy*, 2 May 2007, p. 25.
68 *Financial Times*, 8 September 2006.
69 R. Howard, 'Oil at 100', *The World Today* 64/5, May 2008, 16–18.
70 Oliveira, *Oil and Politics in the Gulf of Guinea*, p. 210.
71 *New Europe*, 22 October 2007.
72 R. Youngs, *International Democracy and the West*, p. 126

Bibliography

Aarts, P. and Nonneman, G. (eds) *Saudi Arabia in the Balance: Political Economy, Society, Foreign Affairs*, London: Hurst and Company, 2005.

AECI, *La Agencia Española de Cooperación Internacional en Cifras*, Madrid: Agencia Española de Cooperación Internacional, 2007.

Aliboni, R., 'Europe's Role in the Gulf: A Transatlantic Perspective', *GRC Gulf Paper*, Dubai: Gulf Research Centre, August 2006.

—— 'Globalization and the Wider Black Sea Area: Interaction with the European Union, Eastern Mediterranean and the Middle East', *Southeast European and Black Sea Studies* 6/2, 2006.

Alieva, L., 'EU and the South Caucasus', *C.A.P Discussion Paper*, Munich: Centre for Applied Policy Research, December 2006.

Al-Rasheed, M., 'Circles of Power: Royals and Society in Saudi Arabia', in Aarts, P. and Nonneman, G. (eds) *Saudi Arabia in the Balance: Political Economy, Society, Foreign Affairs*, London: Hurst and Company, 2005.

Al-Rodhan, K. and Cordesman, A., *The Geopolitics of Energy: Geostrategic Risks and Economic Uncertainties*, Washington, DC: Centre for Strategic and International Studies, 20 March 2006.

Amnesty International, *Human Rights on the Line: The Baku–Tblisi–Ceyhan Pipeline Project*, London: Amnesty International, 2003.

Andrés, A., 'Russia and Europe: Mutual Dependence in the Energy Sector', *Working Paper* 2007/9, Madrid: Real Instituto Elcano, 2007.

Armitage, R., Bloomfield Jr., L. and Kelly, J., 'Preserving US and Allied Interests in a New Era' in Bloomfield Jr., L. (ed.) *Global Markets and National Interests: The New Geopolitics of Energy, Capital, and Information*, Washington, DC: Centre for Strategic and International Studies, 2002.

Austin, G. and Bochkarev, D., 'Energy Sovereignty and Security: Restoring Confidence in a Cooperation International System', in Austin, G. and Schellekens-Gaiffe, M. (eds) *Energy and Conflict Prevention*, Brussels: Madariaga European Foundation, 2007.

Austin, G. and Schellekens-Gaiffe, M. (eds) *Energy and Conflict Prevention*, Brussels: Madariaga European Foundation, 2007.

Baabood, A. and Edwards, G., 'Reinforcing Ambivalence: The Interaction of Gulf States and the European Union', *European Foreign Affairs Review* 12/3, 2007.

Bahgat, G., 'Europe's Energy Security: Challenges and Opportunities', *International Affairs* 82/5, 2006.

Bailes, A., 'The EU and a "Better World": What Role for the European Security and Defence Policy?', *International Affairs* 84/1, 2008.

Baker, P., 'As Democracy Falters, Bush Feels Like a "Dissident"', *Washington Post*, 20 August 2007.

Baltic Council of Ministers' Energy Committee, *Baltic Energy Strategy 1999*, Vilnius, Riga, Tallinn: Baltic Council of Ministers' Energy Committee, 1999.

Baran, Z., 'PESC y Seguridad de los Suministros Eneroéticos', *Política Exterior* 177, May–June 2007.

Barbé, E., Costa, O., Herranz, A., Johansson-Nogués, E., Mestres, L., Natorski, M. and Sabiote, E.M., 'Exporting Rules to the Neighbourhood? A Framework for the Analysis of Emerging Patterns of Europeanisation, Internationalisation and Coordination between the EU and its Neighbours', paper presented at the EUPROX seminar 'Interlocking Dimensions of European Security Neighbourhood: Energy, Borders and Conflict Management', Barcelona, 9 October 2007.

Barnes, J. and Jaffe, A., 'The Persian Gulf and the Geopolitics of Oil', *Survival* 48/1, 2006.

Barroso, J. M., 'The EU: Ending Doubts on Energy and Climate Change', speech at the Energy Security, Environment and Development: Three Issues for the G8 Conference, Institut Français des Relations Internationales (IFRI), Brussels, 24 May 2007.

—— opening speech at the External Energy Policy Conference, Brussels, 20 November 2006.

Barroso, J. M., Putin, V. and Schuessel W., 'Press Conference following the 17th EU-Russia Summit, Sochi, 25 May 2006', in *CEPS Neighbourhood Watch* 16, Brussels: Centre for European Policy Studies, May 2006.

Barysch, K., 'Reciprocity will not Secure Europe's Energy', *CER Bulletin* 55, London: Centre for European Reform, August–September 2007.

—— 'The EU and Russia: From Principle to Pragmatism?', *Policy Brief*, London: Centre for European Reform, November 2006.

Benelux Position Paper, *External Energy Policy for Europe*, February 2007, mimeo.

BG Group, *Annual Report and Accounts 2007*, Reading: BG Group, 2007.

Biscop, S., 'The ABC of European Union Security Strategy: Ambition, Benchmark, Culture', *Egmont Paper* 16, Brussels: Egmont Institute, October 2007.

Blanton, R. and Blanton, S., 'Human Rights and Foreign Direct Investment: A Two-Stage Analysis', *Business and Society* 45/4, 2006.

Bloomfield Jr., L. (ed.) *Global Markets and National Interests: The New Geopolitics of Energy, Capital, and Information*, Washington, DC: Centre for Strategic and International Studies, 2002.

Bochkarev, D., 'El Acceso a los Recursos eneroéticos de Asia Central en el Nuevo Contexto Eneroético Global: Retos y Oportunidades para la Unión Europea', in Claudín, C. and González, A. (eds) *Asia Central y La Seguridad Eneroética Global*, Barcelona: CIDOB, 2008.

Boonstra, J., 'Is the European Union Serious about Promoting Democracy and Human Rights? The Case of Azerbaijan', *FRIDE–ECFR Working Paper*, Madrid: Fundación para las Relaciones Internacionales y el Diálogo Exterior and European Council on Foreign Relations, May 2008.

Bot, B., 'Realistic Multilateralism in the 21st Century: The Netherlands and the EU between International Law, Politics and Power', speech at Roosevelt Academy, Middelburg, 29 January 2007.

BP, *Annual Accounts and Reports 2007*, London: British Petroleum, 2007.

—— *Statistical Review of World Energy* 2007, London: British Petroleum, 2007.

—— *Making Energy More. Annual Review 2005*, London: British Petroleum, 2005.

BP Global Press, 'European Energy Security', speech by Nick Butler at the International Institute for Strategic Studies, Geneva, 17 September 2005. ONLINE. Available HTTP: http://www.bp.com/genericarticle.do?categoryId = 98&contentId = 7010497

Bronsen, R., *Thicker than Oil: America's Uneasy Partnership with Saudi Arabia*, Oxford: Oxford University Press, 2006.

Brown, N., Hamzawy, A., Ottaway, M., Sadjadpour, K. and Salem, P., *The New Middle East*, Washington, DC: Carnegie Endowment for International Peace, 2008.

Browne, J., 'Energy Security: A European Perspective', speech at the European Policy Centre, Brussels, in *EPC Policy Briefing*, Brussels: European Policy Centre, 17 February 2005.

Browning, C. and Joenniemi, P., 'Geostrategies of the European Neighbourhood Policy', *DIIS Working Paper* 2007/9, Copenhagen: Danish Institute for International Studies, 2007.

Burke, E., 'Spain and Equatorial Guinea – Different Views, Same Interest', *FRIDE Comment*, Madrid: Fundación para las Relaciones Internacionales y el Diálogo Exterior, June 2008.

Butler, N., 'European Energy Security', presentation at the International Institute for Strategic Studies, Geneva, 17 September 2005. ONLINE. Available HTTP: http://www.bp.com/genericarticle.do?categoyId = 98&contentId = 7010497

—— 'Energy Security: A New Agenda for Europe', *CER Bulletin* 38, October–November 2004.

Burnell, P., 'The First Two MMD Administrations in Zambia: Millennium Dawn or Millennium Sunset?', *Contemporary Politics* 7/2, 2001.

Burrows, M. and Treverton, G., 'A Strategic View of Energy Futures', *Survival*, 49/3, 2007.

Carothers, T., *US Democracy Promotion during and after Bush*, Washington, DC: Carnegie Endowment for International Peace, 2007.

Clarke, D., *The Battle for Barrels: Peak Oil Myths and World Oil Futures*, London: Profile Books, 2007.

Claudín, C. and González, A. (eds) *Asia Central y La Seguridad Energética Global*, Barcelona: CIDOB, 2008.

CEPS, *CEPS European Neighbourhood Watch* 36, Brussels: Centre for European Policy Studies, March 2008

—— *CEPS European Neighbourhood Watch* 31, Brussels: Centre for European Policy Studies, October 2007.

—— *CEPS European Neighbourhood Watch* 27, Brussels: Centre for European Policy Studies, May 2007.

—— *CEPS European Neighbourhood Watch* 23, Brussels: Centre for European Policy Studies, January 2007.

—— *CEPS European Neighbourhood Watch* 20, Brussels, Centre for European Policy Studies, October 2006.

—— *CEPS European Neighbourhood Watch* 18, Brussels: Centre for European Policy Studies, July 2006.

—— 'G8 Chair's Summary', G8 Summit Saint Petersburg, 17 July 2006 in *CEPS European Neighbourhood Watch* 18, Brussels: Centre for European Policy Studies, July 2006.

—— 'European Commission Approves Terms for Negotiating New EU-Russia Agreement', press release, 3 July 2006, in *CEPS European Neighbourhood Watch* 18, Brussels: Centre for European Policy Studies, July 2006.

—— *CEPS European Neighbourhood Watch* 16, Brussels: Centre for European Policy Studies, May 2006.

CEPS Task Force Report, 'Energy Policy for Europe: Identifying the European Added-Value', Brussels: Centre for European Policy Studies, March 2008.

Cerny, P., 'Political Agency in a Globalizing World: Toward a Structurational Approach', *European Journal of International Relations* 6/4, 2000.

CFR–James A. Baker III Institute for Public Policy, 'Strategic Energy Policy Challenges for the 21st Century', report of an Independent Task Force, Houston: James A. Baker III Institute for Public Policy, Rice University, and the Council on Foreign Relations, 2001.

Chafer, T., 'From Confidence to Confusion: Franco-African Relations in the Era of Globalisation', in Maclean, M. and Szarka, J. (eds) *France in the World*, Basingstoke: Palgrave Macmillan, 2008.

Checkel, J., 'Social Constructivisms in Global and European Politics: A Review Essay', *Review of International Studies* 30, 2004.

—— 'Why Comply? Social Learning and European Identity Change', *International Organization* 55/3, Summer 2001.

Chomsky, N., *World Orders, Old and New*, London: Pluto Press, 1997.

—— *Deterring Democracy*, London: Vintage, 1992.

Christiansen, T. and Tonra, B. (eds) *Rethinking European Union Foreign Policy*, Manchester: Manchester University Press, 2004.

—— 'The Study of EU Foreign Policy: Between International Relations and European Studies', in Christiansen, T. and Tonra, B. (eds) *Rethinking European Union Foreign Policy*, Manchester: Manchester University Press, 2004.

CIEP, *Study on Energy Supply Security and Geopolitics*, The Hague: Clingendael International Energy Programme, January 2004.

Collard-Wexler, S., 'Integration under Anarchy: Neorealism and the European Union', *European Journal of International Relations* 1273, 2006.

Commission of the European Communities, *Implementation of the European Neighbourhood Policy in 2007: Progress Report on Azerbaijan*, COM(2008) 164, Brussels: European Commission, 3 April 2008.

—— *European Energy and Transport Trends to 2030 – Update 2007*, Brussels: European Commission, 2007.

—— *Energy Statistics Pocketbook 2007*, Brussels: European Commission, 2007.

—— *A Strong European Neighbourhood Policy*, COM(2007) 774, Brussels: European Commission, 5 December 2007.

—— *An Energy Policy for Europe*, COM(2007) 1, Brussels: European Commission, 10 January 2007.

—— *Communication from the Commission, Governance in the European Consensus on Development: Towards a Harmonised Approach in the EU*, COM(2006) 421, Brussels: European Commission, 30 August 2006.

—— *Green Paper: A European Strategy for Sustainable, Competitive and Secure Energy*, COM(2006) 105, Brussels: European Commission, 8 March 2006.

—— *Commission Staff Working Document – Annex to the Green Paper, A European Strategy for Sustainable, Competitive and secure Energy*, SEC(2006), 317/2, Brussels: European Commission, 8 March 2006.

—— *An External Policy to Serve Europe's Energy Interests*, paper from the Commission/SG/HR for the European Council, Brussels: European Commission, 2006.

—— *Memorandum of Understanding on a Strategic Partnership between the European Union and the Republic of Azerbaijan in the Field of Energy*, Brussels: European Commission, 2006.

—— *Memorandum of Understanding on Cooperation in the Field of Energy between the European Union and the Republic of Kazakhstan*, Brussels: European Commission, 2006.

—— *EU Strategy for Africa: Towards a Euro-African Pact to Accelerate Africa's Development*, COM(2005) 489, Brussels: European Commission, 12 October 2005.

—— *Communication from the Commission to the Council and European Parliament, Proposal for a Joint Declaration by the Council, the European Parliament and the Commission on the European Development Policy*, COM(2005) 311, Brussels: European Commission, July 2005.

—— *Communication from the Commission to the Council, the European Parliament and the European Economic and Social Committee, Policy Coherence for Development*, COM(2005) 134, Brussels: European Commission, 12 April 2005.

—— *Information Note on the Revision of the Cotonou Agreement*, Brussels: European Commission, 2004.

—— *Strategy Paper 2002–2006 and Indicative Programme 2002–2004 for Central Asia*, Brussels: European Commission, 30 October 2002.

—— *Communication from the Commission on Conflict Prevention*, COM(2001) 211, Brussels: European Commission, 11 April 2001.

—— *The EU's Relations with Turkmenistan*. ONLINE. Available HTTP: http://ec.europa.eu/comm/external_relations/turkmenistan/intro/index.htm (accessed 28 August 2006).

—— *The EU's Relations with Azerbaijan*. ONLINE. Available HTTP: http://ec.europa.eu/comm/external_relations/azerbaijan/intro/index.htm (accessed 28 August 2006).

—— *The EU's Relations with Kazakhstan*. ONLINE. Available HTTP: http://ec.europa.eu/comm/external_relations/kazakhstan/intro/index.htm (accessed 28 August 2006).

—— *The EU's Relations with Uzbekistan*. ONLINE. Available HTTP: http://ec.europa.eu/comm/external_relations/uzbekistan/intro/index.htm (accessed 28 August 2006).

Conservative Party, 'An Unquiet World', submission to the Shadow Cabinet, London: Conservative Party, July 2007.

Cooper, R., *The Breaking of Nations*, Boston: Atlantic Monthly Press, 2003.

Cornell, S., 'Europe's Energy Security: The Role of the Black Sea Region', in Austin, G. and Schellekens-Gaiffe, M. (eds) *Energy and Conflict Prevention*, Brussels: Madariaga European Foundation, 2007.

Cortina, A., 'Welcome and Introduction', in Mossavar-Rahmani, B. (ed.) *Thinking the Unthinkable*, proceedings of XIII Repsol YPF–Harvard Seminar on Energy Policy, Salamanca, 9–10 May 2003.

Council of the European Union, *Climate Change and International Security 7249/08*, paper from the High Representative and the European Commission to the European Council, Brussels: European Council, 3 March 2008.

—— *Conclusions of the Council and the Representatives of the Governments of the Member States Meeting Within the Council on Energy Cooperation between Africa and Europe*, 9562/07, Brussels: European Council, 15 May 2007.

—— *8th EU-Africa Ministerial Troika Meeting, Final Communiqué*, 9678/07, Brussels: European Council, 15 May 2007.

—— *Presidency Conclusions, March 2007, European Council Action Plan (2007–2009): Energy Policy for Europe*, Brussels: European Council, 2 May 2007.

—— *Presidency–Commission Joint Background Paper on Energy Cooperation between Africa and Europe*, 8376/07, Brussels, European Council, 17 April 2007.

—— *8th Euro-Mediterranean Conference of Ministers of Foreign Affairs, Tampere, 27–28 November 2006 – 'Tampere Conclusions'*, Brussels: European Council, 30 November 2006.

—— *Presidency Conclusions 23–24 March 2006* (7775/1/06 REV 1), Brussels: European Council, 18 May 2006.

—— *A Secure Europe in a Better World: European Security Strategy*, Brussels: European Council, 12 December 2003.

Cox, R., 'Global Restructuring: Making Sense of the Changing International Political Economy', in Stubbs, R. and Underhill, G. (eds) *Political Economy and the Changing Global Order*, Basingstoke: Palgrave Macmillan, 1994.

Croft, S., Howarth, J., Krahmann, E., Terriff, T. and Webber, M., 'The Governance of European Security', *Review of International Studies* 30, 2004.

Czech Ministry of Industry and Trade, *State Energy Policy of the Czech Republic 2004*, approved by Government Decision no. 211 of 10 March 2004, Prague: Czech Ministry of Industry and Trade, 2004.

Dannreuther, R., 'Developing the Alternative to Enlargement: The European Neighbourhood Policy', *EFAR* 11/2, 2006.

—— (ed.) *European Union Foreign and Security Policy: Towards a Neighbourhood Strategy*, London: Routledge, 2004.

Dave, B., 'The EU and Kazakhstan: Balancing Economic Cooperation and Aiding Democratic Reforms in the Central Asian Region', *CEPS Policy Brief* 127, Brussels: Centre for European Policy Studies, May 2007.

De Jong, J. and Hanke, S., *Energy as a Bond: Relations with Russia in the European and Dutch context*, The Hague: Clingendael Institute for International Relations, 2007.

Democracy Digest, Washington, DC: National Endowment for Democracy, May 2007.

Denison, M., 'Turkmenistan in Transition: A Window for EU Engagement?', *CEPS Policy Brief* 129, Brussels: Centre for European Policy Studies, April 2007.

Deutch, J., 'Security and Energy: Short-term Implications of a Long-term View', in Mossavar-Rahmani, B. (ed.) *Thinking the Unthinkable*, proceedings of XIII Repsol YPF–Harvard Seminar on Energy Policy, Salamanca, 9–10 May 2003.

DfID, *Governance, Development and Democratic Politics*, London: UK Department for International Development, 2007.

—— *Nigeria, Draft Country Assistance Plan 2004*, London: UK Department for International Development, 2007.

DGCID–MAE, *Governance Strategy for French Development Assistance*, Paris: Direction Générale de la Coopération Internationale et Development, Ministère des Affaires Étrangères, 5 December 2006.

Dimier, V., 'Constructing Conditionality: The Bureaucratization of EC Development Aid', *European Foreign Affairs Review* 11/2, 2006.

Dobson, L., 'Normative Theory and Europe', *International Affairs* 82/3, 2006.

DTI, *Meeting the Energy Challenge: A White Paper on Energy*, London: Department for Business, Enterprise and Regulatory Reform, May 2007.

—— *Energy Act 2004, Second Annual Report to Parliament on the Security of Gas and Electricity Supply in Great Britain by the Secretary of State for Trade and Industry*, London: Department for Business, Enterprise and Regulatory Reform, 11 July 2006.

—— 'Joint Energy Security of Supply Working Group (JESS)', Sixth Report, London: Department for Business, Enterprise and Regulatory Reform, April 2006.

—— *Our Energy Future: Creating a Low Carbon Economy. Energy White Paper*, London: Department for Business, Enterprise and Regulatory Reform, 25 February 2003.

Duke, S. and Ojanen, H., 'Bridging Internal and External Security: Lessons from the European Security and Defence Policy', *Journal of European Integration*, 28/5, 2006.

Dutch Energy Council, The, *Energised Foreign Policy: Security of Energy Supply as a Key Objective*, The Hague: The Dutch Energy Council, December 2005.

Dutch Ministry of Foreign Affairs and Economy Ministry, *Security of Energy Supply and Foreign Policy*, The Hague: Dutch Ministry of Foreign Affairs and Economy Ministry, 19 May 2006.

ECDPM, *Governance Impact Assessment*, SEC(2006) 1021, Maastricht: European Centre for Development Policy Management, March 2006.

—— *InfoCotonou 7: The Review of the Cotonou Partnership Agreement: What's at Stake?*, Maastricht: European Centre for Development Policy Management, 2004.

—— *InBrief* 5, Maastricht: European Centre for Development Policy Management, October 2003.

—— *Cotonou Infokit: Essential and Fundamental Elements (20)*, Maastricht: European Centre for Development Policy Management, 2001.

Echagüe, A., 'The European Union and the Gulf Cooperation Council', *FRIDE Working Paper* 39, Madrid: Fundación para las Relaciones Internacionales y el Diálogo Exterior, May 2007.

Economist, The, Special Report on Iran, London: The Economist, 21 July 2007.

Egenhofer, C., 'Integrating Security of Supply, Market Liberalisation and Climate Change', in Emerson, M. (ed.) *Readings in European Security* 4, Brussels: Centre for European Policy Studies, 2007.

EIA, *US National Oil and Gas Imports by Country*, Washington, DC: Energy Information Administration, 2007. ONLINE. Available HTTP: www.eia.doe.gov

EIU, *Country Monitor*, London: The Economist Intelligence Unit, 24 September 2007.

El-Badri, A. S., keynote address to Chatham House, London, 8 February 2008. ONLINE. Available HTTP: http://www.cfr.org/publication/15701/keynote_address _to_chatham_house_by_he_abdalla_salem_elbari.html

Elgström, O. and Smith, M. (eds), *The European Union's Roles in International Politics. Concepts and Analysis*, London: Routledge, 2006.

Elhefnawy, N., 'The Impending Oil Shock', *Survival*, 50/2, 2008.

Emerson, M., 'Time to Think of a Strategic Bargain with Russia', *Policy Brief* 160, Brussels: Centre for European Policy Studies, May 2008.

—— (ed.) *Readings in European Security* 4, Brussels: Centre for European Policy Studies, 2007.

—— 'From an Awkward Partnership to a Greater Europe? A European Perspective', in Emerson, M., Kobrinskaya, I. and Rumer, E., 'Russia and the West', *Working Paper* 16, Brussels: Centre for European Policy Studies, September 2004.

Emerson, M., Kobrinskaya, I. and Rumer, E., 'Russia and the West', *Working Paper* 16, Brussels: Centre for European Policy Studies, September 2004.

Emerson, M., Tassinari, F. and Vahl, M. 'A New Agreement between the EU and Russia: Why, What and When?', *CEPS Policy Brief* 103, Brussels: Centre for European Policy Studies, May 2006.

Ehteshami, A. and Wright, S., 'Political Change in the Arab Oil Monarchies: From Liberalisation to Enfranchisment', *International Affairs* 83/5, 2007.

ENEL, *Annual Report 2007*, Rome: ENEL, 2007.

—— *Code of Conduct*, Rome: ENEL, 2004

Engdahl, W., *A Century of War: Anglo-American Oil Politics and the New World Order*, London: Pluto, 2004.

ENI, *Sustainability Report 2006*, Milan: ENI, 2006.

ENPI, *Regional Strategy Paper (2007–2103) and Regional Indicative Programme (2007–2010) for the Euro-Mediterranean Partnership*, Brussels: European Neighbourhood and Partnership Instrument.

—— *Azerbaijan Country Strategy Paper 2007–2013*, Brussels: European Neighbourhood and Partnership Instrument.

Estrada, A., 'Argelia: ¿Retorno al Nacionalismo Energético?' *Análisis del Real Instituto*, Madrid: Real Instituto Elcano, September 2006.

Estrada, A. and Lorca, A., 'África del Norte: Su Importancia Geopolítica en el Ámbito Energético', *Working Paper* 11/2007, Madrid: Real Instituto Elcano, April 2007.

EU–Africa Summit, *The Africa–EU Strategic Partnership*, adopted by the Lisbon Summit, 9 December 2007.

EU–Russia Centre, *The Bilateral Relations of Member States with Russia*, Brussels: EU–Russia Centre, January 2008.

EU–Russia Energy Dialogue, *Seventh Progress Report*, presented by Russian Minister of Industry Victor Khristenko and European Commissioner for Energy Andris Piebalgs, Moscow/Brussels, November 2006.

—— 'The Energy Dialogue EU–Russia', presentation of Christian Cleutinx, Director, European Commission Coordinator of the EU–Russia Energy Dialogue, Luxembourg, October 2005.

—— *Sixth Progress Report*, presented by Russian Minister of Industry Victor Khristenko and European Commission Director-General François Lamoureux, Moscow/Brussels, October 2005.

—— *Fifth Progress Report*, presented by Russian Minister of Industry Victor Khristenko and European Commission Director-General François Lamoureux, Moscow/Brussels, November 2004.

European Commission Eurobarometer Unit, *Eurobarometer Survey*, Brussels: European Commission, March 2007.

European Parliament, 'The Future of the European Security Strategy: Towards a White Book on European Defence', paper to the Workshop organised by the EP Sub-Committee on Security and Defence, Brussels, 6 March 2008.

—— *Draft Report on Towards a Common European Foreign Policy on Energy*, Brussels: European Parliament, 22 May 2007.

European Parliament–Council–Commission, *The European Consensus on Development*, 2006/C 46/01, Brussels: European Parliament–Council–Commission, 24 February 2006.

Farés, J. and Pérez, F., 'España en la Génesis de una Nueva Política Europea de Energía', *Working Paper*, Barcelona: Observatorio de Política Exterior Europea, Universidad Autónoma de Barcelona, March 2008.

Farrell, M., 'A Triumph of Realism over Idealism? Cooperation between the European Union and Africa', *Journal of European Integration* 27/3, 2005.

FCO, *UK International Priorities. A Strategy for the FCO*, Foreign Policy White Paper presented to Parliament by the Secretary of State for Foreign & Commonwealth Affairs by Command of Her Majesty, London: Foreign and Common Wealth Office, December 2003.

—— *Good Governance in the Energy Sector,* London: Foreign and Common Wealth Office. ONLINE. [0]Available HTTP: http://www.fco.gov.uk/servlet/Front?pagename = OpenMarket/Xcelerate/ShowPage&c

FCO–DTI–DEFRA–SEPN, *UK International Priorities: The Energy Strategy*, London: Foreign and Common Wealth Office, Department for Business, Enterprise and Regulatory Reform, Department for Environment, Food and Rural Affairs and Sustainable Energy Policy Network, 2004.

Ferrero-Waldner, B., opening speech, European Neighbourhood Policy Conference, Brussels, 3 September 2007. ONLINE. Available HTTP: http://europa.eu/rapid/pressReleasesAction.do?reference = SPEECH/07/500

— 'The European Approach to Democracy Promotion in Post-communist Countries', speech to the Institute for Human Sciences, Vienna, 19 January 2007.

—— opening address at the External Energy Policy Conference, Brussels, 20 November 2006.

—— 'The European Neighbourhood Policy: The EU's Newest Foreign Policy Instrument', *European Foreign Affairs Review* 11/2, 2006.

—— 'Azerbaijan', speech to the European Parliament, Strasbourg, 26 October 2005.

Fischer, S., 'The EU and Russia: Conflicts and Potential of a Difficult Partnership', *SWP Research Paper*, Berlin: Stiftung Wissenschaft und Politik, January 2007.

Financial Times, Special Report: Energy, 9 November 2007. ONLINE. Available HTTP: http://www.ft.com/reports/energynov2007

Fox, L., 'Energy Security and Military Structures', speech at Chatham House, London, 22 May 2006.

Franssen, H., 'Oil Supply Security through 2010', in Bloomfield Jr., L. (ed.) *Global Markets and National Interests: The New Geopolitics of Energy, Capital, and Information,* Washington, DC: Centre for Strategic and International Studies, 2002.

French Ministry of the Economy, Industry and Employment, 'Commentaires de la France sur les propositions du Livre vert', Paris: French Ministry of the Economy, Industry and Employment, March 2006. ONLINE. Available HTTP: www.industrie.gouv.fr/energie

—— *French Memorandum for Revitalising European Energy Policy with a view to Sustainable Development*, Paris: French Ministry of the Economy, Industry and Employment, 17 January 2006.

Friedman, T., 'The First Law of Petropolitics', *Foreign Policy*, May–June 2006.

Frynas, J. and Paulo, M., 'A New Scramble for African Oil? Historical, Political, and Business Perspectives', *African Affairs* 106/243.

Fusaro, P., 'The Future Importance of Oil: Geopolitical Lynchpin or Common Commodity', in Bloomfield Jr., L. (ed.) *Global Markets and National Interests: The New Geopolitics of Energy, Capital, and Information,* Washington, DC: Centre for Strategic and International Studies, 2002.

Garton Ash, T., *Free World: Why a Crisis of the West Reveals the Opportunity of Our Time*, London: Penguin Books, 2005.

Gault, J., 'European Energy Security: Balancing Priorities', *FRIDE Comment*, Madrid: Fundación para las Relaciones Internacionales y el Diálogo Exterior, May 2007. ONLINE. Available HTTP: www.fride.org

—— 'EU energy security and the periphery', in Dannreuther, R. (ed.) *European Union Foreign and Security Policy: Towards a Neighbourhood Strategy*, London: Routledge, 2004.

Ghazvinian, J., *Untapped: The Scramble for Africa's Oil*, Orlando: Harcourt, 2007.

Gheissari, A. and Nasr, V., *Democracy in Iran: History and the Quest for Liberty*, Oxford: Oxford University Press, 2006.

Gibert, M., 'Monitoring a Region in Crisis: the European Union in West Africa', *Chaillot Paper* 98, Paris: European Union Institute for Security Studies, January 2007.

Gills, B., Rocamora, J. and Wilson, R. (eds) *Low Intensity Democracy: Political Power in the New World Order*, London: Pluto Press, 1993.

—— 'Low Intensity Democracy', in Gills, B., Rocamora, J. and Wilson, R. (eds) *Low Intensity Democracy: Political Power in the New World Order*, London: Pluto Press, 1993.

Ginsberg, R., *The European Union in International Politics: Baptism by Fire*, Lanham, MD: Rowman and Littlefield, 2001.

Global Witness, *Oil and Mining in Violent Places: Why Voluntary Codes for Companies Don't Guarantee Human Rights*, London: Global Witness, October 2007.

—— 'EITI on the Right Track: Let's Go Further and Master', press statement, London: Global Witness, March 2005.

Glosemeyer, I., 'Checks, Balances and Transformation in the Saudi Political System', in Aarts, P. and Nonneman, G. (eds) *Saudi Arabia in the Balance: Political Economy, Society, Foreign Affairs*, London: Hurst and Company, 2005.

GMF, *Transatlantic Trends 2007*, Washington, DC: The German Marshall Fund of the United States, 2007.

Grant, C., *Europe's Blurred Boundaries: Rethinking Enlargement and Neighbourhood Policy*, London: Centre for European Reform, 2006.

Grant, C. and Valasek, T., *Preparing for the Multipolar World: European Foreign and Security Policy in 2020*, London: Centre for European Reform, 2007.

GRC, *The GCC Yearbook 2006*, Dubai: Gulf Research Centre, 2006.

Gritsch, M., 'The Nation-state and Economic Globalization: Soft Geo-politics and Increased State Autonomy?', *Review of International Political Economy* 12/1, 2005.

Goldwyn, D. and Kalicki, J. (eds) *Energy and Security: Toward a New Foreign Policy Strategy*, Washington, DC: Woodrow Wilson Center, 2005.

—— 'Introduction: The Need to Integrate Energy and Foreign Policy', in Goldwyn, D. and Kalicki, J. (eds) *Energy and Security: Toward a New Foreign Policy Strategy*, Washington, DC: Woodrow Wilson Center.

Gourlay, C., 'Community Instruments for Civilian Crisis Management', in Nowak, A. (ed.) 'Civilian Crisis Management: The EU Way', *Chaillot Paper* 90, Paris: EU Institute for Security Studies, June 2006.

Guerrero, F., 'Las Relaciones España-África Subsahariana: ¿A Remolque o en la Vanguardia de la UE', *Working Paper*, Barcelona: Observatorio de Política Exterior Europea, Universidad Autónoma de Barcelona, March 2008.

Halliday, F., *100 Myths about the Middle East*, London: Saqi, 2005.

Hamzawy, A., 'The Saudi Labyrinth: Evaluating the Current Political Opening', *Carnegie Working Paper* 68, Washington, DC: Carnegie Endowment for International Peace, April 2006.

Hansen, S., *Pipeline Politics: The Struggle for Control of the Eurasian Energy Resources*, The Hague: Clingendael Institute for International Relations, 2003.

Hay, C. and Rosamond, B., 'Globalization, European Integration and the Discursive Construction of Economic Imperatives', *Journal of European Public Policy* 9/2, 2002.

Heliot, J., 'France and the Arabian Gulf', *GCC–EU Research Bulletin* 5, Dubai: Gulf Research Centre, July 2006.

Henningsen, J., 'Rising to the Energy Challenge: Key Elements for an Effective EU Strategy', *Issue paper* 51, Brussels: European Policy Centre, December 2006.

Hettne, B. and Söderbaum, F., 'Civilian Power or Soft Imperialism? The EU as a Global Actor and the Role of Interregionalism', *European Foreign Affairs Review* 10/4, 2005.

High-Level Task Force on UK Energy Security, Climate Change and Development Assistance, *Energy, Politics and Poverty*, Oxford: Oxford University Press, June 2007.

Hill, C. and Smith, M., *International Relations and the European Union*, Oxford: Oxford University Press, 2005.

—— 'International Relations and the European Union: Themes and Issues', in Hill, C. and Smith, M., *International Relations and the European Union*, Oxford: Oxford University Press, 2005.

Howard, R., 'Oil at 100', *The World Today* 64/5, May 2008.

Howarth, J., *Security and Defence Policy in Europe*, Basingstoke: Palgrave Macmillan, 2007.

Humphreys, M., Sachs, J. and Stiglitz, J. (eds) *Escaping the Resource Curse*, New York: Colombia University Press, 2007.

—— 'Introduction: What is the Problem with Natural Resource Wealth?', in Humphreys, M., Sachs, J. and Stiglitz, J. (eds) *Escaping the Resource Curse*, New York: Colombia University Press, 2007.

Hurrell, A., *On Global Order: Power, Values and the Constitution of International Society*, Oxford: Oxford University Press, 2007.

Hyde-Price, A., 'A "Tragic Actor?" A Realist Perspective on "Ethical power Europe"', *International Affairs* 84/1, 2008.

—— '"Normative" Power Europe: A Realist Critique', *Journal of European Public Policy* 13/2, 2006.

Iberdrola, *Presencia del Grupo Iberdrola en el Mundo*, Madrid: Iberdrola, 2006.

Ibrahim, J., 'Nigeria's 2007 Elections: The Fitful Path to Democratic Citizenship', *Special Report* 182, Washington, DC: United States Institute for Peace, January 2007.

ICG, 'Sudan's Comprehensive Peace Agreement: Beyond the Crisis', *Africa Briefing* 50, Brussels: International Crisis Group, March 2008.

—— 'Nigeria: Ending Unrest in the Niger Delta', *Africa Report* 135, Brussels: International Crisis Group, December 2007.

—— 'Central Asia's Energy Risks', *Asia Report* 133, Brussels: International Crisis Group, 24 May 2007.

—— 'Turkmenistan after Niyazov', *Asia Briefing* 60, Brussels: International Crisis Group, February 2007.

—— 'Uzbekistan: Europe's Sanctions Matter', *Asia Briefing* 54, Brussels: International Crisis Group, November 2006.

—— 'Fuelling the Niger Delta Crisis', *Africa Report* 118, Brussels: International Crisis Group, 28 September 2006.

—— 'Central Asia: What Role for the European Union?', *Asia Report* 113, Brussels: International Crisis Group, April 2006.

International Alert, *Strategising for Peace and Social Justice in West Africa*, London: International Alert, 2004.

Isbell, P., 'Revisiting Energy Security', *Análisis del Real Instituto,* Madrid: Real Instituto Elcano, 23 November 2007.

—— 'La Dependencia Energética y los Intereses de España', *Análisis del Real Instituto*, Madrid: Real Instituto Elcano, 3 March 2006.

Italian Ministry of Foreign Affairs, *Energy.* ONLINE. Available HTTP: http://www. esteri.it/MAE/EN/Politica_Estera/Temi_Globali/Energia/

Jaffe, A., 'The Outlook for Future Oil Supply from the Middle East and Price Implications', speech, Tokyo, 20 July 2005, available from the James Baker III Institute for Public Policy, Rice University.

James A. Baker III Institute for Public Policy, 'The Geopolitics of Natural Gas', *Baker Institute Study* 29, Houston: James A. Baker III Institute for Public Policy, Rice University, March 2005.

Joffé, G., 'The European Union, Democracy and Counter-terrorism in the Maghreb', *Journal of Common Market Studies* 46/1, 2008.

Johnson, D., 'EU-Russia Energy Links', in Johnson, D. and Robinson, P. (eds) *Perspectives on EU–Russia Relations*, London: Routledge, 2005.

Johnson, D. and Robinson, P. (eds) *Perspectives on EU-Russia Relations*, London: Routledge, 2005.

Jonavicius, L., 'The Democracy Promotion Policies of Central and Eastern European States', *FRIDE Working Paper* 55, Madrid: Fundación para las Relaciones Internacionales y el Diálogo Exterior, March 2008.

Kaldor, M., Martin, M. and Selchow, S., 'Human Security: A New Strategic Narrative for Europe', *International Affairs* 83/2, 2007.

Kaldor, M., Karl, T. and Said, Y. (eds) *Oil Wars*, London: Pluto Press, 2007.

—— 'Introduction', in Kaldor, M., Karl, T. and Said, Y. (eds) *Oil Wars*, London: Pluto Press, 2007.

Kassenova, N., 'The New EU Strategy towards Central Asia: A View from the Region', *CEPS Policy Brief* 148, Brussels: Centre for European Policy Studies, January 2008.

Katzenstein, P., Keohane, R. and Krasner, S., 'International Organisation and the Study of World Politics', *International Organization* 52/4, Fall 1998.

Kausch, K., 'Europe and Russia, beyond Energy', *FRIDE Working Paper* 33, Madrid: Fundación para las Relaciones Internacionales y el Diálogo Exterior, March 2007.

Keohane, D., 'The Absent Friend: EU Foreign Policy and Counter-terrorism', *Journal of Common Market Studies* 46/1, 2008.

Kern, S., 'How the Demand for Oil Drives American Foreign Policy', *Análisis del Real Instituto*, Madrid: Real Instituto Elcano, 23 June 2006.

Kirchner, E., 'The Challenge of European Union Security Governance', *Journal of Common Market Studies* 44/5, 2006.

Klare, M., *Blood and Oil*, London: Penguin, 2004.

Kleveman, L., *The New Great Game: Blood and Oil in Central Asia*, London: Atlantic Books, 2004.

Koch, C., 'GCC–EU Relations: The News Again is "No News"', *GCC–EU Research Bulletin* 5, Dubai: Gulf Research Centre, July 2006.

Koenig-Archibugi, M., 'International Governance as New *Raison d'État*? The Case of the EU Common Foreign and Security Policy', *European Journal of International Relations* 10/2, 2004.

Kohler-Koch, B. and Rittberger, B., 'The "Governance Turn" in EU Studies', *Journal of Common Market Studies* 44, Annual Review, 2006.

Kolk, A. and Pinkse, J., 'Multinationals' Political Activities on Climate Change', *Business and Society* 46/2, 2007.

Kolstrad, I.and Wiig, A., 'Transparency in Oil Rich Economies', *U4* 2, Bergen: Chr. Michelsen Institute, 2007.

Konoplyanik, A., 'Energy Charter: The Key to International Energy Security', *Petroleum Economist*, February 2006.

Kotsopoulous, J., 'The EU and Africa: Coming Together at Last?', *EPC Policy Brief*, Brussels: European Policy Centre, July 2007.

Kupchan, C., 'The Rise of Europe, America's Changing Internationalism, and the End of U.S. Primacy', *Political Science Quarterly* 118/2, Summer 2003.

Laïdi, Z. (ed.) *European Union Foreign Policy in a Globalized World: Normative Power and Social Preferences*, London: Routledge, 2008.

Lamy, J., 'Que Signifie Relancer la Politique Énergétique Européenne?', *Revue du marché común et de l'Union européenne* 506, March 2007.

Landaburu, E., European Parliament hearing on 'Towards a Common European Foreign Policy on Energy', Brussels, 28 February 2007.

Lavenex, S. 'EU external governance in "wider Europe"', *Journal of European Public Policy* 11/4, 2004.

Layne, C., 'The Unipolar Illusion Revisited: The Coming of the United States' Unipolar Moment', *International Security* 31/2, 2006.

Leonard, M., *Divided World: The Struggle for Power in 2020*, London: Centre for European Reform, 2006.

Leonard M. and Popescu N. *A Power Audit of EU-Russia Relations*, London, European Council on Foreign Relations, 2007

Linklater, A., 'A European Civilising Process', in Hill, C. and Smith, M., *International Relations and the European Union*, Oxford: Oxford University Press, 2005.

Luciani, G., 'Arab States: Oil Resources and Transparency', *Arab Reform Bulletin* 6/2, Washington, DC: Carnegie Endowment for International Peace, March 2008.

—— 'The Economics and Politics of the "Dire Straits"', *GRC Security and Terrorism Research Bulletin* 6, Dubai: Gulf Research Centre, August 2007.

Lyne, R., 'Russia at the Crossroads: Again?', *The EU–Russia Review*, Brussels: EU–Russia Centre, May 2006.

MacFarlane, S., 'The Caucasus and Central Asia: Towards a Non-strategy', in Dannreuther, R. (ed.) *European Union Foreign and Security Policy: Towards a Neighbourhood Strategy*, London: Routledge, 2004.

Maclean, M. and Szarka, J. (eds) *France in the World*, Basingstoke: Palgrave Macmillan, 2008.

McCormick, J., *The European Superpower*, Basingstoke: Palgrave Macmillan, 2007.

Magen, A., 'Transformative Engagement through Law: The Acquis Communitaire as an Instrument of EU External Influence', *European Journal of Law Reform* 9/3, 2007.

Mañé-Estrada, A., 'European Energy Security: Towards the Creation of the Geoenergy Space', *Energy Policy* 34/18, 2006.

Manners, I., 'Normative Power Europe Reconsidered: Beyond the Crossroads', *Journal of European Public Policy* 13/2, 2006.

Marcel, V., 'Investment in Middle East Oil: Who Needs Whom?', *Chatham House Report*, London: Royal Institute of International Affairs, February 2006.

—— 'Total in Iraq', *Policy Brief*, Washington, DC: Brookings Institution, August 2003.

Martinez, L., 'European Union's Exportation of Democratic Norms: The Case of North Africa', in Laïdi, Z. (ed.) *European Union Foreign Policy in a Globalized World: Normative Power and Social Preferences*, London: Routledge, 2008.

Maynes, C., 'A Soft Power Tool-kit for Dealing with Russia', *Europe's World* 3, Summer 2006.

Marriott J., Rowell, A. and Stockman, L., *The Next Gulf: London, Washington and Oil Conflict in Nigeria*, London: Constable, 2005.

Matveeva, A., 'EU Stakes in Central Asia', *Chaillot Paper* 91, Paris: EU Institute for Security Studies, July 2006.

Melvin, N., 'Building Stronger Ties, Meeting New Challenges: The European Union's Strategic Role in Central Asia', *CEPS Policy Brief* 128, Brussels: European Centre for Policy Studies, March 2007.

Merkel, A. and Putin, V., 'Joint Press Conference Following the Russia-European Union Summit Meeting, Samara, Russia Federation', 18 May 2007, in *CEPS Neighbourhood Watch* 27, Brussels: Centre for European Policy Studies, May 2007.

Meyer, C., 'Convergence Towards a European Strategic Culture? A Constructivist Framework for Explaining Changing Norms', *European Journal of International Relations* 11/4, 2005.

Michel, L., speech at the European Policy Centre, Brussels, 5 December 2007.

Miliband, D., 'New Diplomacy: Challenges for Foreign Policy', speech at the Royal Institute for International Affairs, London, 9 July 2007.

Milov, V. 'The Use of Energy as a Political Tool', *The EU–Russia Review* 1, Brussels: EU-Russia Centre, May 2006.

Missiroli, A., 'Disasters Past and Present: New Challenges for the EU', *Journal of European Integration* 28/5, 2006.

Mitchell, J., 'A New Era for Oil Prices', *Chatham Rouse Report*, London: Royal Institute of International Affairs, August 2006.

—— 'Renewing Energy Security', *RIIA Working Paper*, London: Royal Institute of International Affairs, July 2002.

—— 'Energy Supply Security: Changes in Concepts', speech to the French Ministry of Economy, Finance and Industry, Paris, November 2000.

Mitchell J., Morita K., Selley N. and Stern J., *The New Economy of Oil: Impacts on Business, Geopolitics and Society*, London: Royal Institute for International Affairs, 2001.

Mölling, C., 'EU Battle Groups 2007: Where Next?', *European Security Review* 31, December 2006.

Mommer, B., *The Governance of International Oil: The Changing Rules of the Game*, Oxford: Oxford Institute for Energy Studies, WPM 26, 2000.

Monaghan, A., 'Energy Security: NATO's Limited, Complementary Role', *Research Paper* 36, Rome: NATO Defence College, May 2008.

—— 'EU–Russia Energy Co-operation', *EU–Russia Review* 2, Brussels: EU–Russia Centre, November 2006.

Monaghan, A. and Montanaro-Jankovski, L., 'EU-Russia Energy Relations: The Need for Active Engagement', *EPC Issue Paper* 45, Brussels: European Policy Centre, March 2006.

Mossavar-Rahmani, B. (ed.) *Thinking the Unthinkable*, proceedings of XIII Repsol YPF–Harvard Seminar on Energy Policy, Salamanca, 9–10 May 2003.

Müller, F., 'Energy Security: Demands Imposed on German and European Foreign Policy by a Changed Configuration in the World Energy Market', *SWP Research Paper*, Berlin: Stiftung Wissenschaft und Politik, January 2007.

Murray, C., *Murder in Samarkand: A British Ambassador's Controversial Defiance of Tyranny in the War on Terror*, Edinburgh: Mainstream, 2007.

Neyer, J., 'The Deliberative Turn in Integration Theory', *Journal of European Public Policy* 13/5, 2006.

Niblock, T., *Saudi Arabia: Power, Legitimacy and Survival*, London: Routledge, 2006.

Nigeria–European Community, *Country Support Strategy and Indicative Programme for the Period 2001–2007*, Brussels: European Commission, 2001.

Noël, P., 'Time to Challenge the Myths of Energy security', *Financial Times*, 11 January 2008.

Nonneman, G., 'EU–GCC Relations: Dynamics, Patterns and Perspectives', *International Spectator* 41/3, July–September, 2006.

—— 'Political Reform in the Gulf Monarchies: From Liberalisation to Democratisation? A Comparative Perspective', *Durham Middle East Papers*, Sir William Luce Fellowship Paper 6, Durham: Institute for Middle Eastern and Islamic Studies, August 2006.

—— 'EU–GCC Relations: Dynamics, Patterns and Perspectives', *GRC Working Paper*, Dubai: Gulf Research Centre, June 2006.

Nowak, A. (ed.) 'Civilian Crisis Management: The EU Way', *Chaillot Paper* 90, Paris: EU Institute for Security Studies, June 2006.

Noreng, O., *Oil and Islam: Social and Economic Issues*, Chichester: John Wiley, 1997.

Nuriyev, E., *The South Caucasus at the Crossroads: Conflicts, Caspian Oil and Great Power Politics*, Berlin: Lit Vertag, 2007.

Nye, J., 'The Wrong Way of Thinking About Oil', *The Korea Herald*, 27 February 2006.

Parliament Magazine, 'EU says Russian Oil and Gas Decision "Highly Problematic"', *Parliament Magazine*, 19 September 2006. ONLINE. Available HTTP: http://www.theparliament.com/latestnews/news-article/newsarticle/eu-says-russiannbspoil-and-gasnbspdecision-highly-problematic/

Pascual, C., 'The Geopolitics of Energy: From Security to Survival', Washington, DC: Brookings Institute, January 2008.

Patterson, W., 'Loft Insulation as Foreign Policy', *The World Today* 63/7, July 2007.

Perry, A., 'Africa's Oil Dreams', *Newsweek*, 11 June 2007.

Peterson, J. and Young, A., 'The EU and the New Trade Politics', *Journal of European Public Policy* 13/6, 2006.

Piebalgs, A., 'Energy and Development', speech to the External Energy Policy Conference, Brussels, 21 November 2006.

Polish Ministry of Economy, *Guidelines for Energy Policy of Poland until 2020*, document approved by the Council of Ministers on 22 February 2000, Warsaw: Polish Ministry of Economy, 2000.

Rahr, A., 'Interview with Alexander Lukashenko in *Die Welt*, 25 January 2007', in *CEPS European Neighbourhood Watch* 23, Brussels: Centre for European Policy Studies, January 2007.

Renner, M., 'The New Geopolitics of Oil', *Development* 49/3, 2006.

Repsol-YPF, *Annual Report 2006*, Madrid: Repsol-YPF, 2006.

—— *Áreas de Negocio 2006*, Madrid: Repsol-YPF, 2006.

—— *Informe de Responsabilidad Corporativa 2006*, Madrid: Repsol-YPF, 2006.

Roberts, P., *The End of Oil: The Decline of the Petroleum Economy and the Rise of a New Energy Order*, London: Bloomsbury, 2005.

Robinson, W., *Promoting Polyarchy*, Cambridge: Cambridge University Press, 1996.

Rosamond, B., 'Conceptualizing the EU Model of Governance in World Politics', *European Foreign Affairs Review* 10/4, 2005.

—— 'Babylon and On? Globalization and International Political Economy', *Review of International Political Economy* 10/4, 2003.

Ross, M., 'Blood Barrels: Why Oil Wealth Fuels Conflict', *Foreign Affairs* 87/3, 2008.

Royal Dutch Shell, *Delivery and Growth: Annual Review and Summary of Financial Statements 2007*, The Hague: Royal Dutch Shell plc, 2007.

—— *2004 Royal Dutch/Shell Group of Companies Annual Report*, The Hague: Royal Dutch Shell plc, 2004.

Rutledge, I., *Addicted to Oil: America's Relentless Drive for Energy Security*, London: I.B.Tauris, 2006.

Saferworld–International Alert, *Developing an EU Strategy to Address Fragile States: Priorities for the UK Presidency of the EU in 2005*, London: Saferworld–International Alert, 2005.

Said, Y., 'Political Dynamics in Iraq within the Context of the Surge', submission to the US Senate's Foreign Relations Committee, 2 April 2008.

Sager, A., 'Political Opposition in Saudi Arabia', in Aarts, P. and Nonneman, G. (eds) *Saudi Arabia in the Balance: Political Economy, Society, Foreign Affairs*, London: Hurst and Company, 2005.

Sarkozy, N., 'Press Conference at the European Council Summit in Brussels, 13 March 2008', in *CEPS Neighbourhood Watch* 36, Brussels: Centre for European Policy Studies, March 2008.

Schiffrin A. and Tesalik, S. (eds) *Covering Oil*, New York: Revenue Watch, 2005.

Schimmelfenning, F. and Sedelmeier, U., 'Governance by Conditionality: EU Rule Transfer to the Candidate Countries of Central and Eastern Europe', *Journal of European Public Policy* 11, 2004.

Shaxson, N., *Poisoned Wells: The Dirty Politics of African Oil*, Basingstoke: Palgrave Macmillan, 2007.

Sherr, J., 'Energy Security: At Last, A Response from the EU', *UK Defence Academy* 7/10, March 2007.

Slaughter, A., *A New World Order*, Princeton: Princeton University Press, 2004.

Smith, M., 'Institutionalization, Policy Adaptation and European Foreign Policy Cooperation', *European Journal of International Relations* 10/1, 2004.

—— 'Toward a Theory of EU Foreign Policy Making: Multi-level Governance, Domestic Politics, and National Adaptation to Europe's Common Foreign and Security Policy', *Journal of European Public Policy* 11, August 2004.

Soares de Oliveira, R., *Oil and Politics in the Gulf of Guinea*, London: Hurst, 2007.

Solana, J., 'Energy in the Common Foreign and Security Policy', in Austin, G. and Schellekens-Gaiffe, M. (eds) *Energy and Conflict Prevention*, Brussels: Madariaga European Foundation, 2007.

—— address to the EU External Energy Policy Conference, Brussels, 20 November 2006.

Stanley Foundation, The, 'Africa at Risk or Rising? The Role of Europe, North America and China on the Continent', *Policy Dialogue Brief*, Muscatine: The Stanley Foundation, May 2007.

Steinmeier, F., 'Interaction and Integration', *Internationale Politik* 8/1, Spring 2007.

Stephens, K., 'Oil Companies and the International Oil Market', in Schiffrin A. and Tesalik, S. (eds) *Covering Oil*, New York: Revenue Watch, 2005.

Stern, A., *Who Won the Oil Wars? Why Government Wage War for Oil Rights*, London: Collins and Brown, 2005.

Stern, J., 'Security of European Natural Gas Supplies: The Impact of Import Dependence and Liberalization', *RIIA Working Paper*, London: Royal Institute of International Affairs, July 2002.

Stocking, B., 'Seismic Rupture', *The World Today* 64/1, January 2008.

Stokes, D., 'Blood for Oil? Global Capital, Counter-insurgency and the Dual Logic of American Energy Security', *Review of International Studies* 33/2, 2007.

Stubbs, R. and Underhill, G. (eds) *Political Economy and the Changing Global Order*, Basingstoke: Macmillan, 1994.

Synott, H., *Bad Days in Baghdad: My Turbulent Time as Britain's Man in Southern Iraq*, London: I. B. Tauris, 2008.

Theodorakis, A., keynote speech at the Africa–Europe Energy Forum, Berlin, 6–7 March 2007.

TI Norge, 'Publish What You Pay, New Report Finds Action Needed to Manage Natural Resource Revenues', press release, Oslo: Transparency International Norge, 11 October 2006.

Total, *Registration Document 2007,* Courbevoie: Total, 2007.

—— *Global Report 2005*, Courbevoie: Total, 2005.

Turkmenistan Project, *Turkmenistan News Brief* 12, New York: Open Society Institute, 16–22 March 2007.

Ungar, C., *House of Bush, House of Saud*, London: Gibson Square, 2007, 4th edition.

Vahl, M., 'A Privileged Partnership? EU–Russian Relations in a Comparative Perspective', *Working Paper* 2006/3, Copenhagen: Danish Institute for International Studies, 2006.

Van der Linde, C., 'Energy in a Changing World', inaugural lecture as Professor of Geopolitics and Energy Management at the University of Groningen, *Clingendael Energy Papers* 11, The Hague: Clingendael Institute for International Relations, December 2005.

Van Schaik, L., 'Policy Coherence for Development in the EU Council: Strategies for the Way Forward', *Fiche on EU Energy Policy,* Brussels: Centre for European Policy Studies, June 2006.

Vines, A., 'How Heavy are the Anchors?', *The World Today* , February 2008.

Von Gumppenberg, M., 'Kazakhstan: Challenges to the Booming Petro-Economy', *Working Paper* 2, Bern: Swiss Peace Foundation, 2007.

Vos, S., 'Europe's Infant Energy Strategy Looks Muddled and Unclear', *Europe's World* 4, Autumn 2006.

Walter, A., 'Do They Really Rule the World?', *New Political Economy* 3/2, 1998.

Warkotsch, A., 'The European Union and Democracy Promotion in Bad Neighbourhoods: The Case of Central Asia', *European Foreign Affairs Review* 11/3, 2006.

Wegener, H., 'Central Asia: At Last Europe may be Getting its Act Together', *Europe's World* 5, Spring 2007.

West, J., 'Saudi Arabia, Iraq, and the Gulf', in J. Kalicki and D. Goldwyn (eds) *Energy and Security: Toward a New Foreign Policy Strategy*, Washington, DC: Woodrow Wilson Center, 2005.

White, B., *Understanding European Foreign Policy,* Basingstoke: Palgrave Macmillan, 2001.

Whitman, R., 'Road Map for a Route March? (De-)civilianizing through the EU's Security Strategy', *European Foreign Affairs Review* 11/1, 2006.

Wood, S., 'Energy and Democracy: The European Union's Challenge', *Current History* 107/707, 2008.

Yergin, D., 'Ensuring Energy Security', *Foreign Affairs* 85/2, 2006.

—— 'Energy Security and Markets', in Goldwyn, D. and Kalicki, J. (eds) *Energy and Security: Toward a New Foreign Policy Strategy,* Washington, DC: Woodrow Wilson Center, 2005.

Youngs, R., *Europe and the Middle East: In the Shadow of September 11*, Boulder: Lynne Reinner, 2006.

—— *International Democracy and the West: The Role of Governments, Civil Society and Multinationals*, Oxford: Oxford University Press, 2004.

Zielonka, J., 'Europe as a Global Actor: Empire by Example?', *International Affairs* 84/3, 2008.

—— *Europe as Empire: The Nature of the Enlarged European Union*, Oxford: Oxford University Press, 2006.

Index